OCR Law
for AS

Jacqueline Martin

HODDER
EDUCATION
PART OF HACHETTE

Orders: please contact Bookpoint Ltd, 130 Milton Park, Abingdon, Oxon
OX14 4SB. Telephone: (44) 01235 827720. Fax: (44) 01235 400454. Lines are
open from 9.00 – 5.00, Monday to Saturday, with a 24 hour message
answering service. You can also order through our website
www.hoddereducation.co.uk

If you have any comments to make about this, or any of our other titles,
please send them to educationenquiries@hodder.co.uk

British Library Cataloguing in Publication Data
A catalogue record for this title is available from the British Library

ISBN: 978 0 340 95939 8

First Edition Published 2008
Impression number 10 9 8 7 6 5 4 3 2 1
Year 2012 2011 2010 2009 2008

Illustrations by Barking Dog Art
Cover illustration by Peter Gudynas/Zap Art
Typeset by Dorchester Typesetting Group Ltd
Printed and bound in Italy for Hodder Education, part of Hachette Livre UK,
338 Euston Road, London NW1 3BH

Contents

Preface

This book is aimed at the OCR specification for AS Law. The topics are covered in the order in which they appear in that specification.

The first chapter is an introductory one. It deals with the differences between civil and criminal law and gives a brief introduction to human rights. I have included this chapter as it is important that students grasp that civil and criminal cases are dealt with in different ways and in different courts. A brief account of human rights has been included as they affect so many aspects of our legal system.

The order of topics then starts with those set out for Unit 1 of the AS: civil courts, alternative dispute resolution, police powers, pre-trial matters on criminal cases, the Magistrates' Courts and the Crown Court, appeals in criminal cases, sentencing, the judiciary, the legal profession, lay magistrates, juries and funding. The book then covers the topics needed for Unit 2: judicial precedent, Acts of Parliament, delegated legislation, statutory interpretation, European law and law reform.

Throughout the text I have used my best-selling book, *The English Legal System*, which many teachers of OCR AS Law are already familiar with, as the basis for this textbook. I have kept to the principles of explaining points simply and clearly, but at the same time providing some depth for the more able students. As well as covering the factual material, each chapter contains critical analysis at a level suitable for AS students.

The text is broken up into manageable 'bites' with the use of sub-headings. There are also diagrams and charts to help students with their understanding of topics. Key facts charts are included for each topic to enable students to have an overview of the topics. These charts are also helpful as revision aids.

Newspaper articles, cases and other 'live' material are provided in most chapters to illustrate the legal system at work today. Many of these items are also used as a basis for activities and exercises for students to do. There are also application tasks for students based on scenario-style questions. Examination questions from the new specification for OCR AS Law are also given at the end of most chapters.

Jacqueline Martin

Acknowledgements

The author and publishers would like to thank the following for permission to reproduce copyright material:

Oxford Cambridge and RSA Examinations for OCR examination questions; Courier Media Group Limited for the article on page 5; Telegraph Media Group Limited for the article on page 5; Associated Newspapers for the articles on pages 6, 78 and 87; article on page 6 © NI Syndication Limited, 29 June 2007; article on page 7 © Stewart Tendler, NI Syndication Limited, 2 August 1995; article on pages 9 © Frances Gibb, NI Syndication Limited, 15 March 2007; picture on page 21 © Andrew Holt/Alamy; picture on page 38 © Arthur Turner/Alamy; picture on page 69 © Photofusion Picture Library/Alamy; picture on page 71 © Martyn Hayhow/AFP/Getty Images; picture on page 91 © Dan Atkin/Alamy; extracts on page 93 from 'Taking Responsibility' by Finola Farrant and Joe Leverson from New Law Journal by permission of LexisNexis Butterworths; picture on page 103 © Toby Melville/Reuters/Corbis; picture on page 104 © PSL Images/Alamy; article on page 113 © Frances Gibb, NI Syndication Limited, 31 October 2006; picture on page 121 © age fotostock/SuperStock; picture on page 124 © Horizon International Images Limited/Alamy; article on page 128 © Frances Gibb, NI Syndication Limited, 3 April 2007; picture on page 201 © Jack Sullivan/Alamy; article on page 203 © Copyright Guardian News & Media Ltd 1995; article on page 223 © NI Syndication Limited, 2 November 1990; © Crown copyright material is reproduced with permission of the Controller of HMSO.

Table of Acts of Parliament

Table of Cases

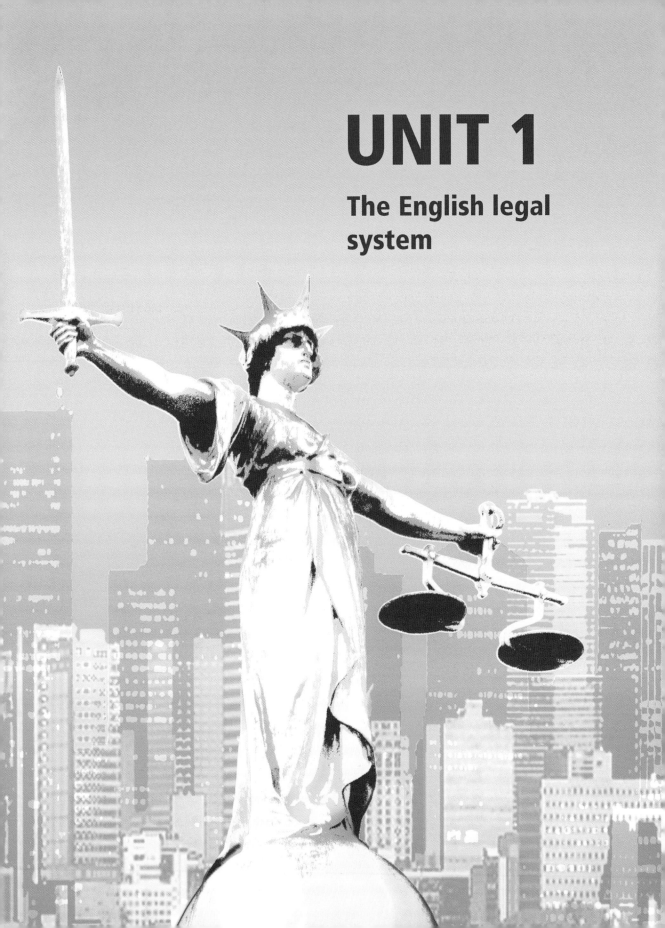

UNIT 1

The English legal system

Chapter 1

Introduction to law

Murderer jailed for life

Burglar caught

Headlines like these in newspapers are what many people think of when 'law' is mentioned. The other main source of information for the ordinary person is television programmes such as *The Bill* and *Crimewatch*. The headlines and these TV programmes all involve criminal cases.

This does not give a complete picture of the law. In fact, the law deals with a very wide variety of different cases and situations. As well as all the criminal cases that we hear so much of, the law also deals with what is called civil law.

The OCR specification you are studying requires you to understand the different ways in which civil and criminal cases are dealt with.

1.1 Civil law

Civil law is about private disputes between individuals and/or businesses. There are several different types of civil law. Some important areas of civil law are:

- contract law
- law of tort
- family law
- employment law
- company law.

This book does not deal with the actual legal rules for any of these areas. It deals only with the system for resolving disputes. However, it is sensible to have some idea of the types of dispute that may be involved in these areas of law, so consider the following situations:

(a) a family complain that their package holiday did not match what was promised by the tour operator and that they were put into a lower grade of hotel than the one they had paid for

(b) a woman has bought a new car and discovers that the engine is faulty

(c) a man who bought a car on hire-purchase has failed to pay the instalments due to the hire-purchase company.

All these situations come under the law of **contract**. There are also many other situations in which contracts may be involved. A contract is an agreement between two or more people and that agreement can be enforced by the courts. If a court case is successfully taken for breach of contract, the court will try to put the parties into the position they would have been in if the contract had not been broken. This is usually done by ordering the person who broke the contract to pay a sum of money in compensation to the other person. This sum of money is called an award of damages. In a very small number of contracts the court may order the person in breach to carry out the contract. This is called specific performance.

Now look at the next list. These also involve disputes between individuals and/or businesses but there is no contract or agreement between them:

(a) a child pedestrian crossing a road is injured by a car whose driver is travelling too fast (the tort of negligence)

(b) a family complain that their health is being affected by the noise and smoke from a factory which has just been built near their house (the tort of nuisance)

(c) a man complains that a newspaper has written an untrue article about him which has damaged his reputation (the tort of defamation).

All these cases come under the law of **tort**. This area of law recognises that there are situations where one person owes a legal responsibility to another. If there is a breach of this responsibility, then the person affected can make a claim under the law of tort. If successful the court will award them damages – a sum of money in compensation for any injury to them, their property or their reputation. Where there is a situation which is continuing (such as in (b) above), it is also possible for the court to order the person causing the problem not to do certain things. The above examples show possible breaches of different torts.

Other divisions of civil law concentrate on specific topics. **Family law** covers all disputes that may arise within families. A major part of this is divorce law and who should have the day-to-day care of any children of the family. **Employment law** covers all aspects of employment. For example, any disputes about unfair dismissal or redundancy come under this area of law. **Company law** is very important in the business world: it regulates how a company should be formed, sets out the formal rules for running a company, and deals with the rights and duties of shareholders and directors.

As well as these areas of civil law, there are also laws relating to land, to copyright, to marine law and many other topics. So it can be seen that civil law covers a wide variety of situations.

1.2 Criminal law

Criminal law sets out the types of behaviour which are forbidden at risk of punishment. A person who commits a crime is said to have offended against the State and so the State has the right to prosecute them. This is so even though there is often an individual victim of a crime as well. For example, if a defendant commits the crime of burglary by getting into someone's house and stealing money and other property, the State will prosecute the defendant for that burglary. But there is also an individual, the person living in the house, who is the victim of the crime. If the State does not prosecute then that individual has the right to prosecute. This happens only rarely in cases where the victim is an individual. There are also other agencies that prosecute such as Trading Standards and Revenue and Customs.

The criminal courts have the right to punish those who break the criminal law. So, at the end of a case when the defendant is found guilty, that defendant will be given a punishment. Such punishments include imprisonment, a community sentence such as unpaid work, a fine, or a ban from driving.

Any individual victim of the crime will not necessarily be given compensation, though where possible the courts do make a compensation order as well as punishing the offender.

Activity

On this page and the next page there are four newspaper articles. Two are about civil cases and two are about criminal cases. Read the articles and answer the questions at the end.

After you have done this activity, read section 1.3 to get a clearer understanding of the differences between the ways civil cases and criminal cases are dealt with in the courts.

Source A

Woman sentenced over benefit fraud worth £3,000

A West Kingsdown woman who used false information to claim more than £3,000 in benefits she was not entitled to has been prosecuted.

Heather Binns pleaded guilty to three charges of benefit fraud at Sevenoaks Magistrates' Court following a tip-off from a member of the public.

Mrs Binns claimed she was a lone parent in receipt of Income Support when she was actually living with a partner who was in full-time employment.

She has now been given a community sentence and ordered to do 50 hours' unpaid work to be completed over a 12-month period and ordered to pay £100 costs.

Adapted from an article in the *Sevenoaks Chronicle* and www.thisiscourier.co.uk, 21 June 2007

Source B

£14,000 for girl whose ear-piercing went wrong

A vicar's daughter has been awarded almost £14,000 compensation after an ear-piercing left her disfigured. Katrina Healey, now 15, lost part of her ear after a piercing gun was used instead of a specialist needle to insert a gold stud near the top of her ear.

. . . Katrina defied her parents to have her ear pierced when she was 12, getting a friend over the age of 18 to sign the consent form in H Warner and Sons jewellers' shop in Barnsley, South Yorks. Afterwards she underwent three hospital operations after her ear swelled and she developed an abscess. A judge at Barnsley County Court has awarded her £13,900 in damages after her parents sued the jewellers.

Adapted from an article by Paul Stokes in the *Daily Telegraph*, 6 October 2001

Source C

Life in jail for shot that rang out

An armed robber whose bullet deflected off the mobile phone in a jeweller's pocket has been jailed for life for attempted murder.

. . . Darren Price, 25, survived being shot by Sean Henry, who ran out of Amore jewellers in Horsham, West Sussex, with £50,000 of diamond rings.

Henry, 35, who was out of jail on licence at the time of the offence in September 2005, was found guilty by a jury of attempted murder, robbery and possession of a gun after a three-week trial at Hove Crown Court. He was ordered to serve at least 15 years.

Adapted from an article in
The Times, 29 June 2007

Source D

Father-of-two awarded £600,000 after wife died following NHS blunders

A man whose wife died after a series of NHS blunders following childbirth yesterday gave a harrowing account of his family's suffering.

Ben Palmer said that his children, Harry, five, and Emily, two, still cry every night for their mother, Jessica, nearly three years after her death.

Mrs Palmer, 35, died less than a week after Emily's birth in June 2004 after medical staff repeatedly failed to spot that she had developed blood poisoning.

Yesterday a judge ordered that the hospital trusts involved pay the family £600,000 in damages.

Speaking after the hearing at London's High Court, Mr Palmer, 36, said: 'My wife died a horrific death six days after giving birth to our daughter. This should not have happened.'

Taken from an article in the
Daily Mail, 13 March 2007

Questions

1. Identify which of these articles is referring to civil cases and which to criminal cases. (If you wish to check that you are right before continuing with the rest of the questions, turn to the Appendix at the back of the book.)

2. Look at the articles which you have identified as civil cases and state in which courts the cases were dealt with.

3. Look at the articles which you have identified as criminal cases and state in which courts the defendants were tried.

4. In one criminal case, the defendant pleaded guilty. In the other case the defendant was found guilty. Who made the decision about whether the defendant was guilty?

5. What did the people taking the civil case receive as a result of winning their case?

6. In the criminal cases the defendants received punishment. List the different punishments used in the cases.

7. In the civil cases, what is the time gap between the event for which the claim is made and the actual award of damages?

1.3 Differences between civil and criminal law

There are many differences between civil cases and criminal cases. The newspaper articles on the previous pages show some of these differences. There are other differences as well and it is important to understand fully the distinctions between civil and criminal cases.

1.3.1 Purpose of the law

Civil law upholds the rights of individuals and the courts can order compensation in an effort at putting the parties in the position they would have been in if there had not been any breach of the civil law.

Criminal law is aimed at trying to maintain law and order. So, when a person is found guilty of an offence, that offender will be punished. There is also the aim of trying to protect society and this is the justification for sending offenders to prison.

1.3.2 Person starting the case

In civil cases the person starting the case is the individual or business which has suffered as a result of the breach of civil law.

Criminal cases are taken on behalf of the State, and so there is a Crown Prosecution Service responsible for conducting most cases. However, there are other State agencies which may prosecute certain types of offence, for example the Environment Agency which prosecutes pollution cases.

The person starting the case is given a different name in civil and criminal cases. In civil cases they are called the claimant, while in criminal cases they are referred to as the prosecutor.

1.3.3 Courts

The cases take place in different courts. In general, civil cases are heard in the High Court or the County Court. The High Court deals with more serious cases while the County Court deals with cases of lower value. (Note that some civil matters, especially family cases, can be dealt with in the Magistrates' Courts – see section 6.1.1 for further details.)

In both the High Court and the County Court a judge will try the case. It is very rare to have a case tried by a jury in a civil matter. See Chapter 12 for details of when a jury might be used in a civil case.

Criminal cases will be tried in either the Magistrates' Courts or the Crown Court. The Magistrates' Courts deal with less serious offences and the case is tried by a panel of lay magistrates or by a single legally qualified District Judge. Serious offences are tried in the Crown Court. The case is tried by a judge sitting with a jury. The judge decides points of law and the jury decide the verdict of 'guilty' or 'not guilty'.

1.3.4 Standard of proof

Criminal cases must be proved 'beyond reasonable doubt'. This is a very high standard of proof, and is necessary since a conviction could result in the defendant serving a long prison sentence.

Civil cases have to be proved 'on the balance of probabilities'. This is a much lower standard of proof, where the judge decides who is more likely to be right. This difference in the standard of proof means that it is possible for a defendant who has been acquitted in a criminal case to be found liable in a civil case based on the same facts. Such situations are not common, but one is illustrated in the following article.

Judgment overtakes Brink's-Mat accused 11 years later

Eleven years after a man was acquitted of the £26 million Brink's-Mat bullion robbery, a High Court Judge ruled that he was involved and must repay the value of the gold.

Anthony White, acquitted at the Old Bailey in 1984 of taking part in Britain's biggest gold robbery, was ordered to repay the £26,369,778 value and £2,188,600 in compensation. His wife Margaret was ordered to pay £1,084,344.

Insurers for Brink's-Mat had sued the couple for the value of the proceeds.

Mr Justice Rimmer told Mr White that his acquittal did not mean that the Old Bailey jury had been satisfied he was innocent; only that he was not guilty according to the standard of proof required in criminal cases . . .

The case against the Whites is the latest and almost the last in a series of actions since the 1983 robbery brought by insurers for Brink's-Mat against people either convicted or suspected of taking part in the robbery.

Using the lower standards of proof in civil courts and in actions for seizure of assets, lawyers believe that they will recoup at least £20 million.

Taken from an article by Stewart Tendler
in *The Times*, 2 August 1995

1.3.5 Outcome of case

A defendant in a civil case is found 'liable' or 'not liable'. A defendant in a criminal case is found 'guilty' or 'not guilty'. Another way of stating this in criminal cases is to say that the defendant is 'convicted' or 'acquitted'.

At the end of a civil case, anyone found liable will be ordered to put right the matter as far as possible. This is usually done by an award of money in compensation, known as damages, though the court can make other orders such as an injunction to prevent similar actions in the future or an order for specific performance (where the defendant who broke a contract is ordered to complete that contract).

At the end of a criminal case a defendant found guilty of an offence may be punished.

	CIVIL CASES	CRIMINAL CASES
Purpose of the law	To uphold the rights of individuals	To maintain law and order; to protect society
Person starting the case	The individual whose rights have been affected	Usually the State, through Crown Prosecution Service
Legal name for that person	Claimant	Prosecutor
Courts hearing cases	County Court or High Court Some cases dealt with in tribunals	Magistrates' Court or Crown Court
Standard of proof	The balance of probabilities	Beyond reasonable doubt
Person/s making the decision	Judge Very rarely a jury	Magistrates in Magistrates' Courts OR A judge and jury at the Crown Court
Decision	'Liable' or 'not liable'	'Guilty' (convicted) or 'not guilty' (acquitted)
Powers of the court	Usually an award of damages. Also possible: injunction, specific performance of a contract, rescission or rectification	Prison, community sentence fine, discharge, driving ban

Figure 1.1 Differences between civil and criminal cases

1.4 Double liability

It is possible for the same incident to give rise to both civil and criminal liability. This occurs most often where someone is injured as a result of another person's bad driving. The driver can then be prosecuted in the criminal courts for a driving offence and also the injured person can claim against the driver in the civil courts. This next newspaper article shows a case where this happened.

Record £8.5 million for woman hit by car

A 22-year-old woman who suffered serious brain damage in a road accident nine years ago has been awarded £8.5 million, believed to be a record for a personal injury case (Frances Gibb writes).

Leanne Evans was hit by a 79-year-old driver on a pelican crossing in Birmingham when she was 13. The driver was fined £75 and convicted of careless driving.

Leanne now needs round-the-clock attention from eight carers, has severe memory impairment and uses a wheelchair.

Her father, Ivor Evans, said: 'We are very pleased for Leanne. This award will at least give her a limited quality of life and allow her to enjoy some of the things that every other 22-year-old likes to do, like going to pop concerts, going to the theatre and having a holiday, as well as making sure she has all the medical care that she needs.'

The Times, 15 March 2007

In this article the criminal case was the one in which the driver was convicted of careless driving. The civil case is the one in which the injured girl was awarded £8.5 million.

1.5 Human rights and the English legal system

The Human Rights Act 1998 incorporated the European Convention on Human Rights into our law. This is important, as it has affected many areas of the English legal system. This section explains key rights under the Convention and also gives a brief summary of some of the effects on our legal system.

1.5.1 The European Convention on Human Rights

The Convention sets out the rights that the people of Europe should have. These are:

- the right to life (Art 2), though it is recognised that states may impose the death penalty for certain crimes
- the right not to be tortured or subjected to inhumane or degrading treatment (Art 3)
- slavery is forbidden (Art 4)
- the right to liberty (Art 5), although limitations on this right are permitted so that people who are lawfully arrested or held in custody for trial or given a prison sentence by a court can be detained
- the right to a fair trial (Art 6)
- the right not to be punished except according to law (Art 7)
- the right to respect for private and family life (Art 8).

Activity

Look through newspapers to find articles about court cases. When you have found an article, use your knowledge about civil and criminal cases to decide what type of case it is.

If you are having difficulty finding civil cases, try searching for the phrase 'High Court' or 'County Court' in newspapers online. Easy sites to search are:

www.dailymail.co.uk
www.telegraph.co.uk

The Convention also sets out freedoms which people should be able to enjoy. These include:

- freedom of thought, conscience and religion
- freedom of expression and
- freedom of assembly and association.

1.5.2 Effect on the English legal process

Before the Convention was incorporated into our law by the Human Rights Act 1998, anyone who wanted to complain of a breach of human rights had to take their case to the European Court of Human Rights. If the United Kingdom was found to be in breach of the Convention, the Government did not have to change the law. However, in some cases it did do so. An example is *T v United Kingdom; V v United Kingdom* (1999) (see Criminal trials, below).

Since the Convention was incorporated, people can rely on the rights it gives in our courts. In addition, there have been some changes in our legal system in order to comply with the Convention. Some of these are explained below. These points are not the only way in which the English legal system has been affected by the European Convention on Human Rights. However, they give some illustration of how wide-ranging the effect has been on our legal system.

Civil cases

An appeal route for small claims cases was created. Previously there had been no appeal for small claims cases. This would have breached Art 6 of the Convention – the right to a fair trial.

Criminal trials

In the case of *T v United Kingdom; V v United Kingdom* (1999), the European Court of Human Rights had ruled that there was a breach of Art 6. In the case, a boy of 10 and a boy of 11 were tried in the Crown Court for murder. The European Court of Human Rights held that the formality of a Crown Court trial would have made it difficult for the boys to understand what was happening.

This meant that the trial was not fair and there was a breach of the European Convention.

Following this decision, trials of juveniles at the Crown Court were altered to make the trial process less formal.

Sentencing

Where an offender is sentenced to prison for life, it is usual to set a minimum period which must be served before the offender can be considered for parole. This minimum sentence used to be set by the Home Secretary (a Government Minister). The European Court of Human Rights held that this was a breach of the European Convention. This has been changed so that judges are now responsible for setting any minimum period.

Judicial appointment

Part-time judges in this country used to be appointed for a period of three years. After this time they could then be appointed for further periods of three years. In addition, the appointment was made by the Lord Chancellor (a Government Minister). The length of appointment was changed to five years as it was thought that the shorter period meant that there was a risk of the judges not being sufficiently independent from the Government. This would have been a breach of the European Convention.

1.5.3 Effect on sources of law

As well as affecting our legal system, the Human Rights Act 1998 sets out three important matters for the way our law is made and interpreted. These affect the making of Acts of Parliament, decisions on points of law by judges and the way in which judges interpret new laws. Each of these is explained below.

Acts of Parliament

When a new potential Act of Parliament (known as a Bill) is put before Parliament, there must be a statement as to whether it is compatible with the Convention rights or not.

Precedent

Section 2(1)(a) of the Human Rights Act 1998 states that our courts must take into account any judgment or decision of the European Court of Human Rights. This means that judges, when deciding a case, must look at human rights cases, as well as our own English law.

Statutory interpretation

Section 3 of the Act states that, so far as it is possible to do so, all legislation (that is, Acts of Parliament and other laws made in this country) must be given effect so that it is compatible with the European Convention. For example, if the wording of an Act of Parliament has two possible meanings, then the meaning which fits with the European Convention is the one that must be used.

Chapter 2

Civil cases

As already stressed in Chapter 1, it is important to understand the differences between civil cases and criminal cases. Civil cases cover a wide range of matters, so there cannot be a very specific definition which will cover all of them. However, a basic definition for civil claims is to say that these arise when an individual or a business believes that their rights have been infringed in some way. Some of the main areas of civil law are contract law, the law of tort, family law, employment law and company law.

As well as dealing with different areas of law, the types of dispute that can arise within the field of civil law are equally varied. A company may be claiming that money is owed to it (contract law); this type of claim may be for a few pounds or for several million. An individual may be claiming compensation for injuries suffered in an accident (the tort of negligence), while in another tort case the claim might not be for money but for another remedy: such as an injunction to prevent someone from building on disputed land. Other types of court orders include the winding-up of a company which cannot pay its debts or a decree of divorce for a marriage that has failed. The list is almost endless.

2.1 Negotiation

In most civil matters people regard a court case as a last resort and will try to resolve the problem without going to court, so that when a dispute arises it is likely that some form of negotiation will take place. The most usual situation is that the person making the complaint will either go to see the other side and explain the problem (this is common where shoppers take back sub-standard goods) or they will write to the other side, setting out the complaint. Many cases will be resolved at this stage by the other party agreeing to refund money, change goods, pay the debt or take some other desired action.

In fact, research in 2007 found that 89 per cent of people try some form of alternative way of resolving the dispute before starting a court case.

hmcs
GWASANAETH LLYSOEDD EI MAWRHYDI
HER MAJESTY'S COURTS SERVICE

EX301

Making a claim? Some questions to ask yourself

Making a claim?

Some questions to ask yourself.

This leaflet suggests some questions you ought to ask yourself before making a claim (called 'issuing a claim') in a county court. The answers to the questions will help you decide if going to court is going to be worthwhile for you.

Do I have to make a claim? Are there any alternatives to court?

Until recently, if you had a legal problem, you would normally have gone to a court or tribunal in what is often called 'litigation'. While this is still a common way of sorting out such problems, individuals often find that going to court is expensive and can be stressful.

There are now a number of other ways of sorting out complaints and legal problems, including things like arbitration, mediation and ombudsmen schemes. These are often called 'alternative dispute resolution' (ADR) schemes.

Court rules require you to think about whether alternative dispute resolution is a better way to reach an agreement before going to court. If you refuse to consider this, you may not get your costs back, or the court may order you to pay the other party's costs, even if you win the case.

You may find it helpful to read information leaflet 23 Alternatives to court, published by the Community Legal Service, which explains these schemes in more detail, how they work and when you can use them. A copy of the leaflet can be obtained free from www.legalservices.gov.uk or viewed on the Internet at www.clsdirect.org.uk

F2

Why should I use an alternative dispute resolution scheme instead of going to court?

Alternative schemes are not meant to replace the courts. But they can have advantages over going to court. The advantages include:

- being more flexible;
- solving your problem faster;
- being less stressful; and
- costing you less money.

If you have a problem with a person regularly (a neighbour for example) or organisation you deal with, an alternative process such as mediation could mean a better, longer-lasting solution to your problem.

You can find out more about mediation by contacting the National Mediation Helpline on 0845 60 30 809 or by visiting the website www.nationalmediationhelpline.com

How do I decide whether to use an alternative dispute resolution scheme?

How you choose to solve your problem depends on:

- the result you want;
- what you can expect to achieve;
- how you want to go about solving your problem; and
- how willing the other party is to try and solve the problem.

By going to court, you might get:

- an order that something be done or stopped;
- compensation; or
- a judgment from the court about who is right and who is wrong.

3

www.hmcourts-service.gov.uk

Figure 2.1 Making a claim? Some questions to ask yourself

The need to try to settle any dispute is stressed in the leaflets issued by the Court Service on taking action in court. See Figure 2.1.

Legal advice

If the other party will not settle the claim, then the aggrieved person must decide whether they are prepared to take the matter further. The most common next stage is to get legal advice and perhaps have a solicitor write to the other person. This may lead to a 'bargaining' situation where a series of letters is written between the parties and eventually a compromise is reached. However, if, after all this, the other side refuses to pay the debt or compensation or whatever else is claimed, then the aggrieved person must decide if the matter is worth pursuing any further. This may involve starting a court case or an alternative form of dispute resolution may be used (these alternatives to going to court are considered in the next chapter).

Going to court

Taking a case to court can be an expensive exercise, even if you decide to 'do it yourself' and not use a lawyer. There will be a court fee based on the type and size of the claim, which can be claimed back from the other party if you win the case, but there is always the risk that you will lose the case and have to pay the other side's costs. Even if you win, your problems may not be over as the other person may not have enough money to pay the claim and refund your costs. If the case is complicated it could take years to complete and may cost hundreds or thousands of pounds.

Given these problems, it is not surprising that many people who believe they have a good claim decide not to take court action.

However, starting a court case does not mean that it will actually go to court. The vast majority of cases are settled out of court, so that fewer than 5 per cent of all cases started in the civil courts get as far as a court hearing. This is because the dispute is a private one between the parties involved and they can settle their own dispute at any time, even after court proceedings have been started.

2.2 Starting a court case

The civil justice system was reformed in 1999 following the Woolf Report (see section 2.6).

Parties are encouraged to give information to each other, in an attempt to prevent the need for so many court cases to be started. So, before a claim is issued, especially in personal injury cases, a pre-action 'protocol' should be followed. This is a list of things to be done and if the parties do not follow the procedure and give the required information to the other party, they may be liable for certain costs if they then make a court claim.

The information is usually in a letter explaining brief details of how the claim arises; why it is claimed that the other party is at fault; details of injury or other damage; and any other relevant matters. The defendant is then given three months to investigate the claim and must then reply, setting out if liability is admitted or if it is denied, with the reasons for the denial. If expert evidence is going to be needed, then the parties should try to agree to use one expert. This should lead to many claims being settled, but there will still be some which need to go to court.

2.2.1 Which court to use?

Where the decision is made to go to court, then the first problem is which court to use. The two courts which hear civil cases are:

- the County Court and
- the High Court.

For cases where the claim is for £15,000 or less, the case must be started in the County Court. For larger claims the claimant can usually choose to start a case in either the County Court or the High Court. This is still the position after the Woolf reforms. However, there are some restrictions laid down in the High Court and County Courts Jurisdiction Order 1991. These are that:

- personal injury cases for less than £50,000 must be started in the County Court and
- defamation actions must be started in the High Court.

So, for most cases over £15,000 a claimant will be able to choose the most convenient court for starting the case. The main points to consider in making the decision are the amount that is being claimed and whether the case is likely to raise a complex issue of law. The fact that a case is started in one court does not necessarily mean that the trial will be there; cases may be transferred from one court to the other for the actual trial, if this is thought necessary. Once a case is defended, the case is allocated to the appropriate track and at the same time it is possible for it to be transferred to another court.

Jurisdiction

If the High Court is chosen, then there is the question of which division to use. There are three divisions dealing with different types of law. These are:

- the Queen's Bench Division
- the Chancery Division and
- the Family Division.

The type of case a court deals with is referred to as the jurisdiction of the court. The jurisdiction of the County Court is very wide, as it can hear cases of any amount if the parties agree to that. Also, it can hear claims about almost every type of civil law. This means it can hear contract cases, tort cases and land law cases (such as a claim for unpaid rent or a claim to get possession of land back from a tenant). The court can also deal with family cases, especially divorce and any related disputes about custody of the children, property or maintenance. Jurisdiction of the County Court is dealt with further in section 2.4.

The jurisdiction of the three divisions of the High Court is explained in section 2.5. The jurisdiction of all the courts is also shown in Figure 2.4.

2.2.2 Issuing a claim

If you are using the County Court, then you can choose to issue the claim in any of the 230 or so County Courts in the country. If you are using the High Court, then you can go to one of the 20 District Registries or the main court in London. You need a claim form called 'N1' (see Figure 2.2). The court office will give you notes explaining how to fill in the form.

Court staff can help to make sure that you have filled in the claim form properly, or you may get help from advice centres or a Citizens' Advice Bureau. Once the form is filled in you should photocopy it so that you have a copy for the court, a copy for yourself and a copy for each defendant. Then take the form to the court office. A court fee for issuing the claim has to be paid. This fee varies according to how much the claim is for.

In 2007 the fee for a claim of up to £300 was £30, with the maximum fee for a small claim (under £5,000) being £108. Claims of £5,000 to £15,000 had a fee of £225, while at the top end of the scale claims of over £300,000 had a fee of £1,530.

 Internet Research

Look up court forms such as N1 on the website **www.courtservice.gov.uk**.

Also use that website to find guidance on starting cases in the County Court.

2.2.3 Defending a claim

When the defendant receives the claim form there are several routes which can be taken. The defendant may admit the claim and pay the full amount. Where this happens, the case ends. The claimant has achieved what was wanted. In other cases the defendant may dispute the claim. If the defendant wishes to defend the claim, he must send either an acknowledgement of service (Form

Claim Form

In the

	for court use only
Claim No.	
Issue date	

Claimant

SEAL

Defendant(s)

Brief details of claim

Value

		£
Defendant's name and address	Amount claimed	
	Court fee	
	Solicitor's costs	
	Total amount	

The court office at

is open between 10am and 4pm Monday to Friday. When corresponding with the court, please address forms or letters to the Court Manager and quote the claim number.

NI Claim form (CPR Part 7) (01.02)   *Printed on behalf of The Court Service*

	Claim No.	

Does, or will, your claim include any issues under the Human Rights Act 1998?   ☐ Yes   ☐ No

Particulars of Claim (attached)(to follow)

Statement of Truth
*(I believe)(The Claimant believes) that the facts stated in these particulars of claim are true.
*I am duly authorised by the claimant to sign this statement

Full name _____

Name of claimant's solicitor's firm _____

signed_____   position or office held _____
*(Claimant)(Litigation friend)(Claimant's solicitor)   (if signing on behalf of firm or company)

*delete as appropriate

Claimant's or claimant's solicitor's address to which documents or payments should be sent if different from overleaf including (if appropriate) details of DX, fax or e-mail.

Figure 2.2 Form N1

Value of claim	Court in which case will usually be tried
Under £5,000	County Court small claims procedure
£5,000–£15,000	County Court fast-track procedure
£15,000–£25,000	County Court multi-track procedure
£25,000–£50,000	Either High Court or County Court multi-track procedure
Over £50,000	High Court multi-track procedure

Figure 2.3 Summary of where cases are likely to be tried

N9) or a defence to the court within 14 days of receiving the claim. If only an acknowledgement of service is sent, then the defendant has an extra 14 days in which to serve the defence.

If the defendant does not do either of these things, then the claimant can ask the court to make an order that the defendant pays the money and costs claimed. This is called an order in default. Once a claim is defended the court will allocate the case to the most suitable 'track' or way of dealing with the case.

2.2.4 The three tracks

The decision on which track should be used is made by the District Judge in the County Court or the Master (a procedural judge) in the High Court. The tracks are:

1. **The small claims track**
   This is normally used for disputes under £5,000, except for personal injury cases and housing cases where the limit is usually £1,000.

2. **The fast track**
   This is used for straightforward disputes of £5,000–£15,000.

3. **The multi-track**
   This is for cases over £15,000 or for complex cases under this amount.

NB A Government consultation paper in 2007 suggested raising the fast track limit to £25,000.

To help the judge consider to which track a claim should be allocated, both parties are sent an allocation questionnaire. If it is thought necessary, the judge can allocate a case to a track which normally deals with claims of a higher value. Alternatively, if the parties agree, the judge can allocate a case to a lower-value track.

For claims over £15,000 there may also be a decision to transfer the case from the County Court to the High Court or *vice versa*. Usually, claims of less than £25,000 are tried in the County Court, while claims for between £25,000 and £50,000 are generally tried in the court in which the proceedings were started. Claims for over £50,000 are usually tried in the High Court. This is shown in Figure 2.3.

We will now go on to consider the different courts and tracks.

2.3 Small claims

Clearly, it is important to have a relatively cheap and simple way of making a claim for a small amount of money, otherwise the costs of the action will be far more than the amount in dispute. For that reason, the small claims procedure was started in 1973, and originally only claims of up to £75 could be made there. The limit has since been raised several times, especially after the Woolf Report when the limit was increased to £3,000; and in 1999 it became £5,000.

In 2007 the limit was still £5,000 for most cases and £1,000 for personal injury and housing cases.

A Government consultation paper issued in 2007 recommended that the limits should remain at those levels.

2.3.1 Small claims procedure

People are encouraged to take their own case so that costs are kept low. However, under the present rules small claims cases are started in the same way as all other cases. This makes it more difficult for the ordinary person. The use of lawyers is discouraged, as, though it is possible to have a lawyer to represent you at a small claims hearing, the winner cannot claim the costs of using a lawyer from the losing party. An alternative to using a lawyer is to have a 'lay representative', that is a non-legally qualified person, to help put your case.

Small claims cases are usually heard in private, but they can be heard in an ordinary court. The procedure allows the District Judge to be flexible in the way he hears the case. District Judges are encouraged to be more inquisitorial and are given training in how to handle small claims cases, so that they will take an active part in the proceedings, asking questions and making sure that both parties explain all their important points.

2.3.2 Advantages of small claims

1. The cost of taking proceedings is low, especially for claims under £1,000.
2. If you lose, you will not have to pay the other person's lawyers' costs.
3. People do not have to use lawyers, but can take the case themselves.
4. The procedure is quicker than for other cases.
5. The District Judge should help the parties to explain their case.

2.3.3 Disadvantages of small claims

1. For cases over £1,000, an allocation fee of £100 has to be paid.

2. Legal funding for paying for a lawyer is not available, though it may be possible to fund the case through a 'no win, no fee' arrangement (see Chapter 13).
3. Where the other side is a business, they are more likely to use a lawyer. This can put an unrepresented claimant at a disadvantage.
4. Research by John Baldwin has shown that District Judges are not always very helpful to unrepresented claimants.
5. Even when you win your case, it does not mean that you will get your money from the defendant. Only about 60 per cent of successful claimants actually received all the money awarded by the court.

2.4 County Court

There are about 230 County Courts, so that most major towns will have a court. The courts can try nearly all civil cases. The main types of cases are:

*   all contract and tort claims
*   all cases for the recovery of land
*   disputes over partnerships, trusts and inheritance up to a value of £30,000.

In addition, some County Courts have the jurisdiction to hear divorce cases, bankruptcy cases, admiralty cases (normal limit £5,000 or £15,000 for salvage cases) and matters under the Race Relations Act 1976.

The County Court can try small claims, fast-track and multi-track cases and its workload is much greater than that of the High Court. About two million cases are started in the County Courts each year. This figure includes small claims.

Despite the large total of cases started, only a small number of cases actually proceed to a trial. Most cases, especially those involving claims in contract or tort, settle. This means that the parties come to an agreement, so there is no need for the case to continue.

Cases will nearly always be heard in open court and members of the public are entitled to attend; the exceptions to this are cases involving family matters, for example maintenance hearings, and proceedings under the Children Act 1989, which are heard in private. The whole hearing is more formal and many claimants and defendants will be represented, usually by a solicitor but sometimes by a barrister. The winner of a case may claim costs, including the cost of legal representation. All this makes a case in the County Court much more expensive than one in the small claims track. John Baldwin's research found that 40 per cent of those taking cases in the main County Court viewed it as 'an inappropriate and disproportionately expensive way of resolving' their dispute.

Cases are usually heard by Circuit Judges, although District Judges may hear lower-value cases. In rare cases it is possible for a jury of eight to sit with the judge. (For further information on the use of juries in civil cases, see Chapter 12.)

2.4.1 Fast-track cases

Claims between £5,000 and £15,000 need a faster and cheaper method of dealing with them. In 1998, before the Woolf reforms, the statistics for the year show that the average wait for cases in the County Court was 85 weeks from the issue of the claim to the actual hearing in court. As well as delay, cases were too expensive. Indeed, the Woolf Report found that the costs of cases were often higher than the amount claimed.

As a result of this, the new fast-track idea was brought in. Once a case is defended, the District Judge at the County Court will send out the allocation questionnaire and then make the decision of whether the case is suitable for the fast track. Personal injury cases and housing cases over £1,000 and up to £15,000 are also dealt with as fast-track cases.

'Fast track' means that the court will set down a very strict timetable for the pre-trial matters. This is aimed at preventing one or both sides from wasting time and running up unnecessary costs. Once a case is set down for hearing, the aim is to have the case heard within 30 weeks. The new timetables have lessened the delays a

little. In 2005 the wait from issue of claim to hearing was 58 weeks. This is a six-month improvement on the pre-Woolf era. However, the total time of 58 weeks is still a long time to wait for a trial of what is meant to be a fast-track case. The actual trial will usually be heard by a Circuit Judge and take place in open court with a more formal procedure than for small claims. In order to speed up the trial itself, the hearing will be limited to a maximum of one day and the number of expert witnesses restricted, with usually only one expert being allowed.

2.4.2 Multi-track cases

Claims for more than £15,000 are usually allocated to the multi-track. If the case was started in a County Court then it is likely to be tried there, though it can be sent to the High Court, especially for claims of over £50,000. The case will be heard by a Circuit Judge who will also be expected to 'manage' the case from the moment it is allocated to the multi-track route. The judge can set timetables. It is even possible to ask the parties to try an alternative method of dispute resolution in an effort to prevent waste of costs.

2.5 High Court

The High Court is based in London but also has judges sitting at 26 towns and cities throughout England and Wales. It has the power to hear any civil case and has three divisions each of which specialises in hearing certain types of case. These divisions are the Queen's Bench Division, the Chancery Division and the Family Division.

2.5.1 Queen's Bench Division

The President of the Queen's Bench Division is the Lord Chief Justice and there are about 70 judges sitting in the division. It deals with contract and tort cases where the amount claimed is over £50,000, though, as seen earlier in this chapter, a claimant can start an action for any amount of £15,000 and above. The intention is that only multi-track cases should be dealt with

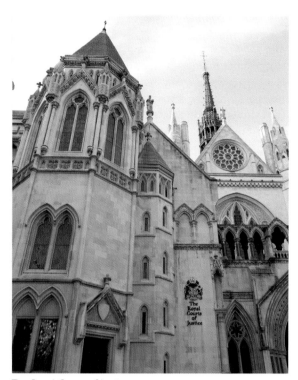

The Royal Courts of Justice

in the High Court. Also, certain types of action are thought to be more suitable for the High Court than the County Court.

Usually cases are tried by a single judge but there is a right to jury trial for fraud, libel, slander, malicious prosecution and false imprisonment cases. When a jury is used there will be 12 members.

Cases in the High Court are expensive and can take a long time. The average time between issuing a claim and the trial is about three years. Cases are expensive because of the need to use lawyers and also because of court fees. As well as fees for issuing the claim and other preliminary stages, hourly trial fees were brought in for High Court cases from April 2005.

Commercial Court

This is a special court which is part of the Queen's Bench Division. This court has specialist judges to deal with insurance, banking and other commercial matters, for example the problems of

the Lloyd's 'names' for the losses caused by large insurance claims. In this court a simplified speedier procedure is used and the case may be decided on documentary evidence.

Admiralty Court

There is also an Admiralty Court dealing with shipping and deciding such matters as claims for damage caused by collision at sea. It also decides disputes over salvage rights when a ship has sunk or been stranded. The judge in the Admiralty Court sits with two lay assessors, who are chosen from Masters of Trinity House, and who are there to advise the judge on questions of seamanship and navigation.

Technology and Construction Court

In 1998 the Technology and Construction Court was set up to take over from what had been called the Official Referee's Court. This court deals with any cases in the Chancery or the Queen's Bench Division which involve technically complex issues, such as building and engineering disputes or litigation over computers.

Judicial review

The Queen's Bench Division also has important supervisory functions over inferior courts and other bodies with decision-making powers, such as Government Ministers or local councils. Judicial review is concerned with whether a decision-making process has been carried out legally, as distinct from the merits of the decision in question.

2.5.2 Chancery Division

The Chancellor of the High Court is the head of the division. There are about 17 High Court Judges assisting in the division. The main business of this division involves disputes concerned with such matters as insolvency, for both companies and individuals, the enforcement of mortgages, disputes relating to trust property, copyright and patents, intellectual property matters and contested probate actions. There is also a special Companies Court in the division which deals mainly with winding up companies.

Juries are never used in the Chancery Division and cases are heard by a single judge. The criticisms of cost and delay which apply to the Queen's Bench Division apply equally to the Chancery Division.

2.5.3 Family Division

The head of this division is the President and 17 High Court Judges are assigned to the division. It has jurisdiction to hear wardship cases and all cases relating to children under the Children Act 1989. It also deals with other matters regarding the family, such as declarations of nullity of

Key facts

County Court	Financial limits	• small claims – usually under £5,000 • fast-track – between £5,000 and £15,000 • multi track – usually under £50,000 but parties can agree to a claim for any amount being heard in County Court.
	Types of case	• contract claims, eg for failure to pay agreed amount • tort claims, eg personal injury caused through negligence • land law cases, especially for recovery of possession of land • disputes over partnerships, trusts and inheritance up to a value of £30,000. Some County Courts also have jurisdiction to hear: • divorce cases • bankruptcy cases • admiralty cases (normal limit £5,000 or £15,000 for salvage cases) • matters under the Race Relations Act 1976.
High Court	Financial limits	• only claims over £15,000 • personal injury cases over £50,000 • any other multi-track claim.
	The three divisions	**Queen's Bench Division** • mainly contract and tort cases • applications for judicial review • Commercial Court • Admiralty Court • Technology and Construction Court. **Chancery Division** • insolvency, for both companies and individuals • enforcement of mortgages • disputes relating to trust property • copyright and patents • intellectual property matters • contested probate cases. **Family Division** • wardship cases • all cases relating to children under the Children Act 1989 • declarations of nullity of marriage • grants probate in non-contested probate cases.

Figure 2.4 Key facts chart on the jurisdiction of the County Court and High Court

marriage, and grants probate in non-contentious probate cases.

Cases are heard by a single judge and, although juries were once used to decide defended divorce cases, juries are not now used in this division.

Activity

Advise the people in the following situations:

1. Sarah has bought a DVD player costing £70 from a local electrical superstore. The DVD player has never worked properly, but the store has refused to replace it or to refund the purchase price to Sarah. She wishes to claim against the store. Advise her as to which court to start the case in and how she should go about this. Also explain to her the way in which the case will be dealt with if the store defends it and there is a court hearing.
2. Thomas has been badly injured at work and alleges that the injuries were the result of his employer's failure to take proper safety precautions. He has been advised that his claim is likely to be worth £200,000. Advise him as to which court or courts could hear his case.
3. Imran wishes to start an action for defamation against a national newspaper. Advise him as to which court he should use and explain to him who tries defamation cases.

2.6 The Woolf reforms

The present system of civil justice is based on the reforms recommended by Lord Woolf in his report *Access to Justice* (1996).

In 1995 Lord Woolf stated that a civil justice system should:

- be just in the results it delivers
- be fair in the way it treats litigants

- offer appropriate procedures at a reasonable cost
- deal with cases at a reasonable speed
- be understandable to those who use it
- provide as much certainty as the nature of particular cases allows
- be effective, adequately resourced and organised.

The Report found that virtually none of these points was being achieved in the civil courts, and criticised the system for being unequal, expensive, slow, uncertain and complicated. The Report contained 303 recommendations. The most important ones proposed were:

- extending small claims up to £3,000
- a fast track for straightforward cases up to £10,000
- a multi-track for cases over £10,000, with capping of costs
- encouraging the use of alternative dispute resolution
- giving judges more responsibility for managing cases
- more use of information technology
- simplifying documents and procedures and having a single set of rules governing proceedings in both the High Court and the County Court
- shorter timetables for cases to reach court and for lengths of trials.

The proposal to increase the small claims limit to £3,000 was implemented before the full report was issued. Before committing itself to the remainder of the reforms, the Labour Government, which came to power in 1997, commissioned the Middleton Report as a 'second opinion'. This supported most of the Woolf proposals, but suggested that the small claims limit should be raised to £5,000 and the fast-track route to £15,000. As a result of the Woolf and Middleton Reports, the civil justice system was radically reformed in April 1999.

2.6.1 The Civil Procedure Rules

From 26th April 1999, new Civil Procedure Rules were brought into effect. These use much simpler language than previous rules. They also changed the vocabulary used in court cases. For example, anyone starting a civil case is now called the 'claimant'; previously the term used in most cases was the 'plaintiff'. The document used to start cases is a 'claim form', rather than a 'writ' or a 'summons'. The new terms are used in this book, but the old terms still appear in reports of cases decided before April 1999.

Overriding objective

Rule 1.1 of the Civil Procedure Rules states that the overriding objective is to enable the court to deal with cases justly. This means that courts should try to:

- ensure that the parties in any case are on an equal footing
- save expense
- deal with cases in a way which is proportionate to:
  - the amount involved (that is avoid the costs of the case being more than the amount claimed)
  - the importance of the case (for example, is there a major point of law involved?)
  - the complexity of the issues in the case
- ensure that the case is dealt with quickly and fairly
- allocate an appropriate share of the court's resources (so smaller claims do not take up more time than they justify).

Comment

It is now nine years since the Woolf reforms came into effect. What effect have the reforms had? Suzanne Burn, in an article in *Legal Action*, July 2003, considered all the available evidence and research and pointed out that it is difficult to isolate the 'Woolf factor' because there were a number of other factors that came into effect either at the same time as the Woolf reforms or shortly afterwards.

These included:

- the withdrawal of legal aid from certain types of civil claim, in particular personal injury cases
- the widening of the scope of conditional fee agreement together with the ability to recover success fees and insurance premiums (see Chapter 13 for detailed information) and
- the implementation of the Human Rights Act 1998 in October 2000.

With the overlapping effects of these other changes and also the fact that there has been only limited research, Burn pointed out that measuring the success or otherwise of the Woolf reforms is difficult. However, she found there had been some positive effects:

- the total volume of litigation has fallen since April 1999 (although it had also been decreasing before the Woolf reforms)
- the number of fast-track trials, in particular, has dropped sharply in many courts
- the rate of settlement of cases has increased.

However, there are still problems. These include:

- the time taken for cases to get to trial has improved, but not as much as hoped for
- the fact that the new Civil Procedure Rules are very lengthy and too many amendments have been issued
- small claims listings seem to have suffered, as priority has been given to fast-track and multi-track conferences and trials
- increases in court fees and problems in the enforcement of judgments may also have played a part in reducing the number of small claims cases
- there are claims that case management 'takes extra time and cost, but adds little value'.

Another problem is that many County Courts are under-resourced. This leads to delays in issuing, allocation, listing and production of court orders.

Key facts

Courts dealing with civil cases	● County Court ● High Court
Different tracks for claims	● Small claims ● Fast track ● Multi-track
Problems of civil cases	● Cost ● Delay ● Complexity
1999 reforms	● Encourage use of ADR ● Simpler forms and language ● Increase small claims limit to £5,000 ● Fast track for claims between £5,000 and £15,000 ● Judges responsible for case management ● Strict timetables
Effect of 1999 reforms	● Cases settle earlier ● Initial costs are high ● Delays are getting shorter ● Courts strict on timetables

Figure 2.5 Key facts chart on civil justice

Judges have more control over proceedings than previously. They can set timetables and make sure that the parties do not drag out a case unnecessarily. Rule 1.4 of the Civil Procedure Rules explains that as well as fixing timetables, 'active case management' by judges includes:

- identifying the issues at an early stage
- deciding which issues need investigation and trial
- encouraging the parties to use alternative dispute resolution if this is appropriate
- dealing with any procedural steps without the need for the parties to attend court
- giving directions to ensure that the trial of a case proceeds quickly and efficiently.

2.7 Appellate courts

These are courts which hear appeals from lower courts. The main appellate courts are the Divisional Courts, the Court of Appeal and the House of Lords.

2.7.1 Divisional Courts

Each division of the High Court has what is called a Divisional Court which has the power to hear appeals from inferior courts and tribunals. For most appeals, two or three of the judges from the particular division will sit together to hear the case.

Queen's Bench Divisional Court

The most important of the Divisional Courts is the Queen's Bench Divisional Court. This has two main functions:

1. It hears appeals by way of case stated from criminal cases decided in the Magistrates' Court. This is dealt with more fully in Chapter 11.

2. It has supervisory powers over inferior courts and tribunals and also over the actions and decisions of public bodies and Government Ministers. This process is known as 'judicial review' and for this purpose the court has the power to make what are called 'prerogative orders'. These orders are a mandatory order, which is a command to perform a duty; a prohibition order, which is an order to prevent an inferior court from hearing a case which it has no power to deal with; and a quashing order, which removes the decision to the Queen's Bench Division so that its legality can be enquired into and the decision quashed if it is found to be invalid.

The Queen's Bench Divisional Court also hears applications for *habeas corpus* from those who allege that they are being unlawfully detained. This is an important way of protecting the right to liberty.

Chancery Divisional Court

This deals with only a small number of appeals, mainly from decisions made by Tax Commissioners on the payment of tax and appeals from decisions of the County Court in bankruptcy cases.

Family Divisional Court

The main function of this court is to hear appeals from the decisions of the magistrates regarding family matters and orders affecting children.

2.7.2 Court of Appeal (Civil Division)

The Court of Appeal was set up by the Judicature Act 1873 and was initially intended to be the final court of appeal. However, the position of the House of Lords as the final appellate court was re-instated by the Appellate Jurisdiction Act 1876. Today the Court of Appeal has two divisions: civil and criminal. There are 37 Lords Justices of Appeal and each division is presided over by its own head. The Civil Division is the main

appellate court for civil cases and it is headed by the Master of the Rolls.

The Court of Appeal (Civil Division) mainly hears appeals from the following courts:

- all three divisions of the High Court
- the County Court for multi-track cases
- the Immigration Appeal Tribunal
- some tribunals, especially the Lands Tribunal.

Permission to appeal

Permission to appeal is required in most cases. It can be granted by the lower court where the decision was made or by the Court of Appeal. Permission to appeal will only be granted where the court considers that an appeal would have a real prospect of success or that there was some other compelling reason why the appeal should be heard.

Permission to appeal is not required in cases where the liberty of the individual is in issue; for example in an appeal against a committal to prison for breaking an injunction.

2.7.3 House of Lords

This is the final court of appeal in the English legal system. It hears appeals from the Court of Appeal, the Divisional Courts and, on rare occasions, direct from the High Court under what are called the 'leapfrog' provisions. Appeals are heard by the Lords of Appeal in Ordinary (the Law Lords), usually by a panel of five, but on some occasions by a panel of seven. A panel of seven was used in the case of *Pepper v Hart* (1993) which involved the question of whether *Hansard* could be used as an aid to statutory interpretation (see Chapter 17).

Permission to appeal

On an appeal from the Court of Appeal or the Divisional Courts it is necessary to be given permission or leave to appeal to the House of Lords. Under the Administration of Justice (Appeals) Act 1934 this leave can be given by either the House of Lords or the lower court. It is difficult to get leave to appeal, with only about one in three cases being granted leave.

In leapfrog cases from the High Court under the Administration of Justice Act 1969, not only must the House of Lords give permission to appeal, but the trial judge must also grant a certificate of satisfaction. This will be done only if the case involves a point of law of general public importance which *either* involves the interpretation of a statute *or* is one where the trial judge is bound by a previous decision of the Court of Appeal or House of Lords. This would mean that an appeal to the Court of Appeal would be of no effect as it would also be bound by that previous decision. Leapfrog appeals are rare, with permission to appeal being asked for in only two or three cases each year.

The number of appeals heard by the House of Lords is small; usually about 60 cases per year involving civil law with about three-quarters of these involving a question of statutory interpretation.

 Internet Research

Use the Internet to look up cases in which there has been an appeal to the House of Lords and which are waiting for the appeal to be heard. This can be found on **www.parliament.uk**.

2.7.4 The Supreme Court

The Constitutional Reform Act 2005 has provision for the Judicial Committee of the House of Lords to be replaced by a Supreme Court. This Supreme Court will not be part of Parliament. This will make the judiciary completely separate from the legislature.

The first members of the Supreme Court will be the existing judges from the House of Lords. It is intended that the Supreme Court will start work in 2009.

The role of the court will be the same as that of the House of Lords.

2.8 Appeal routes in civil cases

Although the detail on the appellate courts is given in section 2.7, it is probably helpful to have a list of the normal appeal routes from both the County Court and the High Court.

2.8.1 Appeals from the County Court

Since May 2000, the appeal routes from the County Court are as set out in Part 52 of the Civil Procedure Rules. This means that generally:

- for fast-track cases dealt with by a District Judge the appeal is heard by a Circuit Judge
- for fast-track cases dealt with by a Circuit Judge the appeal is heard by a High Court Judge
- for final decisions in multi-track cases heard in the County Court (whether by a Circuit Judge or by a District Judge) the right of appeal is to the Court of Appeal.

Appeals from small claims

Since October 2000 appeals against decisions in small claims cases have been possible. This right of appeal was introduced in order to comply with Art 6 (the right to a fair trial) of the European Convention on Human Rights. The appeal routes are the same as for fast-track cases. This means that the appeal is to the next judge up in the hierarchy, so if the case was tried by a District Judge the appeal is to a Circuit Judge; if the case was dealt with by a Circuit Judge then the appeal is to a High Court Judge.

Second appeals

Where the first appeal is heard by a Circuit Judge or a High Court Judge, then there is a possible further appeal to the Court of Appeal. However, this will only happen in exceptional cases, as s 55 of the Access to Justice Act 1999 states that:

> *no appeal may be made to the Court of Appeal . . . unless the Court of Appeal considers that*
> *(a) the appeal would raise an important point of principle or practice, or*
> *(b) there is some other compelling reason for the Court of Appeal to hear it.*

These appeal routes are shown in Figure 2.6.

Figure 2.6 Appeal routes from the County Court

2.8.2 Appeals from the High Court

1. From a decision in the High Court the appeal usually goes to the Court of Appeal (Civil Division).
2. In rare cases there may be a 'leapfrog' appeal direct to the House of Lords under the Administration of Justice Act 1969. Such an appeal must involve a point of law of general public importance which either concerns the interpretation of a statute or involves a binding precedent of the Court of Appeal or the House of Lords which the trial judge must follow. In addition, the House of Lords has to give permission to appeal.

These appeal routes are shown in Figure 2.7.

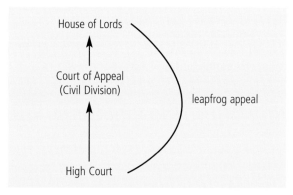

Figure 2.7 Appeal routes from the High Court

2.8.3 Further appeals

From a decision of the Court of Appeal there is a further appeal to the House of Lords, but only if the House of Lords or Court of Appeal gives permission to appeal. Also note that if a point of European law is involved, the case may be referred to the European Court of Justice under Art 234 of the Treaty of Rome. Such a referral can be made by any English court.

2.9 Tribunals

As well as courts, there are also tribunals for specific types of dispute. For example, employment disputes over unfair dismissal or redundancy are dealt with in employment tribunals. Social security tribunals deal with disputes over eligibility to social security benefits.

Tribunals are not part of the court system, but operate alongside it. Tribunals are more informal and cheaper than courts. Decisions are usually made by a panel of three. The chairman is usually legally qualified, while the other two have some connection with the type of disputes being dealt with. For example, in an employment tribunal one person will be involved in management while the other will be a worker.

Examination Questions

(a) Describe the jurisdiction of both the High Court and the County Court in civil cases, including the track system.

(b) Discuss the problems of using the civil courts to solve disputes.

OCR G141 January 2007

Chapter 3

Alternative methods of dispute resolution

I n Chapter 2 we saw that using the courts to resolve disputes can be costly, in terms of both money and time. It can also be traumatic for the individuals involved and may not lead to the most satisfactory outcome for the case. An additional problem is that court proceedings are usually open to the public and the press, so there is nothing to stop the details of the case being published in local or national newspapers. It is not surprising, therefore, that more and more people and businesses are seeking other methods of resolving their disputes. Alternative methods are referred to as 'ADR', which stands for 'Alternative Dispute Resolution', and include any method of resolving a dispute without resorting to using the courts. There are many different methods which can be used, ranging from very informal negotiations between the parties to a comparatively formal commercial arbitration hearing.

3.1 Negotiation

Anyone who has a dispute with another person can always try to resolve it by negotiating directly with them. This has the advantage of being completely private, and is also the quickest and cheapest method of settling a dispute. If the parties cannot come to an agreement, they may decide to take the step of instructing solicitors, and those solicitors will usually try to negotiate a settlement. In fact, even when court proceedings have been commenced, the lawyers for the parties will often continue to negotiate on behalf of their clients, and this is reflected in the high number of cases which are settled out of court. Once lawyers are involved, there will be a cost element – clearly, the longer negotiations go on, the higher the costs will be. One of the worrying aspects is the number of cases that drag on for years, only to end in an agreed settlement literally 'at the door of the court' on the morning that the trial is due to start. It is this situation that other alternative dispute resolution methods are aimed at avoiding.

To encourage more use of ADR, the judges in the civil courts can ask the parties to consider using an alternative method.

3.2 Mediation

This is where a neutral mediator helps the parties to reach a compromise solution. The role of a mediator is to consult with each party and see how much common ground there is between them. He will explore the position with each party, looking at their needs and carrying offers to and fro, while keeping confidentiality. A mediator will not usually tell the parties his own views of the merits of the dispute; his job is to act as a 'facilitator', so that an agreement is reached by the parties. However, a mediator can be asked for an opinion of the merits, and in this case the mediation becomes more of an evaluation exercise, which again aims at ending the dispute.

Mediation is only suitable if there is some hope that the parties can co-operate. Companies which are used to negotiating contracts with each other are most likely to benefit from this approach. Mediation can also take different forms, and the parties will choose the exact method they want. The important point in mediation is that the parties are in control: they make the decisions.

3.2.1 Formalised settlement conference

This is a more formal method of approaching mediation. It involves a 'mini-trial' where each side presents its case to a panel composed of a decision-making executive from each party, and a neutral party. Once all the submissions have been made, the executives, with the help of the neutral adviser, will evaluate the two sides' positions and try to come to an agreement. If the executives cannot agree, the neutral adviser will act as a mediator between them. Even if the whole matter is not resolved, this type of procedure may be able to narrow down the issues so that if the case does go to court, it will not take so long.

An advantage of mediation and mini-trials is that the decision need not be a strictly legal one sticking to the letter of the law. It is more likely to be based on commercial commonsense and compromise. The method will also make it easier for companies to continue to do business with each other in the future, and it may include agreements about the conduct of future business between the parties. This is something that cannot happen if the court gives judgment, as the court is only concerned with the present dispute. It avoids the adversarial conflict of the court room and the winner/loser result of court proceedings – it has been said that with mediation, everyone wins.

3.2.2 Mediation services

There are a growing number of commercial mediation services. One of the main ones is the Centre for Effective Dispute Resolution which was set up in London in 1991. It has many important companies as members including almost all of the big London law firms. Businesses say that using the Centre to resolve disputes has saved several thousands of pounds in court costs. The typical cost of a mediator is about £1,200 to £3,000 a day. This compares with potential litigation costs which are frequently over £100,000 and sometimes may even come to more than £1 million, especially in major commercial cases.

The main disadvantage of using mediation services is that there is no guarantee the matter will be resolved, and it will then be necessary to go to court after the failed attempt at mediation. In such situations there is additional cost and delay through trying mediation. However, the evidence is that a high number of cases will be resolved; the Centre for Effective Dispute Resolution claims that over 80 per cent of cases in which it is asked to act are settled. There is also the possibility that the issues may at least have been clarified, and so any court hearing will be shorter than if mediation had not been attempted.

There are also mediation services aimed at resolving smaller disputes, for example those between neighbours. An example of such a service is the West Kent Independent Mediation Service. This offers a free service that will try to help resolve disagreements between neighbours arising from such matters as noise, car-parking, dogs or boundary fence disputes. The Service is run by trained volunteers who will not take sides or make judgements on the rights and wrongs of an issue. They will usually visit the party who has made the complaint to hear their side of the matter, then, if that party agrees, ask to visit the other person and get their point of view. Finally, if both parties are willing, the mediator arranges a meeting between them in a neutral place. The parties are in control and can withdraw from the mediation process at any time.

The latest idea is Online Dispute Resolution. There are an increasing number of websites offering this, eg www.theclaimroom.com and www.mediate.com/odr.

Comment

Research into mediation has found some interesting facts showing that it has advantages and disadvantages. On the positive side it has been noted that, even if the actual mediation session did not resolve the dispute, the parties were more likely to settle the case without going to court than in non-mediated cases. However, there are also disadvantages. Amounts paid in mediated settlements are often lower than the amounts agreed in other settlements and considerably lower than amounts awarded by the courts.

Another problem is that successful mediation requires a skilled mediator with 'natural talent, honed skills and accumulated experience'. If these qualities are not present mediation can become a bullying exercise in which the weaker party may be forced into a settlement. This was recognised by one person who said:

'*Leaning on people is the only way that you will get a settlement. If you lean on two halves of a see-saw it is usually the weaker half that will break and that is where you should apply your effort.*'

However, overall it appears that voluntary mediation can promote early settlement and can lead to a situation in which the sense of grievance is reduced and an acceptable settlement reached.

3.3 Conciliation

This has similarities to mediation in that a neutral third party helps to resolve the dispute, but the main difference is that the conciliator will usually

Negotiation	Parties themselves
Mediation	Parties with help of neutral third party
Conciliation	Parties with help of neutral third party who plays an active role in suggesting a solution
Arbitration	Parties agree to let third party make a binding decision
Litigation	Parties go to court and a judge decides the case

Figure 3.1 Methods of dispute resolution

play a more active role. He will be expected to suggest grounds for compromise, and the possible basis for a settlement. In industrial disputes ACAS can give an impartial opinion on the legal position. As with mediation, conciliation does not necessarily lead to a resolution and it may be necessary to continue with a court action.

3.4 Arbitration

The word 'arbitration' is used to cover two quite different processes. The first is where the courts use a more informal procedure to hear cases; this is the way proceedings in the Commercial Court of the Queen's Bench Division are described. The second meaning of the word 'arbitration' is where the parties agree to submit their claims to private arbitration; this is the type of arbitration that is relevant to alternative dispute resolution, as it is another way of resolving a dispute without the need for a court case.

Private arbitration is now governed by the Arbitration Act 1996 and s 1 of that Act sets out the principles behind it. This says that:

> (a) the object of arbitration is to obtain the fair resolution of disputes by an impartial tribunal without unnecessary delay or expense;
>
> (b) the parties should be free to agree how their disputes are resolved, subject only to such safeguards as are necessary in the public interest.

So, arbitration is the voluntary submission by the parties, of their dispute, to the judgment of some person other than a judge. Such an agreement will usually be in writing, and indeed the Arbitration Act 1996 applies only to written arbitration agreements. The precise way in which the arbitration is carried out is left almost entirely to the parties' agreement.

3.4.1 The agreement to arbitrate

The agreement to go to arbitration can be made by the parties at any time. It can be before a dispute arises or when the dispute becomes apparent. Many commercial contracts include what is called a *Scott v Avery* clause, which is a clause where the parties in their original contract agree that in the event of a dispute arising between them, they will have that dispute settled by arbitration. Figure 3.2 shows a *Scott v Avery* clause in the author's contract for writing this book.

Where there is an arbitration agreement in a contract, the Arbitration Act 1996 states that the court will normally refuse to deal with any dispute; the matter must go to arbitration as agreed by the parties. However, the rules are different for consumer claims where the dispute is for an amount which can be dealt with in the small claims track. In such circumstances the consumer may choose whether to abide by the agreement to go to private arbitration, or whether to insist that the case be heard in the small claims track.

An agreement to go to arbitration can also be

Arbitration

24. If any difference shall arise between the PROPRIETOR and the PUBLISHERS touching the meaning of this Agreement or the rights and liabilities of the parties hereto, the same shall in the first instance be referred to the informal Disputes Settlement Scheme of the Publishers' Association, and failing agreed submission by both parties to such Scheme shall be referred to the arbitration of two persons (one to be named by each party) or their mutually agreed umpire in accordance with the provisions of the Arbitration Act 1996, or any amending or substituted statute for the time being in force.

Figure 3.2 Arbitration clause from author's contract

made after the dispute arises. Arbitration is becoming increasingly popular in commercial cases.

3.4.2 The arbitrator

Section 15 of the Arbitration Act 1996 states that the parties are free to agree on the number of arbitrators, so that a panel of two or three may be used or there may be a sole arbitrator. If the parties cannot agree on a number then the Act provides that only one arbitrator should be appointed. The Act also says that the parties are free to agree on the procedure for appointing an arbitrator. In fact most agreements to go to arbitration will either name an arbitrator or provide a method of choosing one. In commercial contracts it is often provided that the president of the appropriate trade organisation will appoint the arbitrator.

There is also the Institute of Arbitrators which provides trained arbitrators for major disputes. In many cases the arbitrator will be someone who has expertise in the particular field involved in the dispute, but if the dispute involves a point of law the parties may decide to appoint a lawyer. If there is no agreement on who or how to appoint, then, as a last resort, the court can be asked to appoint an appropriate arbitrator.

3.4.3 The arbitration hearing

The actual procedure is left to the agreement of the parties in each case, so that there are many forms of hearing. In some cases the parties may opt for a 'paper' arbitration, where the two sides

put all the points they wish to raise into writing and submit this, together with any relevant documents, to the arbitrator. He will then read all the documents, and make his decision. Alternatively, the parties may send all these documents to the arbitrator, but before he makes his decision both parties will attend a hearing at which they make oral submissions to the arbitrator to support their case. Where necessary, witnesses can be called to give evidence. If witnesses are asked to give evidence orally then this will not normally be given on oath, ie the person will not have to swear to tell the truth. However, if the parties wish, then the witness can be asked to give evidence on oath and the whole procedure will be very formal. If witnesses are called to give evidence, the Arbitration Act 1996 allows for the use of court procedures to ensure the attendance of those witnesses.

The date, time and place of the arbitration hearing are all matters for the parties to decide in consultation with the arbitrator. This gives a great degree of flexibility to the proceedings; the parties can choose what is most convenient for all the people concerned.

3.4.4 The award

The decision made by the arbitrator is called an 'award' and is binding on the parties. It can even be enforced through the courts if necessary. The decision is usually final, though it can be challenged in the courts on the grounds of serious irregularity in the proceedings or on a point of law (s 68 Arbitration Act 1996).

D Complaints

3. Disputes arising out of, or in connection with, this contract which cannot be amicably settled may (if you so wish) be referred to arbitration under a special scheme devised by arrangement with the Association of British Travel Agents (ABTA) but administered independently by the Chartered Institute of Arbitrators. The scheme provides for a simple and inexpensive method of Arbitration on documents alone, with restricted liability on you in respect of costs. The scheme does not apply to claims greater than £1,500 per person or £7,500 per booking form or to claims which are solely or mainly in respect of physical injury or illness or the consequences of such injury or illness. If you elect to use the scheme, written notice requesting arbitration must be made within 9 months after the scheduled date of return from holiday.

Figure 3.3 Optional arbitration clause in a consumer contract

3.4.5 Advantages of arbitration

There are several advantages which largely arise from the fact that the parties have the freedom to make their own arbitration agreement, and decide exactly how formal or informal they wish it to be. The main advantages are:

- the parties may choose their own arbitrator, and can therefore decide whether the matter is best dealt with by a technical expert or by a lawyer or by a professional arbitrator
- if there is a question of quality this can be decided by an expert in the particular field, saving the expense of calling expert witnesses and the time that would be used in explaining all the technicalities to a judge
- the hearing time and place can be arranged to suit parties
- the actual procedure used is flexible and the parties can choose that which is most suited to the situation; this will usually result in a more informal and relaxed hearing than in court
- the matter is dealt with in private and there will be no publicity
- the dispute will be resolved more quickly than through a court hearing
- arbitration proceedings are usually much cheaper than going to court
- the award is normally final and can be enforced through the courts.

3.4.6 Disadvantages of arbitration

However, there are some disadvantages of arbitration, especially where the parties are not on an equal footing as regards their ability to present their case. This is because legal aid is not available for arbitration and this may disadvantage an individual in a case against a business; if the case had gone to court, a person on a low income would have qualified for legal aid and so had the benefit of a lawyer to present their case. The other main disadvantages are that:

- an unexpected legal point may arise in the case which is not suitable for decision by a non-lawyer arbitrator
- if a professional arbitrator is used, his fees may be expensive
- it will also be expensive if the parties opt for a formal hearing, with witnesses giving evidence and lawyers representing both sides
- the rights of appeal are limited
- the delays for commercial and international arbitration when a professional arbitrator and lawyers are used may be nearly as great as those in the courts.

This problem of delay and expense has meant that arbitration has, to some extent, lost its popularity with companies as a method of dispute resolution. More and more businesses are turning to the alternatives offered by centres such as the Centre for Dispute Resolution or, in the case of international disputes, are choosing to have the matter resolved in another country. One of the problems was that the law on arbitration had become complex and the Arbitration Act 1996 is an attempt to improve the process. In general it can be said that certain types of dispute are suitable for arbitration. This especially includes commercial disagreements between two businesses where the parties have little hope of finding sufficient common ground to make mediation a realistic prospect, and provided there is no major point of law involved.

Activity

Find an arbitration clause in a consumer contract, for example for a package holiday or insurance or for a mobile phone.

 ## Internet Research

Look up websites for ADR organisations. Try:

www.adrgroup.co.uk
www.cedr.com

Examination Questions

(a) Describe the different methods of Alternative Dispute Resolution available to deal with civil disputes.

(b) Discuss the advantages of using Alternative Dispute Resolution rather than using the courts.

OCR G141 June 2007

Chapter 4

Police powers

The police need to have powers to investigate crimes. So Parliament has given them special powers which can be used in certain circumstances. These powers include the right to stop suspects, to search them, to arrest and interview people, and to take fingerprints and DNA samples.

Without these powers it would be impossible to investigate crimes. However, it is important that people are not unnecessarily harassed by the police and that suspects are protected from unfair treatment. The law, therefore, also sets out certain rights that all suspects have.

Most of the police powers are set out in the Police and Criminal Evidence Act 1984. This is usually abbreviated to PACE. There are eight codes of practice giving more detail on the use of the various powers. These Codes are:

- Code A on stop and search powers
- Code B on powers to search premises and seize property
- Code C dealing with the detention and questioning of suspects
- Code D on the rules for identification procedures
- Code E on the tape-recording of interviews with suspects
- Code F on visual recording with sound of interviews (ie videoing interviews)
- Code G on powers of arrest
- Code H on detention, treatment and questioning of those arrested under s 41 of the Terrorism Act 2000.

4.1 Powers to stop and search

The purpose of stop and search powers is to enable police officers to check out their suspicions without having to arrest the suspect. If the stop and search does not find anything then it has been a quick way of checking, rather than having to arrest the individual and take them to a police station.

4.1.1 Powers under PACE

The main police power to stop and search people is given under s 1 of PACE. This gives the police the right to stop and search people and vehicles in a public place. 'Public place' not only means the street, but also includes areas such as car parks. It can even include a garden if the police officer has a good reason for believing that the person does not live at that address.

To stop and search under PACE, a police officer must have reasonable grounds for suspecting that the person is in possession of (or the vehicle contains) stolen goods or prohibited articles. Prohibited articles include items such as offensive weapons (this includes knives and other sharp objects) and articles for use in connection with burglary or theft or criminal damage.

As these powers are very wide there are safeguards. PACE states that the police officer must give his name and station. If this is not done then the search may be unlawful. This was shown in *Osman v DPP* (1999) where the officers did not give their names or station. The Queen's Bench Divisional Court held this made the search of Mr Osman unlawful and so he could not be guilty of assaulting the police in the execution of their duty. Also, if the officer fails to give the reason for the search, then that search is unlawful.

If the search is in public, the police can only request that the suspect removes outer coat, jacket and gloves (s 2(9) of PACE). The police officer must also make a written report as soon as possible after the search.

If the officer wishes to make a more thorough search, for example asking the suspect to take off their shoes or their T-shirt, then this must be done out of public view. It can be done in a police van.

Detention for the purposes of a search must take place at or near the location of the stop.

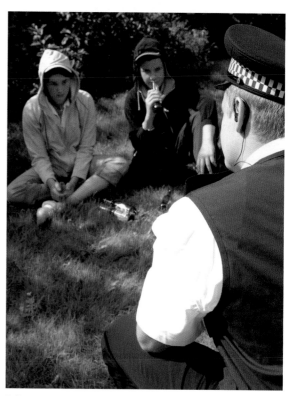

Police questioning some teenagers

4.1.2 Code A

Police Code of Practice A under PACE contains guidance on when the powers to stop and search should be used. The Code stresses that powers to stop and search must be used fairly, responsibly, with respect for people being searched and without unlawful discrimination.

Paragraph 2.2 of the code says:

 Reasonable suspicion can never be supported on the basis of personal factors alone without reliable supporting intelligence or some specific behaviour by the person concerned.

> For example, a person's race, age, appearance, or the fact that the person is known to have a previous conviction cannot be used alone or in combination with each other as the reason for searching that person. ""

The Code stresses that there must be an objective basis for stopping and searching someone. This will normally be from information, such as information that the person is carrying a knife, or the fact that a person has been seen carrying a type of article known to have been stolen recently in the area. Reasonable suspicion can also come from the behaviour of the suspect, for example if an officer encounters someone on the street at night who is obviously trying to hide something.

Appearance

There is one situation when a police officer may base his suspicions on appearance. This is where there is reliable information that members of a group or gang habitually carry knives unlawfully or weapons or controlled drugs, and wear a distinctive item of clothing or other means of showing that they are members of the group or gang. In these circumstances that distinctive item of clothing or other means of showing membership may provide reasonable grounds to stop and search a person.

4.1.3 Other powers to stop and search

As well as PACE there are also other Acts of Parliament which give the police the right to stop and search people. Two important powers are

- under the Misuse of Drugs Act 1971 which gives the police the power to stop and search for controlled drugs and
- under the Terrorism Act 2000 which gives the police powers to stop and search where there is reasonable suspicion that the person is involved in terrorism.

Under the Terrorism Act the police have more powers of search than under PACE. The police can ask a suspect to remove their headgear and their shoes.

In addition, s 60 of the Criminal Justice and Public Order Act 1994 gives the police the right to stop and search in anticipation of violence. This type of stop and search can only take place where it has been authorised by a senior police officer who reasonably believes that serious violence may take place in the area. An interesting feature of this right to stop and search is that once it has been authorised, any police officer acting under it does not have to have reasonable suspicion about the individual he stops. Section 60(5) says that: 'A constable may, in the exercise of those powers, stop any person or vehicle and make any search he thinks fit whether or not he has any grounds for suspecting that the person or vehicle is carrying weapons or (dangerous) articles . . . '

This right to stop and search without any reason to suspect the individual who is stopped can be seen as an infringement of civil liberties. However, at least such rights are of limited duration as the senior police officer authorising such stop and search powers can only do so for a period of 24 hours.

Another interesting power is given by s 60AA of the Criminal Justice and Public Order Act 1994. This allows police officers to ask a person to remove any item that they have reasonable grounds for believing is being worn to conceal that person's identity. This would include asking for the removal of a scarf or any item covering the face.

Voluntary searches

A voluntary search is where a person is prepared to be searched voluntarily. Since 2004, Code of Practice A has made it clear that a voluntary search can only be made where a power to search already exists. All voluntary searches must be made in accordance with the law and the provisions of Code A. This includes the fact that voluntary searches must be recorded in writing.

Find out which other Acts of Parliament give the police the right to stop and search people. These are listed towards the end of Code A.

Look up Code A on the Internet. Try **http://police.homeoffice.gov.uk** and search for PACE Codes of Practice.

4.1.4 Problems of stop and search powers

Home Office statistics show that following the introduction of PACE rules the police made increasing use of the power to stop and search. The number of stops and searches rose from just over 100,000 in 1986 to well over a million in 1998.

In 1999 the MacPherson Report on the Stephen Lawrence case was published. Stephen Lawrence was a black youth who was stabbed to death in South London. The police investigation into the case was very badly handled. The report found that there was 'institutionalised racism' in the Metropolitan Police.

Following this report the police reviewed their methods of working and one of the changes was to try to limit the use of stops and searches. In the year immediately after the publication of the MacPherson Report there was a 21 per cent decrease in stops and searches nationwide. In the Metropolitan Police force area the decrease was even higher, at 41 per cent.

Despite this, it still appears that certain groups are more likely to be stopped and searched than others. In particular, a Home Office publication, *Statistics on Race and the Criminal Justice System, 2005*, shows that black people are six times more likely to be stopped and searched than any other group. This figure is calculated on the resident population in each police area.

However, research by Miller, Quinton and Bland in 2000 considered the population 'available' at sites where stops and searches were carried out. 'Available' meant the type of people actually out in public places at the time. They found that there were high numbers of young men and people from ethnic minority groups in such places. The research showed that when comparing those stopped and searched with the 'available' population, there were no significant

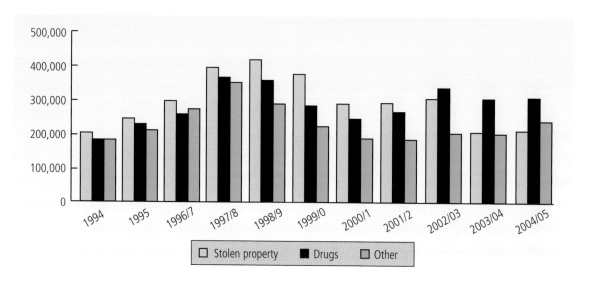

Figure 4.1 Number of stops and searches by reasons for search

Source: Home Office Statistical Bulletin 21/05

differences between racial groups in the number of stops and searches made.

Since 2000 there have been about 850,000 stops and searches each year. This is shown in Figure 4.1.

Balance of interests

The main difficulty with using stop and search powers is achieving the balance between crime prevention and interfering with human rights. A very sensitive area is in relation to items worn for religious reasons. This is why the normal stop and search powers under PACE do not allow the police to ask for the removal of headgear in public.

However, the importance of being able to ask people to remove items that may be concealing their identity was shown by the case of one of the failed bombers in the London bombing of July 2005. It was discovered that the man had initially avoided detection by leaving the city dressed in a burka which covered him completely.

Does stop and search lead to arrest?

Before 1999, only 10 per cent of those stopped and searched were then arrested. In these 10 per cent of cases the search was justified as it revealed that the suspect was indeed in possession of stolen goods or prohibited items. However, in the other 90 per cent of cases it appears that over 900,000 people were stopped and searched unnecessarily each year.

In 2000, when the number of stops and searches went down, 13 per cent ended with an arrest. This shows that a more targeted approach to stop and search is more likely to produce an arrest.

Early statistics also show this. In 1996, the number of stops and searches in the Tottenham area of London was reduced by over 50 per cent from the previous year. The proportion of arrests increased from 10 per cent to 17 per cent. However, there was also an increase of 17 per cent in crimes such as burglary and street robbery in the area. So, fewer stops and searches may not be as effective in crime prevention.

Activity

State whether there has been a lawful stop and search in the following situations. Give reasons for your answers.

1. A member of the public tells a police officer that Zak has been holding a shiny object which looked like a knife. The officer stops Zak and tells Zak he will be searched as the officer believes he is carrying a knife. The officer does not tell Zak his identity or station.

2. Yan, who has six previous convictions for theft and burglary, is stopped by a police officer when he is walking home late one night. The officer tells Yan that he is going to be searched. When Yan asks why, the officer says 'With your history, there's always a reason'.

3. The police have a report of a burglary late at night. As two officers drive to the scene of the burglary, they see Sean walking along a nearby road carrying a holdall. The police stop Sean. They identify themselves and tell Sean they want to search him for stolen goods. They look in the holdall, but find it only has clothes in it. Then they tell Sean to take off his jacket and his shoes. Sean does this. The police find nothing and let Sean go.

4.2 Powers of arrest

Where an offence has been or may have been committed, or is being or may be being committed, or is about to be committed, then the police have powers to arrest anyone they reasonably suspect of the offence. The powers of arrest under PACE were completely changed at the end of 2005. Powers to arrest are clearly necessary for protection of the public and prevention of crime. The problem is whether the powers introduced at the end of 2005 are too wide. The powers are explained in the next section.

4.2.1 Powers of arrest under PACE

Section 24 of PACE sets out the powers the police have to arrest suspects. These powers were completely changed at the end of 2005 by the Serious Organised Crime and Police Act 2005 (SOCPA). Section 110 of SOCPA substituted a new s 24 into PACE.

Previously there had to be an arrestable offence, but now an arrest can be made for any offence. The new s 24 of PACE says:

> s 24(1) 'A constable may arrest without a warrant –
>
> (a) anyone who is about to commit an offence;

(b) anyone who is in the act of committing an offence;

(c) anyone whom he has reasonable grounds for suspecting to be about to commit an offence;

(d) anyone whom he has reasonable grounds for suspecting to be committing an offence.'

s 24(2) 'If a constable has reasonable grounds for suspecting that an offence has been committed, he may arrest anyone without a warrant whom he has reasonable grounds to suspect of being guilty of it.'

TIMING	EVENT	SECTION
PAST **Actual offence**	anyone who is guilty of the offence	24(3)(a)
	anyone whom the constable reasonably suspects to be guilty	24(3)(b)
PAST **Suspected offences**	where a constable has reasonable grounds for suspecting that an offence has been committed he can arrest anyone whom he reasonably suspects to be guilty of it	24(2)
PRESENT	anyone who is in the act of committing an offence	24(1)(b)
	anyone whom the constable has reasonable grounds for suspecting to be committing an offence	24(1)(d)
FUTURE	anyone who is about to commit an offence	24(1)(a)
	anyone whom the constable has reasonable grounds for suspecting to be about to commit an offence	24(1)(c)

Figure 4.2 Police powers of arrest

s 24(3) 'If an offence has been committed, a constable may arrest without a warrant –

(a) anyone who is guilty of the offence;

(b) anyone whom he has reasonable grounds for suspecting to be guilty of it.'

It is easier to think of these powers by considering whether the offence (or possible offence) has been committed in the past, is being committed in the present or is about to be committed in the future. Figure 4.2 gives a summary showing this.

These are very wide powers of arrest, but there is a 'necessity' test which sets limits on when an officer has the power to arrest. However, these limitations are not thought to be adequate.

Necessity test

An arresting officer can only arrest if he has reasonable grounds for believing that it is necessary to make the arrest for one of the following reasons:

- to enable the person's name or address to be ascertained
- to prevent the person:
  - causing physical injury to himself or any other person
  - suffering physical injury
  - causing loss of or damage to property
  - committing an offence against public decency
  - causing an unlawful obstruction of the highway
- to protect a child or other vulnerable person
- to allow the prompt and effective investigation of the offence or of the conduct of the person
- to prevent any prosecution for the offence from being hindered by the disappearance of the person in question.

These last two grounds are themselves open to abuse as they could be claimed to exist in most cases.

4.2.2 PACE Code of Practice G

Code of Practice G gives guidelines for arrest under these powers. It stresses that a lawful arrest requires two elements:

- a person's involvement or suspected involvement or attempted involvement AND
- reasonable grounds for believing that the person's arrest is necessary.

The Code also states that arresting officers are 'required to inform the person arrested that they have been arrested, even if this fact is obvious and of the relevant circumstances in respect to both elements'.

The Code points out that the power to arrest is only exercisable if the constable has reasonable grounds for believing that it is necessary to arrest the person. It remains an operational decision at the discretion of the arresting officer as to:

- what action he may take at the point of contact with the individual
- the necessity criteria, if any, which apply
- whether to arrest, report for summons, grant street bail, issue a fixed penalty notice or take any other action open to the officer.

This part of the Code shows how much discretion is given to police officers.

4.2.3 Other powers of arrest

Arrest for breaching police bail

The Criminal Justice and Public Order Act 1994 added an extra power of arrest into PACE. This is now in s 46A of PACE and gives the police the right to arrest without a warrant anyone who, having been released on police bail, fails to attend at the police station at the set time.

Arrest for breach of the peace

As well as rights given by Acts of Parliament, the police retain a common law right to arrest where there has been or is likely to be a breach of the peace. This applies even if the behaviour complained of was on private premises as demonstrated by the case of *McConnell v Chief Constable of the Greater Manchester Police* (1990). In this case the manager of a carpet store had asked McConnell to leave, but he had refused to do so. A police officer had then taken McConnell outside, but he attempted to re-enter, so the office arrested him for conduct whereby a breach of the peace might be occasioned. McConnell later sued the police for false imprisonment arguing that the arrest was unlawful as a breach of the peace could not occur on private premises, but the Court of Appeal held that it could do so and the arrest was lawful.

In *Bibby v Chief Constable of Essex Police* (2000), the Court of Appeal summarised the conditions that must apply for this common law power of arrest to be used. The conditions are:

- there must be a sufficiently real and present threat to the peace
- the threat must come from the person to be arrested
- the conduct of that person must clearly interfere with the rights of others and its natural consequence must be 'not wholly unreasonable' violence from a third party
- the conduct of the person to be arrested must be unreasonable.

Arrest with a warrant

The police may make an application to a magistrate for a warrant to arrest a named person. Such a warrant is issued under s 1 of the Magistrates' Court Act 1980 which requires written information, supported by evidence on oath showing that a person has committed or is suspected of committing an offence.

A warrant for arrest allows the police to enter and search the suspect's home for the purpose of making the arrest.

Arrest by private citizens

The Serious Organised Crime and Police Act 2005 also created a new s 24A in PACE. This sets out

the rights of private citizens to make an arrest. The first point is that private citizens can only make an arrest in respect of indictable offences.

The arrest can be made if someone is in the act of committing an indictable offence or where the citizen has reasonable grounds for suspecting the person to be committing an indictable offence. A private citizen can also arrest where there has been an indictable offence and there are reasonable grounds for suspecting the person to be guilty of it.

However, there are also limitations. It must appear that it is not reasonably practicable for a constable to make the arrest and it must be necessary because the citizen has reasonable grounds to believe the arrest is necessary to prevent the person:

- causing physical injury to himself or any other person
- suffering physical injury
- causing loss of or damage to property
- making off before a constable can assume responsibility for him.

4.2.4 Comment on powers of arrest

Manner of arrest

Whenever the police make an arrest they should at the time of, or as soon as practicable afterwards, tell the person arrested that they are under arrest and the reason for it, even if it is perfectly obvious why they are being arrested. There is no set form of words to be used and, as is often portrayed in television dramas, it is sufficient if the arresting officer says something like 'You're nicked for theft'.

Where necessary, both the police and private citizens making an arrest may use reasonable force.

Lawful arrest

In *Taylor v Chief Constable of Thames Valley Police* (2004) the Court of Appeal held that the test whether the words of arrest were sufficient is:

was the person arrested told in simple non-technical language that they could understand the essential legal and factual grounds for his arrest?

Taylor was a 10-year-old boy who had been throwing stones during an anti-vivisection demo. When he was present at a later protest he was identified by a police officer who said: 'I am arresting you on suspicion of violent disorder on April 18, 1998 at Hillgrove Farm.'

The Court of Appeal held that this was understandable and so there was a lawful arrest.

The right to search an arrested person

Where a person has been arrested the police have a right to search that person for anything which might be used to help an escape or anything which might be evidence relating to an offence. If such a search takes place in public the police can only require the suspect to remove outer coat, jacket and gloves.

4.3 Powers of detention

Once a person has been arrested and taken to a police station, there are rules setting out very strict time limits on how long they may be held there. There are also rules about the treatment of people in detention; these are contained in PACE and Code of Practice C.

Anyone brought to a police station must be brought before the custody officer as soon as practicable after their arrival at the police station. The custody officer must start a custody record in which all events at the police station in relation to the suspect must be written down. This will include the time of arrival and the reason why they have been brought to the police station and any reviews of the detention. The custody officer must also record any visits to the detainee in the cell in which he is detained or any other event which occurs.

4.3.1 Time limits under PACE

The general rules on detention are that the police may detain a person for 24 hours. After that the police can detain the suspect for another 12 hours (making a total of 36 hours), but only with the permission of a senior officer (superintendent or above).

After 36 hours those being detained must be released unless they are detained in connection with an indictable offence. In these circumstances the police have the right to apply to the Magistrates' Court for permission to hold the detainee for a longer period. The magistrates can order detention for a maximum total of 96 hours.

Where the police apply to magistrates for the right to detain a suspect beyond 36 hours, the suspect has the right to be legally represented in order to oppose the police application. Applications for the right to detain someone

Activity

State whether there has been a lawful arrest in the following situations. Give reasons for your answers.

1. After an incident in which a man was stabbed and seriously hurt, a police officer grabs hold of Damon. When Damon protests and asks why, the police officer says 'You know what it's for'. The police officer did not see the incident but was told by someone else at the scene that Damon was responsible.
2. Tony, a taxi driver, sees Gary climbing out of the window of a house. Tony catches hold of Gary and takes him to a nearby police station.
3. Amanda is stopped by the police for speeding. When one of the police officers asks for her name, she replies 'Superwoman'. She is then asked for her address and refuses to give it. The police officer arrests her and takes her to the police station.

TIME FACTOR	EVENT(S)
Start of detention	Arrested person arrives at police station and the custody officer decides there is reason to detain him
Six hours	First review by custody officer
15 hours and every nine hours thereafter	Second and subsequent reviews by custody officer
24 hours	After 24 hours the permission of a superintendent or above is needed to extend the period of detention
36 hours	For summary and triable either way offences the police may NOT detain a suspect beyond 36 hours For indictable offences the police may apply to magistrates to extend the period of detention
96 hours	Maximum time for detaining an arrested person (except under the Terrorism Act 2000) Police must charge or release the suspect

Figure 4.3 Time limits on detention of a suspect

beyond the 36 hour period are only made in about 1 per cent of cases.

During the period of detention there must be regular reviews by the custody officer. The first review must be not later than six hours after the detention. Then reviews must take place at intervals of not less than nine hours. If at any time the custody officer decides that there are no grounds for continuing the detention, he is under a duty to order that the detainee be immediately released from custody.

Terrorism cases have different rules about periods of detention. See section 4.3.3.

Figure 4.3 sets out the time limits on detention of suspects.

4.3.2 Rights of a detained person

Detainees must be told their rights by the custody officer. These rights include:

- having someone informed of his arrest
- being told that independent legal advice is available free and being allowed to consult privately with a solicitor
- being allowed to consult the Code of Practice.

Code C states that each detainee must be given a written notice setting out these three rights.

The right to have someone informed of the arrest

The right to have someone informed of the arrest is given by s 56 of PACE. The arrested person can nominate any friend, relative or any other person who is likely to take an interest in their welfare. The person nominated by the detainee must be told of the arrest and where the person is being held.

This should normally be done as soon as practicable, but, in the case of an indictable offence, a senior police officer may authorise that there be a delay of up to 36 hours. This can only be done if there are reasonable grounds for believing that telling the named person will lead to interference with or harm to evidence or to other persons or the alerting of others involved in the offence or hinder the recovery of property obtained through the offence.

Code C states that, in addition to the right to have someone informed of the arrest, a detained person should be allowed to speak on the telephone 'for a reasonable time to one person'. If the suspect is under the age of 17 the police must also contact a person 'responsible for his welfare' and inform them of the arrest.

The right to legal advice

A detained person may either contact their own solicitor or they can use the system of duty solicitors which is provided free for anyone under arrest. In fact, the Code of Practice tries to make sure that detained people are aware of their right to legal advice. Under the Code the custody officer, when he authorises the detention of someone at the police station, must ask the suspect to sign the custody record at that time saying whether he wishes to have legal advice. Police stations must have posters 'prominently

displayed' advertising the right to free legal advice and an arrested suspect must not only be told orally of this right, but also given a written notice of it.

It is possible for a senior police officer to authorise a delay to a suspect's right to see a solicitor in the case of an indictable offence for up to 36 hours. However, this can only occur if there are reasonable grounds for believing that giving access to a solicitor will lead to interference with, or harm to, evidence or to other persons or the alerting of others involved in the offence or hinder the recovery of property obtained through the offence. The case of *R v Samuel* (1988) stressed that it would only be on rare occasions that such a delay was justified and that it must be based on specific aspects of the case, not a general assumption that access to a solicitor might lead to the alerting of accomplices.

Key facts

Right	Source	Comment
To have someone informed of detention	s 56 PACE	Can be delayed for up to 36 hours for an indictable offence
To be told of right to legal advice	s 58 PACE	Can be delayed for up to 36 hours for an indictable offence BUT only in exceptional circumstances *R v Samuel* (1988)
To consult the Codes of Practice	Code C	
Suspect must be given written notice of these three rights listed above		
To have an appropriate adult present at interview	Code C	Applies to those under 17 and also to mentally ill or handicapped *R v Aspinall* (1999)
To speak to someone on the telephone	Code C	Not compulsory – police can refuse this
To have adequately lit and ventilated accommodation To have regular meals To be allowed a continuous period of 8 hours rest in 24 hours	Code C	

Figure 4.4 Key facts chart on rights of suspects in police detention

In Samuel's case, the defendant was a 24-year-old man, whose mother had already been informed of her son's arrest some hours before he was refused access to a solicitor. The Court of Appeal felt that if anyone was likely to be alerted then it would already have happened and that there was no reason to deny Samuel his 'fundamental freedom' of consulting with a solicitor. As his final interview with the police had taken place after his solicitor had been refused access, the evidence of what was said at that interview was inadmissible in court and so Samuel's conviction for robbery was quashed.

In *R v Grant* (2005) the Court of Appeal held that the court would not tolerate illegal conduct by the police. In this case there had been deliberate interference by the police with the detained suspect's right to the confidence of privileged communication with his solicitor. This was such a serious abuse of process that it justified his conviction for murder being quashed.

Other rights

Code C states that cells must be adequately heated, cleaned, lit and ventilated. A suspect should be offered at least two light meals and one main meal in any 24 hours. Drinks should be provided at mealtimes and upon reasonable request between meals. In any period of 24 hours a detainee must also be allowed a continuous period of at least eight hours' rest.

4.3.3 Terrorism cases

Longer periods of detention are allowed where the suspect has been arrested for terrorism offences.

Sections 23–25 of the Terrorism Act 2006:

- enable prosecutors to apply for an extension of the detention warrant
- require approval by a magistrate for up to 14 days and by a senior judge for warrants over 14 days

- extend the maximum period of detention to 28 days
- amend the grounds for detention to include detention which is necessary pending the results of an examination or analysis of relevant evidence, or of anything which is being examined or analysed with a view to obtaining relevant evidence.

The Home Office want to extend the maximum time of detention to 42 days. Check the Internet (www.homeoffice.gov.uk) to see if this has happened.

Those detained in relation to terrorism have the same rights as other detainees to:

- have someone informed of his arrest
- be told that independent legal advice is available free and be allowed to consult privately with a solicitor
- be allowed to consult the relevant Code of Practice (Code H).

Where a suspect is held for more than 96 hours, then he must be visited by a healthcare professional at least once every 24 hours.

4.4 Police interviews of suspects

Any detained person may be questioned by the police. All interviews at a police station must be tape-recorded and some are video-recorded rather than just audio-taped.

Suspects have the right to have a solicitor present at any interview, unless it is one of the rare occasions referred to in *R v Samuel* (see section 4.3.2). However, if the suspect does not ask for a solicitor, the police may conduct the interview without one being present. In addition, if the matter is urgent or the solicitor is likely to be delayed for some time, the police have the right to start questioning a suspect before a solicitor arrives.

Interviews should take place in interview rooms which are adequately heated, lit and ventilated. The person being interviewed must be offered a seat. PACE Code C points out that they shall not be required to stand. There must be breaks from interviews at mealtimes and also short refreshment breaks about every two hours.

4.4.1 Tape recording

Two copies of the tape recording are made. One is a master copy which is sealed. The other is the working copy which can be checked by the suspect or his lawyers.

At the start of each interview the police must start the tape by recording the time and who is present at the interview. At the end of the recording, the police must state the time it finishes.

4.4.2 Appropriate adult

If the suspect is under the age of 17 or is mentally handicapped then there must be an 'appropriate adult' present during all interviews. This right is in addition to the right to legal advice.

In *R v Aspinall* (1999), the Court of Appeal ruled that a defendant who was suffering from schizophrenia should have had an appropriate adult present when interviewed by the police. This was so even though the defendant appeared to be able to understand the police questions. As no appropriate adult had been present, the interview was not admissible as evidence.

4.4.3 Right to silence

Until the Criminal Justice and Public Order Act 1994 was enacted, defendants could refuse to answer any questions without any adverse conclusion being drawn on their silence. In fact, the previously used caution given before a police interview commenced contained the phrase 'you do not have to say anything'. However, the Government decided that this rule was allowing guilty people to go free and that the right to silence should be restricted. This was done by ss 34–39 of the Criminal Justice and Public Order Act 1994.

These sections allow inferences to be made from the fact that a defendant has refused to answer questions. As a result, the wording of the caution given to a suspect before interviewing commences now states:

> You do not have to say anything. But it may harm your defence if you do not mention when questioned something which you later rely on in court. Anything you do say may be given in evidence.

This change in the law does not mean that the defendant can be forced to speak; he can still remain silent. However, at any trial which follows the judge may comment on the defendant's failure to mention a crucial matter and this failure can form part of the evidence against him. It is argued that this alters the basic rule of criminal trials that the prosecution must prove the defendant's guilt.

However, a defendant's silence is not enough for a conviction on its own; there must be prosecution evidence as well.

4.4.4 Protection of suspects

The law gives some protection to suspects as to the way they should be treated whilst being detained and questioned. Section 76 of PACE states that the court shall not allow statements which have been obtained through oppression to be used as evidence.

'Oppression' is defined as including torture, inhuman or degrading treatment and the use of or threat of violence. As pointed out above, Code C also gives protection to suspects who are being questioned in regard to the physical conditions of the interview. For example, the Code states that interview rooms must be adequately lit, heated and ventilated and that suspects must be given adequate breaks for meals, refreshments and sleep.

In theory, the treatment of a suspect is monitored by the custody officer who is supposed to keep accurate records of all happenings during the detention period. This should include the length and timing of interviews and other matters such as visits of police officers to the defendant's cell, so that if there are any breaches of the rules this will be obvious. However, research by Sanders and Bridge suggests that a substantial minority of custody records (about 10 per cent) are falsified.

4.5 Searches, fingerprints and body samples

4.5.1 Searches

When a person is being held at a police station the police have no automatic right to search them. However, the custody officer has a duty to record everything a person has with him when he is brought to the police station, and if the custody officer thinks a search is necessary to carry out this duty, then a non-intimate search may be made.

Strip searches

These are defined in Code C as searches 'involving the removal of more than outer clothing'. The Code stresses that a strip search may only take place if it is necessary to remove an article which a person in detention should not be allowed to keep, and there is reasonable suspicion that the person might have such an article concealed on their person.

Such searches should not take place in an area where the search can be seen by any person who does not need to be present. No member of the opposite sex should be present during a strip search. Suspects should not normally be required to remove all their clothing at the same time. A man should be allowed to put his shirt back on before he removes his trousers and a woman should be given a robe or similar garment to wear once she has removed her top garment.

Intimate searches

In addition, a high-ranking police officer can authorise an intimate search if there is reason to believe that the person has with him an item which he could use to cause physical injury to himself or others or that he is in possession of a Class A drug.

An intimate search is defined as 'a search which consists of the physical examination of a person's body orifices other than the mouth'. If it is a drugs-related search then it may only be carried out by a suitably qualified person, for example a doctor or nurse. If it is a search for other items then, if practicable, it should be carried out by a suitably qualified person, but can be by another person if a high-ranking police officer authorises it.

4.5.2 Fingerprinting

Taking of fingerprints prior to arrest

Fingerprints can be taken prior to arrest away from the police station as it is now possible to check against the National Automated Fingerprint Identification System in a matter of minutes. This power can only be used where:

- the officer reasonably suspects that the person is committing or attempting to commit an offence, or has committed or attempted to commit an offence and
- either the name of the person is unknown to, and cannot be readily ascertained by, the officer or the officer has reasonable grounds for doubting whether the name given by the person is his real name.

At the police station, fingerprints can be taken by the police. The police will ask the detainee to agree to this, but if they do not consent the police have the right to use reasonable force to take fingerprints.

Records of any fingerprints taken can be kept on the police databases, even if the defendant is not charged with an offence.

4.5.3 Samples

Non-intimate samples

At the police station, non-intimate samples can be taken by the police. As with fingerprints, the police will try to get the person's consent to this, but if they do not consent then the police have the right to use reasonable force to take the samples.

Intimate samples

There are different rules for intimate samples. These are defined by PACE as:

 (a) a sample of blood, semen or any other tissue fluid, urine or pubic hair;

(b) a dental impression;

(c) a swab taken from any part of a person's genitals or from a person's body orifice other than the mouth.

These can only be taken by a doctor or a nurse. Although a sample will only be taken where there is reasonable ground for suspecting involvement in a particular recordable offence, the sample may

Key facts

Power	Sections in PACE or other Act	Code of Practice	Comments
Stop and search	ss 1–7 of PACE Also other Acts, eg Misuse of Drugs Act 1971	A	Must be in a public place and must have reasonable grounds for suspecting person
Arrest	With a warrant OR under s 24 of PACE	C	Magistrates issue warrant Must have reasonable grounds for suspicion and must believe arrest is necessary
Detention	ss 34–46 PACE Normal limit 24 hours Can be extended to 36 hours by senior police officer Can be extended to 96 hours for indictable offence	C	Detainee has rights to: ● have someone told; ● be told of availability of legal advice; ● see Code of Practice
Searches	ss 54, 55 PACE	C	Intimate search must be by person of same sex
Fingerprints	ss 61 PACE		
Samples	ss 62, 63 PACE		Intimate samples must be taken by qualified person
Police interviews	s 53 PACE Also ss 34–39 Criminal Justice and Public Order Act 1994 re 'silence'	D	● Police must caution ● Must be tape-recorded ● Appropriate adult present for those under 17

Figure 4.5 Key facts chart on police powers

then be checked against information held on other crimes.

This has led to solving of old crimes. In one case a woman who was arrested for drink-driving had a DNA sample taken. When the sample was checked against the database, it was a close match to the DNA profile of a rape suspect. This meant that the rapist was likely to be a close relative of the woman. The police checked her

Activity

Advise whether or not in the following situations there have been breaches of the rules in PACE and the Codes of Practice.

1. Leroy, aged 23, has been arrested on suspicion of murder. He is taken to the police station at 7.00 am on 6 June. The custody officer tells him that he will not be allowed to see a lawyer. Leroy is interviewed for eight hours that day about the alleged murder. He continually denies any involvement and demands to see a lawyer. The police take his fingerprints and a sample of saliva for DNA testing. Leroy spends the night in the police station cells. The following morning the police finally allow him to make a telephone call to his brother at 11.00 am (7 June).

2. Martin, aged 16, has been arrested for breaking into an office and stealing money. The police believe he may have been responsible for several other burglaries and that he has an accomplice. On the way to the police station they question him about this. At the police station he is taken into an interview room and told that the police have enough evidence 'to lock him up for years' but that if he tells them who was with him, the police will only caution him. Martin asks if he can see his father but the police refuse to call his father until Martin signs an admission.

family and this led to the arrest of the rapist.

Samples can be kept on police databases even though the person was not charged with an offence or, if charged, was later found not guilty of the offence.

4.6 The balance between police powers and individual rights

As seen in this chapter the police have a wide variety of powers to help them investigate crime. These powers are necessary otherwise it would not be possible to solve crimes and convict offenders. For example, the vast majority of people would agree that a DNA test ought to be taken from a suspected rapist. However, it is also important that the rights of the individual are protected.

In the previous sections of this chapter we have seen that, for each of the powers the police have, there are also limits on when and how they can use these powers. We have also seen that suspects are given rights, particularly when being detained by the police. It is important that there is a reasonable balance between the police having powers to investigate crime and protecting the rights of the individual.

The chart in Figure 4.7 summarises the police powers, limits on the power and the relevant rights of the suspect. The final column then gives comments on the balance between the two. Note that this is only a summary. Fuller details are given in the earlier sections.

4.7 Complaints against the police

Citizens who believe that the police have exceeded their powers can complain to the police authorities. Any complaint about police behaviour must be recorded.

The type of complaint determines how it is dealt with. In all instances, the police are under a duty to take steps to obtain and/or preserve

POLICE POWER	LIMITATIONS ON POWER	SUSPECT'S RIGHTS	COMMENT
Stop and search	Must have reasonable grounds for suspecting possession of stolen goods or prohibited articles. Must not stop only on basis of personal factors (eg age, race, known previous convictions). Must have real reason.	Police must give name and station. Police must state reason for search. If search is in public, can only ask suspect to remove outer coat, jacket and gloves.	If these are breached the search is unlawful. Only about 13 per cent of those stopped are arrested, suggesting that too many stop and searches are made. When there are fewer searches crime rates go up.
Arrest	There must be involvement or suspected involvement in an offence AND the police officer must have reasonable ground for believing the person's arrest is necessary.	Suspect must be told of arrest and reason for it. Police can only use reasonable force in making the arrest. Suspect must be taken to a police station as soon as possible after arrest.	The powers of arrest now apply to all offences. The necessity test is very wide. The police have considerable discretion in making the decision of whether to arrest or not.
Detention	Normally can only detain for 36 hours. For indictable offences must apply to magistrates for an extension to 96 hours. In terrorism cases the limit is 28 days.	Right to: ● have someone informed of detention ● have legal advice ● consult the Code of Practice. Cells must be adequately heated, cleaned, lit and ventilated. Must be given food and drink.	Custody officer reviews detention regularly. Custody record is kept BUT it is believed that 10 per cent of records are not accurate. The police need to be allowed to hold a suspect while investigations are on-going, eg waiting for results of a DNA test or while premises are searched.
Interview	Must tape-record interview.	Right to have solicitor present. Suspects under 17 or mentally ill must have an appropriate adult present. Must be given a break about every two hours. Must be allowed eight hours continuous rest in 24-hour period.	If urgent, interview can be started without solicitor present. Suspect can remain silent but this can be commented on at any later trial. Main protection is s76 PACE under which courts do not allow statements obtained through oppression to be used as evidence.

Figure 4.7 Police powers and the rights of the suspect

Searches	Custody officer can carry out a search if he thinks it is necessary. An intimate search must be authorised by a high-ranking officer if there is reason to believe the suspect has an item which could cause him damage or that he is in possession of Class A drugs.	Strip search must be by member of same sex and suspects should not have to remove all their clothing at the same time. An intimate search should be carried out by a suitably qualified person, eg a doctor or nurse.	Right to privacy is reasonably protected.
Fingerprinting	Fingerprints prior to arrest can only be taken where there is reasonable suspicion of involvement in an offence and the name of the person is not known or there are reasonable grounds for believing the name given is false. After arrest police have right to fingerprint.	Suspect will be asked to consent to fingerprinting. If he does not consent, reasonable force can be used to take the prints.	Fingerprints may be kept even if the person is not charged.
Samples	After arrest police have the right to take samples.	Suspect will be asked to consent to samples being taken. If he does not consent, reasonable force can be used to take the samples. Intimate samples must be taken by a doctor or a nurse.	DNA records obtained from samples may be kept on the national database even if the person is not charged.

Figure 4.7 Police powers and the rights of the suspect (continued)

evidence which is relevant to the complaint. Minor complaints will be dealt with informally, and if the complaint is proved, the individual will receive an apology and that will probably be an end of the matter. If disciplinary action is thought to be necessary, then the complaint should be investigated by the police force concerned, or by the Independent Police Complaints Commission.

4.7.1 The Independent Police Complaints Commission

The Independent Police Complaints Commission (IPCC) was set up in April 2004 to supervise the handling of complaints against the police and

police staff such as Community Support Officers. The IPCC sets down standards for the police to follow when dealing with complaints. They also monitor the way that complaints are dealt with by local police forces.

In addition, the IPCC itself investigates serious issues. These include:

- any incident involving death or serious injury
- allegations of serious or organised corruption
- allegations against senior officers
- allegations involving racism
- allegations of perverting the course of justice.

An example of the IPCC investigating was in relation to the death of Jean Charles de Menezes at Stockwell tube station. The police mistakenly believed that Menezes was a terrorist, but they had made mistakes in their conduct of the case.

The fact that the IPCC can carry out its own investigations into such matters is an improvement on the previous system where police from one area would be asked to investigate complaints about police in another area. This was felt not to be sufficiently independent. The IPCC is totally independent of the police.

Who can make a complaint?

Any member of the public who:

- has been a victim of misconduct by a person serving with the police
- was present when the alleged misconduct took place and suffered loss, damage, distress or inconvenience, or was put in danger or at risk
- is a friend or relative of the victim of the alleged misconduct or
- has witnessed the alleged misconduct.

A complaint can be made directly to the police force concerned or through the IPCC or any advice organisation such as the Citizens Advice Bureau or the Council for Racial Equality or a Youth Offending Team. Instead of making the complaint direct, it is also possible to ask a solicitor or your MP to make the complaint for you.

4.7.2 Court actions

Where the police have committed a crime in the unlawful execution of their duties, criminal proceedings may be brought against them. Such proceedings are usually for assault and may be commenced by a private prosecution or, as seen above, by the State.

If there is a breach of civil rights, citizens may also be able to take proceedings in the civil courts against the police. This can be done under a claim in tort for trespass to property, as would be the case if the police entered premises without a search warrant or other permission, or for trespass to the person where any arrest is unlawful. There can also be civil proceedings for false arrest or malicious prosecution.

Examination Questions

(a) Describe the powers the police have to stop and search an individual on the street.

Tyrone, aged 16, has missed the last bus and has to walk home. It is 2 am and a police officer driving past in a police car sees Tyrone and stops. The police officer tells Tyrone to empty his pockets and Tyrone refuses. The police officer then grabs Tyrone's shoulder, and pushes him into the police car and takes him to the local police station.

(b) Advise Tyrone on whether the police officer acted lawfully with regard to the stop and search and the arrest.

OCR Specimen Paper

Chapter 5

Pre-trial procedure in criminal cases

The criminal law is set down by the State. A breach of the criminal law can lead to a penalty, such as imprisonment or a fine, being imposed on the defendant in the name of the State. Therefore, bringing a prosecution for a criminal offence is usually seen as part of the role of the State. Indeed, the majority of criminal prosecutions are conducted by the Crown Prosecution Service which is the state agency for criminal prosecutions (the role of the Crown Prosecution Service is dealt with in section 5.3).

Other agencies also bring prosecutions. These include Trading Standards and Revenue and Customs. Also, bodies like the RSPCA may bring prosecutions. However, it is unusual for a private individual to bring a prosecution. This will probably only happen where the police have refused to act to investigate a complaint, or where the Crown Prosecution Service has decided to drop a case after the police had brought charges.

5.1 Pre-trial hearings

All criminal cases will first go to the Magistrates' Court. It is unusual for a case to be completed at this first hearing, although it is possible for minor offences to be dealt with at this point. For most driving offences there is a special procedure which allows the defendant to plead guilty by post, so that no attendance at court is necessary. Even in these cases the magistrates may need to adjourn the case to get further information about the defendant.

5.1.1 Categories of offences

The type of offence that is being dealt with affects the number and type of pre-trial hearings, and where the final trial will take place. Criminal offences are divided into three main categories. These are:

1. Summary offences
   These are the least serious offences and are always tried in the Magistrates' Court. They include nearly all driving offences, common assault and criminal damage which has caused less than £5,000 worth of damage.
2. Triable either way offences
   These can be regarded as the middle range of crimes and they include a wide variety of

offences, such as theft and assault causing actual bodily harm. As the name implies, these cases can be tried in either the Magistrates' Court or the Crown Court.

3. Indictable offences
   These are the more serious crimes and include murder, manslaughter and rape. All indictable offences must be tried at the Crown Court, but the first hearing is dealt with at the Magistrates' Court. After this the case is transferred to the Crown Court.

Figure 5.1 summarises the three categories of offence.

5.1.2 Pre-trial procedure for summary offences

It is possible for cases to be dealt with on a first appearance in court but often an adjournment may be needed. This could be because the Crown Prosecution Service has not got all the information required to complete the case, or because the defendant wants to get legal advice. Another reason for adjourning a case is where the magistrates want pre-sentence reports on a defendant who pleads guilty, before they decide what sentence to impose. When a defendant wishes to plead not guilty, there will almost

CATEGORY OF OFFENCE	PLACE OF TRIAL	EXAMPLES OF OFFENCES
Summary	Magistrates' Court	Driving without insurance Taking a vehicle without consent Common assault
Triable either way	Magistrates' Court OR Crown Court	Theft Assault causing actual bodily harm
Indictable	Crown Court	Murder Manslaughter Rape

Figure 5.1 The three categories of offence

always have to be an adjournment, as witnesses will have to be brought to court. One of the main points to be decided on an adjournment is whether the defendant should be remanded on bail or in custody (see section 5.2).

Early administrative hearings

In order to prevent unnecessary delays, the first hearing is now an early administrative hearing (EAH). The hearing can be dealt with by a single lay magistrate, or even by the clerk of the court. The hearing is aimed at discovering if the defendant wants to apply for legal aid and, if so, enquiring into whether he is eligible for it; requesting pre-sentence or medical reports if these are appropriate; and deciding if the defendant should be remanded in custody or on bail.

5.1.3 Pre-trial procedure for triable either way offences

Plea before venue

The plea before venue procedure applies only to triable either way offences. Under this procedure, the defendant is first asked whether he pleads guilty or not guilty. If the plea is guilty then the defendant has no right to ask for the case to be heard at the Crown Court. However, the magistrates may decide to send the defendant to the Crown Court for sentence.

Mode of trial

If the defendant pleads not guilty then the magistrates must carry out 'mode of trial' proceedings to decide whether the case will be tried in the Magistrates' Court or the Crown Court.

The magistrates first decide if they think the case is suitable for trial in the Magistrates' Court and whether they are prepared to accept jurisdiction (they have the power to deal with the case).

Under s 19 of the Magistrates' Court Act 1980 they must consider the nature and seriousness of the case, their own powers of punishment and any representations of the prosecution and defence.

Cases involving complex questions of fact or law should be sent to the Crown Court. Other relevant factors which may make a case more suitable for trial at the Crown Court include:

- where there was a breach of trust by the defendant
- where the crime was committed by an organised gang
- where the amount involved is more than twice the amount that the magistrates can fine the defendant.

In rare cases where the Attorney-General, Solicitor-General or the Director of Public Prosecutions is the prosecutor, the magistrates, under s 19(4) of the Magistrates' Court Act 1980, must send the case to the Crown Court if that is what the prosecution wants. In other cases the prosecution's wishes are just part of the matters to be considered by the magistrates before they decide whether they are prepared to hear the case or whether it should be tried at the Crown Court.

Defendant's election

If the magistrates are prepared to accept jurisdiction, the defendant is then told he has the right to choose trial by jury, but may be tried by the magistrates if he agrees to this course. However, he is also warned that if the case is tried by the magistrates and at the end of the case he is found guilty, the magistrates can send him to the Crown Court for sentence if they feel their powers of punishment are insufficient.

A main point for discussion is whether defendants should be allowed to choose where they will be tried. This involves the right to trial by jury.

5.1.4 The right to trial by jury

Cases where the defendant pleads not guilty to a summary offence can never be tried by a jury. These are always tried by magistrates.

Cases where the defendant pleads not guilty to an indictable offence are always tried by jury.

The only offences for which there is a choice of who should try the case are triable either way offences. The choice is made at the mode of trial proceedings (explained at section 5.1.3) in cases where the defendant is pleading not guilty to a triable either way offence. If the magistrates decide that the case is suitable for them to try, then they must offer the defendant the choice of court for the trial.

In this type of case most defendants choose to be tried by magistrates in the Magistrates' Courts. However, there are some reasons why defendants may prefer to be tried by a jury in the Crown Court.

Reasons for choosing trial by jury

Defendants are more likely to be acquitted (that is, found not guilty) at the Crown Court than in the Magistrates' Court. Only 20 per cent of

defendants who plead not guilty in the Magistrates' Courts are found not guilty. At the Crown Court, over 60 per cent of defendants are acquitted.

An interesting point on the number of acquittals in the Crown Court is that most are as a result of the judge discharging the case or directing that the defendant be found not guilty. This will happen where the prosecution drop the case or witnesses fail to attend court, so there is no evidence against the defendant.

However, juries do acquit in more cases than magistrates. They acquit in about 35 per cent of cases compared with the 20 per cent acquittal rate in the Magistrates' Courts.

Research conducted into the reasons why defendants chose trial at the Crown Court found that most did so on the advice of their lawyers. The main factor in the choice was the higher chance of an acquittal.

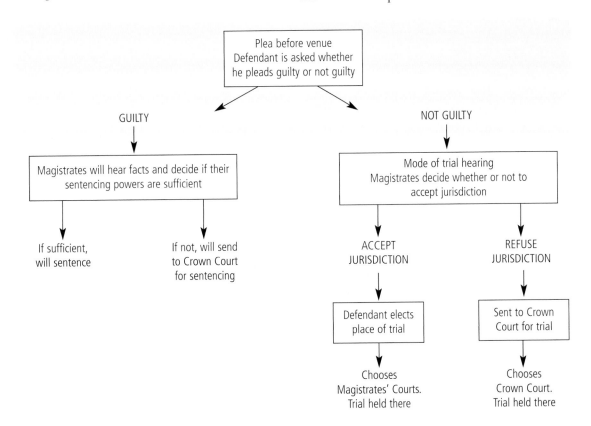

Figure 5.2 Flow chart of procedure for triable either way offences

There were other factors influencing the choice, including (where defendants were held in custody awaiting trial) a wish to serve part of the sentence in a remand prison!

Another reason for choosing trial at the Crown Court is that the defendant is more likely to get legal aid. This means that the State will pay for his legal representation.

The legal representative at the Crown Court must have a certificate of advocacy giving the right to do cases at the Crown Court. This is likely to mean that the lawyer is more experienced at presenting cases in court.

Disadvantages of trial by jury

There will usually be a longer wait before the case is dealt with than for cases in the Magistrates' Courts. If the defendant is not given bail, this waiting period is spent in prison. However, waiting times for trials in the Crown Court have been reduced in recent years. Nearly half of cases where the defendant is pleading not guilty are now dealt with within 16 weeks from the case being sent to the Crown Court.

The costs of the case are much greater than those in the Magistrates' Court. If the defendant has to pay for their own lawyers, this will be expensive. In addition, if the defendant is ordered to pay part of the prosecution costs, this will be more than in the Magistrates' Court.

The other disadvantage is that, for defendants who are found guilty, the judge at the Crown Court has the power to give a greater sentence than the magistrates.

5.1.5 Pre-trial procedure for indictable offences

Even for the most serious offences, the first hearing is in the Magistrates' Court. This deals with whether the defendant wants to apply for legal aid and issues of bail. All indictable offences are then sent to the Crown Court immediately after the early administrative hearing in the Magistrates' Court.

All other pre-trial matters are dealt with by a judge at the Crown Court.

5.2 Bail

An important pre-trial matter to be decided is whether the defendant should stay in custody while awaiting the trial or whether bail should be granted. A person can be released on bail at any point after being arrested by the police. Being given bail means that the person is allowed to be at liberty until the next stage in the case.

5.2.1 Police powers to grant bail

The police may release a suspect on bail while they make further enquiries. This means that the suspect is released from police custody on the condition that they return to the police station on a specific date in the future.

The police can also give bail to a defendant who has been charged with an offence. In this case the defendant is bailed to appear at the local Magistrates' Court on a set date. The decision on whether to grant bail or not is made by the custody officer.

The custody officer can refuse bail if the suspect's name and address cannot be discovered, or if there is a doubt as to whether the name and address given are genuine. Apart from this, the normal principles as to when bail should be granted apply. These are set out in the Bail Act 1976 and are given in section 5.2.2.

If any person granted bail by the police fails to surrender to that bail, (ie attend at the next stage of the case) then the police are given the right to arrest them. About 84 per cent of those charged with offences are given bail by the police.

Conditional bail

The police have the power to impose conditions on a grant of bail. The types of conditions include asking the suspect to surrender his passport, report at regular intervals to the police station or ask another person to stand surety for him. These conditions can only be imposed in order to make sure that the suspect surrenders to bail, does not commit an offence while on bail and does not interfere with witnesses or interfere in any other way with the course of justice.

No police bail

Where, having charged a defendant with a crime, the police are not prepared to allow bail, they must bring the defendant in front of the Magistrates' Court at the first possible opportunity. If (as usually happens) the magistrates cannot deal with the whole case at that first hearing, the magistrates must then make the decision as to whether the defendant should be given bail or remanded in custody. The question as to whether bail should be given can also be considered by a court at any later stage of the criminal proceedings.

Statistics published by the Home Office show that the majority of those prosecuted are summonsed to court, rather than charged. This means that the question of bail or custody is not relevant: they are automatically at liberty. Of those who are charged, about five out of every six are released on bail by the police pending the court proceedings, so in fact only a small number of defendants are refused bail by the police. In these cases the courts must then decide whether to grant bail.

5.2.2 The Bail Act 1976

This is the key Act. It starts with the assumption that an accused person should be granted bail, though this right is limited for certain cases (see section 5.2.3). Section 4 of the Bail Act 1976 gives a general right to bail. However, the court need not grant a defendant bail if it is satisfied that there are substantial grounds for believing that the defendant, if released on bail, would:

1. fail to surrender to custody

2. commit an offence while on bail

3. interfere with witnesses or otherwise obstruct the course of justice.

The court can also refuse bail if it is satisfied that the defendant should be kept in custody for his own protection.

In deciding whether to grant bail, the court will consider various factors including:

- the nature and seriousness of the offence (and the probable method of dealing with it)
- the character, antecedents (that is, past record), associations and community ties of the defendant
- the defendant's record as respects the fulfilment of his obligations under previous grants of bail in criminal proceedings; in other words whether he has turned up (surrendered to his bail) on previous occasions
- the strength of the evidence against him.

If a defendant is charged with an offence which is not punishable by imprisonment, bail can only be refused if the defendant has previously failed to surrender to bail and there are grounds for believing that he will not surrender on this occasion.

A court can make conditions for the granting of bail. These are similar to conditions which can be set by the police and may include the surrender of passport and/or reporting to a police station. The court can also make a condition as to where the accused must reside while on bail; this could be at a home address or at a bail hostel.

The court can also order that the defendant is placed on a curfew. This means that he has to be at his home address at set times, for example for the evening and night. As part of the curfew order the defendant is usually required to wear an electronic tag so that it is known where he is at all times.

Sureties

The court (and the police) can require a surety for bail. A surety is another person who is prepared to promise to pay the court a certain sum of money if the defendant fails to attend court. Note that no money is paid unless the defendant fails to answer to his bail. This system is different from

Key facts

Bail can be granted by	● police ● magistrates ● Crown Court
Bail Act 1976	There is a presumption in favour of bail BUT ● for an offence while already on bail, bail can only be given if the court is satisfied there is no significant risk of further offending ● must be exceptional circumstances for bail to be granted for murder, attempted murder, manslaughter, rape or attempted rape where the defendant has already served a custodial sentence for such an offence.
In all cases bail can be refused if there are reasonable grounds for believing the defendant:	● would fail to surrender ● would commit further offences ● would interfere with witnesses.
Conditions can be imposed	● sureties ● residence in bail hostel ● curfew ● hand in passport, etc.
Comment	Many of those in prison are awaiting trial and could have been given bail Problem of balancing this against need to protect public

Figure 5.3 Key facts chart on bail

those of other countries. For example, in the USA the surety must pay the money into court before the defendant is released on bail, but gets the money back when the defendant attends court as required.

Renewed applications and appeals

If bail is refused, then normally only one further application can be made to the magistrates, unless there is a change of circumstance. The defendant can appeal against a refusal to grant bail. Such an appeal is made to a judge at the Crown Court. A defendant who has been sent for trial to the Crown Court can also apply there for bail.

5.2.3 Restrictions on bail

The right to liberty is a human right and the right to bail is therefore part of that right. This means

that, even for serious offences, bail must be available in suitable cases. However, in some situations the public need to be protected from a potentially dangerous person. In such circumstances the right to bail is restricted.

Repeat serious offences

Where a person is charged with murder, attempted murder, manslaughter, rape or attempted rape and they have already served a custodial sentence for a similar offence, they only have the right to bail if the court thinks that there are exceptional circumstances.

Offence committed while on bail

Where a defendant, aged 18 or over, was on bail when the present alleged offence was committed, s 14 of the Criminal Justice Act 2003 amended the

Bail Act 1976 to read:

> he may not be granted bail unless the court is satisfied that there is no significant risk of his committing an offence on bail (whether subject to conditions or not).

Restrictions on bail for adult drug users

Section 19 of the Criminal Justice Act 2003 amended the Bail Act 1976 to place restrictions on bail for adult offenders who have tested positive for specified Class A drugs where:

- the offender is either charged with possession or possession with intent to supply a Class A drug or
- the court is satisfied that there are substantial grounds for believing that the misuse of a Class A drug caused or contributed to the offence OR that the offence was motivated wholly or partly by his intended misuse of such a drug and
- the defendant has refused to agree to participate in an assessment or follow-up in relation to his dependency upon or propensity to misuse specified Class A drugs.

Such a defendant may not be granted bail unless the court is satisfied that there is no significant risk of his committing an offence on bail (whether subject to conditions or not).

5.2.4 Prosecution appeals

The Bail (Amendment) Act 1993 gave the prosecution the right to appeal to a judge at the Crown Court against the granting of bail. Originally this only applied where the offence involved carried a maximum of at least five years' imprisonment. However, the Criminal Justice Act 2003 extended the prosecution's power to appeal to all offences punishable with imprisonment.

5.2.5 Balancing conflicting interests

Denying people bail is an interference with their right to liberty. This is why there is a presumption in favour of bail. However, it is important to protect the public from potentially dangerous criminals. This is why there are restrictions on the use of bail. Getting the right balance between these two conflicting interests can be difficult.

Prisoners on remand account for 10 per cent of the prison population, with about 6,000 to 7,000 being held in custody at any one time. Only about 50 per cent of those remanded in custody are actually sent to prison at the end of the case. Of these, 18 per cent are found not guilty and the other 32 per cent are given non-custodial sentences. These figures suggest that too many people are being remanded in custody.

However, there has been a steady decrease in the percentage being held on remand in custody over the last 10 or so years. At one point remand prisoners accounted for 20 per cent of the prison population.

Public protection

To protect the public, there are methods of trying to make sure that someone who is given bail will not commit offences while on bail. There are bail hostels where those on bail who have no home address can live and be supervised.

Recently there has been an increased use of curfews enforced by electronic tagging for those released on bail. However, there are doubts as to whether this is always successful in preventing re-offending. A *Panorama* programme in July 2007 claimed that there had been six murders committed by people who were tagged and over 1,000 violent crimes. But it must be noted that, as tagging is also used for early release prisoners, not all these offences will have been committed by those on bail.

There are also a number of offenders who fail to answer to bail (ie attend at court when required). In 2004, 180,000 people were prosecuted for failing to answer to bail. In 2005, 157,000 were prosecuted.

These figures suggest that the balance may be tipping too far in favour of the individual who has been charged, so you can see how difficult it is to get the balance right.

Activity

Consider each of the following situations and explain with reasons whether you think bail would be granted or not.

1. Alex, aged 19, is charged with a robbery in which he threatened a shopkeeper with a gun and stole £2,000. He has no previous convictions and lives at home with his mother.
2. Homer, aged 43, is charged with three offences of burglary. He has been convicted of burglary on two occasions in the past.
3. Melanie, aged 21, is charged with theft of items from a sportswear shop. She is currently unemployed and living rough. She has no previous convictions.

5.3 Crown Prosecution Service (CPS)

Before 1986, prosecutions brought by the State were normally conducted by the police. This led to criticism as it was thought that the investigation of crime should be separate from the prosecution of cases. The Royal Commission on Criminal Procedure (the Phillips Commission), whose report led to the enactment of PACE, had also pointed out that there was no uniform system of prosecution in England and Wales. The Commission thought it was desirable to have an independent agency to review and conduct prosecutions. Eventually, the Crown Prosecution Service (CPS) was established by the Prosecution of Offences Act 1985 and began operating in 1986.

5.3.1 Organisation of the CPS

The head of the CPS is the Director of Public Prosecutions (DPP), who must have been qualified as a lawyer for at least 10 years. The DPP is appointed by, and is subject to supervision by, the Attorney-General. Below the DPP are Chief Crown Prosecutors who each head one of the 42 areas into which the country is divided up. Each area is sub-divided into branches, each of which is headed by a Branch Crown Prosecutor. Within the branches there are several lawyers and support staff, who are organised into teams and given responsibility for cases.

5.3.2 The functions of the CPS

These involve all aspects of prosecution and can be summarised as:

- deciding on what offence(s) should be charged. This used to be done by the police, but sometimes inappropriate charges were brought which meant that the case had to be discontinued
- reviewing all cases passed to them by the police to see if there is sufficient evidence for a case to proceed, and whether it is in the public interest to do so; this is to avoid weak cases being brought to court
- being responsible for the case after it has been passed to them by the police
- conducting the prosecution of cases in the Magistrates' Court; this is usually done by lawyers working in the Crown Prosecution Service as Crown Prosecutors or lay presenters
- conducting cases in the Crown Court. This can either be by instructing an independent lawyer to act as prosecuting counsel at court or a Crown Prosecutor with the appropriate advocacy qualification.

On a practical level, once a defendant has been charged or summonsed with an offence the police role is at an end. They must send the papers for each case to the CPS – each case is then assigned to a team in the local branch of the CPS, and that team will be responsible for the case throughout the prosecution process. This is aimed at ensuring continuity and better communication in each case.

Examination Questions

(a) Describe how matters relating to the granting of bail to a person awaiting trial are decided.

(b) Charlie is charged with criminal damage. He has three previous convictions for criminal damage, one which was committed whilst on bail. He does not live locally and he has no contact with his family.

Explain which factors and conditions are likely to be considered when making a decision whether on not to grant bail to Charlie.

OCR G141 June 2007

Chapter 6

Criminal courts

The two courts which hear criminal trials are the Magistrates' Court and the Crown Court. As already explained in Chapter 5, the actual court for the trial is decided by the category of crime involved in the charge. Summary offences can only be tried at the Magistrates' Court; indictable offences can only be tried at the Crown Court; and triable either way offences may be tried at either court.

At the Magistrates' Courts, cases are always tried by magistrates. At the Crown Court, cases are tried by a judge and jury.

In both the Magistrates' Court and the Crown Court, the majority of defendants plead guilty to the charge against them. In these cases the role of the court is to decide what sentence should be imposed on the defendant. Where the accused pleads not guilty, the role of the court is to try the case and decide whether the accused is guilty or not guilty; the burden of proof is on the prosecution who must prove the case beyond reasonable doubt. The form of the trial is an adversarial one, with prosecution and defence presenting their cases and cross-examining each other's witnesses, while the role of the magistrate or judge is effectively that of referee, overseeing the trial and making sure that legal rules are followed correctly. Magistrates and judges cannot investigate the case nor ask to see additional witnesses.

6.1 Magistrates' Courts

There are about 430 Magistrates' Courts in England and Wales. They are local courts, so there will be a Magistrates' Court in almost every town, while big cities will have several courts. Each court deals with cases that have a connection with its geographical area and they have jurisdiction over a variety of matters involving criminal cases. Cases are heard by magistrates, who may be either qualified District Judges or unqualified lay justices (see Chapter 11 for further details on magistrates). There is also a legally qualified clerk attached to each court to assist the magistrates.

6.1.1 Jurisdiction of the Magistrates' Courts

So far as criminal cases are concerned, the Magistrates' courts have jurisdiction in a variety of matters. Jurisdiction means that the court has the legal right to hear the case. They have a very large workload and they do the following:

1. Try all summary cases.
2. Try any triable either way offences which it is decided should be dealt with in the Magistrates' Court (see section 6.1.3). (These first two categories account for about 97 per cent of all criminal cases.)
3. Deal with the first hearing of all indictable offences. These cases are then sent to the Crown Court.
4. Deal with all the side matters connected to criminal cases, such as issuing warrants for arrest and deciding bail applications.
5. Try cases in the Youth Court where the defendants are aged 10–17 inclusive.

Civil jurisdiction

The Magistrates' Courts also have some civil jurisdiction. Strictly speaking, this side of their work belongs in Chapter 2 – however, for completeness, and to illustrate the wide variety of work carried out by Magistrates' Courts, this side of their work is listed below. It includes:

- enforcing council tax demands and issuing warrants of entry and investigation to gas and electricity authorities
- family cases including orders for protection against violence and maintenance orders (NB Magistrates' Courts cannot grant divorces)
- proceedings concerning the welfare of children under the Children Act 1989
- hearing appeals against the refusal of a licence to sell alcohol.

6.1.2 Summary trials

These are the least serious criminal offences and are sub-divided into offences of different 'levels' – level one being the lowest level and level five the highest. The use of levels allows a maximum fine to be set for each level which is increased in line with inflation from time to time. The current maximum fines date from the Criminal Justice Act 1991 and are level one: maximum £200; level two: £500; level three: £1,000; level four: £2,500; and level five: £5,000. However, for certain breaches of environmental law and health and safety legislation, businesses can be fined up to £20,000 by the magistrates. The maximum prison sentence that can be given on summary trial is six months, but the Criminal Justice Act 2003 gives power for this to be increased to 15 months in future.

At the start of any case, the clerk of the court will check the defendant's name and address and then ask whether he pleads guilty or not guilty. Over 90 per cent of defendants in the Magistrates' Court plead guilty and the process is then concerned with establishing an appropriate penalty for the case.

Guilty plea

The usual sequence of events where the defendant pleads guilty to a summary offence is as follows:

1. The Crown Prosecutor or lay presenter from the CPS will give the court a resumé of the facts of the case.

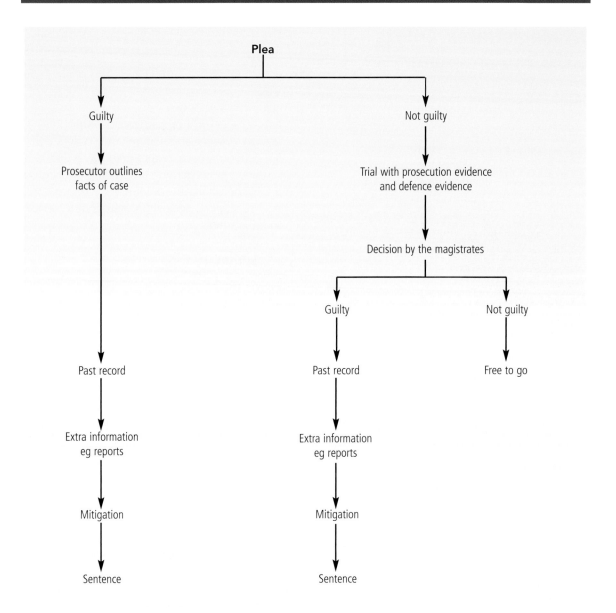

Figure 6.1 Flow chart of proceedings for a summary offence in the Magistrates' Court

2. The defendant is asked if he agrees with those facts (if he does not, the magistrates may have to hold an inquiry, called a Newton hearing, to establish the facts).

3. The defendant's past record of convictions, if any, is given to the court.

4. Other information about the defendant's background, especially his financial position, is given to the court.

5. Any relevant reports are considered by the magistrates; these may include a pre-sentence report prepared by a probation officer and/or a medical report on the defendant's mental health.

6. The defendant or his lawyer can then explain any matter which might persuade the

Giving evidence to a Magistrates' Court

magistrates to give a lenient sentence. This is called making a speech in mitigation.

7. The magistrates decide the sentence.

This is shown in flow chart form in Figure 6.1.

Not guilty plea

When a defendant pleads not guilty, the procedure is longer and more complicated, as both sides produce evidence to the court. Since the burden of proof is on the prosecution, it will begin the case – usually by making a short speech outlining what the case is about and what it hopes to prove. The prosecution witnesses will then be called one at a time to give evidence, and the prosecutor will question each to establish what he or she saw and heard. This is called the examination-in-chief. After the prosecution finishes the examination-in-chief of a witness, the defence will then cross-examine that witness to test their evidence and try to show that it is not reliable. The prosecution may also produce

relevant exhibits, such as property found in the possession of the defendant or documents which help establish the case.

No case to answer

At the end of the prosecution case the defence can submit to the magistrates that there is no case to answer and that the case should be dismissed at this point. This is because the prosecution has to prove the case and if its evidence does not establish that case, then it must be dismissed.

Only a very small number of cases will be dismissed at this stage. In the vast majority the case will continue and the defence will have to give their evidence to the court.

Defence case

The defendant himself will usually give evidence, though he does not have to. However, since the Criminal Justice and Public Order Act 1994, the magistrates can draw their own conclusions from the fact that the accused stays silent and does not explain his side of the matter. If the defendant does give evidence, he can be cross-examined by the prosecutor, as can any defence witnesses. The defence can call any witnesses and produce any evidence that it believes will help to disprove the prosecution's case.

Once all the evidence has been given, the defence has the right to make a speech pointing out the weaknesses of the case to the magistrates and try to persuade them to acquit the defendant. Further speeches are not usually allowed unless there is a point of law to be argued. The magistrates then decide whether the defendant is guilty or not guilty. If they convict, they will then hear about his past record and may also look at reports and hear a speech in mitigation from the defence. They will then pass sentence.

If the magistrates dismiss the case, the defendant is free to go and cannot usually be tried for that offence again. There is, however, one exception when the defendant can be retried. This is where the prosecution successfully appeals against the acquittal in a 'case stated' appeal (see section 7.1.2 for the rules on these).

6.1.3 Triable either way offences

As already explained in Chapter 5, two preliminary matters have to be decided before there can be a trial in a triable either way offence. These are, first, whether the defendant pleads guilty or not guilty.

Guilty plea

If the defendant pleads guilty, then the case will be dealt with in the Magistrates' Court using the same procedure as for a guilty plea to a summary offence (see section 6.1.2). The only difference is that at the end of hearing all the facts the magistrates can decide to send the defendant to the Crown Court for sentencing. The magistrates can only do this if they feel that their powers of punishment are not sufficient.

Not guilty plea

If the defendant pleads not guilty then the magistrates have to decide where the trial should take place – Magistrates' Court or Crown Court? The case will only be tried by the magistrates if they accept that it is a suitable case for them to try AND the defendant elects to be tried in the Magistrates' Court.

If the case is tried in the Magistrates' Court, the procedure is then the same as for a not guilty plea to a summary offence.

6.1.4 Sending cases to the Crown Court

Where the trial is going to be held at the Crown Court, the magistrates must officially send the case to the Crown Court.

For indictable offences the case is transferred to the Crown Court immediately after the first hearing at the Magistrates' Court. This is under s 51 of the Crime and Disorder Act 1998.

For triable either way offences, magistrates will hold a plea before venue and, if the defendant pleads not guilty, a mode of trial hearing. If, at this hearing, it is decided that the case is to be tried in the Crown Court, the magistrates will then transfer the case to the Crown Court.

6.1.5 The role of the clerk

Every bench of magistrates is assisted by a clerk who is also known as legal adviser. The senior clerk in each Magistrates' Court area has to be a barrister or solicitor of at least five years' standing. The role of the clerk is to guide the magistrates on questions of law, practice and procedure. The clerk makes sure that the correct procedure is followed in court. For example, at the start of a case it is the clerk who will ask the defendant whether he pleads guilty or not guilty. The clerk is not meant to take part in the decision-making process; that is the magistrates' role. This means that the clerk should not retire with the justices when they leave the court at the end of a case to consider their verdict.

The senior clerk has been granted greater powers to deal with routine matters which previously had to be done by magistrates. For example, clerks can now issue warrants for arrest, extend police bail, adjourn criminal proceedings (where the defendant is on bail and the terms of the bail are not being changed) and conduct early administrative hearings.

6.2 Youth Courts

Young offenders aged from 10 to 17 are dealt with in the Youth Court which is a branch of the Magistrates' Court. Children under the age of 10 cannot be charged with a criminal offence.

There are some exceptional cases in which young offenders can be tried in the Crown Court. These are cases where the defendant is charged with murder or manslaughter, rape and causing death by dangerous driving. In addition, it is possible for those aged 14 and over to be sent to the Crown Court for trial in any case where they are charged with a serious offence (usually one which for an adult carries a maximum prison sentence of at least 14 years).

The Youth Court sits in private, with only those who are involved in the case allowed into the court room. Members of the press may be present, but they cannot publish the name of any young offender or other information which could identify him, such as address or school.

The magistrates who sit on the bench in these courts must be under 65 and have had special training to deal with young offenders. There must be at least one female magistrate and one male magistrate on the bench. The procedure in the court is less formal than in the adult courts and the parents or guardian of any child under 16 are required to be present for the proceedings. The court can also ask parents of those aged 16 or 17 to attend.

6.3 The Crown Court

The Crown Court currently sits in 90 different centres throughout England and Wales. There are three kinds of centre:

Maidstone Crown Court

1. **First tier**

   These exist in main centres throughout the country, for example there are first-tier Crown Courts in Bristol, Birmingham, Leeds and Manchester. At each court there is a High Court and a Crown Court with separate judges for civil and criminal work. The Crown Court is permanently staffed by High Court Judges as well as Circuit Judges and Recorders, and the court can deal with all categories of crime triable on indictment.

2. **Second tier**

   This is a Crown Court only, but High Court Judges sit there on a regular basis to hear criminal cases, as well as Circuit Judges and Recorders. All categories of crime triable on indictment can be tried here.

3. **Third tier**

   This is staffed only by Circuit Judges and Recorders. The most serious cases, such as murder, manslaughter and rape, are not usually tried here as there is no High Court Judge to deal with them.

DONBRIDGE CROWN COURT

The Queen v John Wilkie charged as follows:

STATEMENT OF OFFENCE

Murder contrary to the common law

PARTICULARS OF OFFENCE

John Wilkie on the 4th day of April 2007 murdered
Abraham Lincoln

Figure 6.2 Sample indictment

6.3.1 Preliminary matters

The indictment

This is a document which formally sets out the
charges against the defendant. Although the
defendant will have been sent for trial charged
with specific crimes, the indictment can be drawn
up for any offence that the witness statements
reveal. In more complicated cases the indictment
may be for several counts. Figure 6.2 shows a
sample indictment.

Criminal Procedure Rules

Criminal Procedure Rules to deal with all aspects
of criminal cases came into force in April 2005.
The overriding objective of the Rules is that
'criminal cases be dealt with justly'.

Disclosure by prosecution and defence

The Criminal Procedure and Investigations Act
1996 places a duty on both sides to make certain
points known to the other. The prosecution, who
have already given the defence statements of all
the evidence they propose to use at the trial, must
also disclose previously undisclosed material
'which in the prosecutor's opinion might
reasonably be considered capable of undermining
the case for the prosecution against the accused'.

The 1996 Act also imposes a duty on the
defence in cases which are to be tried on
indictment. In these, after the prosecution's
primary disclosure, the defence must give a
written statement to the prosecution, setting out:

- the nature of the accused's defence, including
  any particular defences on which he intends to
  rely
- the matters of fact on which he takes issue
  with the prosecution and why he takes issue
- any point of law which he wishes to take, and
  the case authority on which he will be relying.

The defendant also has to give details about any
alibi and the witnesses he intends calling to
support that alibi. This information allows the
prosecution to run police checks on the alibi
witnesses.

Plea and case management hearing

Under the Criminal Procedure Rules, most cases
sent to the Crown Court are dealt with first at a
plea and case management hearing (PCMH). The
first purpose of a PCMH is to find out whether
the defendant is pleading guilty or not guilty. All
the charges on the indictment are read out to the
defendant in open court, and he is asked how he
pleads to each charge. This process is called the
'arraignment'.

Guilty plea

If the defendant pleads guilty, the judge will, if
possible, sentence the defendant immediately.
This means that defendants who plead guilty will
not have an unnecessarily long wait for their case
to come to court.

Not guilty plea

Where a defendant pleads not guilty, the judge
will require the prosecution and defence to
identify the key issues, both of fact and law, that
are involved in the case. He will then give any
directions that are necessary to organise the
actual trial; for instance, the prosecution and

defence may agree that certain witnesses need not attend court as their evidence is not in dispute. Other points, such as whether it will be necessary to use a video link for any witnesses, are also agreed on. The aim of the PCMH is to speed up the actual trial process and to ensure that time will not be wasted on unnecessary points. It also allows the court to plan its lists.

The Criminal Procedure Rules encourage active case management. Case management in the Crown Court includes:

- the early identification of the real issues
- the early identification of the needs of witnesses
- achieving a certainty as to what must be done, by whom, and when, in particular by the early setting of a timetable for the progress of a case
- monitoring the progress of the case and compliance with directions
- ensuring that the evidence, whether disputed or not, is presented in the shortest and clearest way
- discouraging delay, dealing with as many aspects of the case as possible on the same occasion, and avoiding unnecessary hearings
- encouraging the participants to co-operate in the progression of the case and
- making use of technology.

The full Criminal Procedure Rules are available online on the Ministry of Justice website: www.justice.gov.uk

6.3.2 The trial

It is normal for a defendant appearing at the Crown Court to be represented, usually by a barrister, although solicitors who have a certificate of advocacy can also appear at the Crown Court. Defendants can represent themselves.

At the trial where the defendant pleads not guilty, the order of events will normally be:

1. The jury is sworn in to try the case (for further information on juries, see Chapter 12).

2. The prosecution will make an opening speech to the jury explaining what the case is about and what they intend to prove.

3. The prosecution witnesses give evidence and can be cross-examined by the defence; the prosecution will also produce any other evidence such as documents or video recordings.

4. At the end of the prosecution case the defence may submit that there is no case to go to the jury; if the judge decides there is no case, he will direct the jury to acquit the defendant.

5. The defence may make an opening speech provided they intend calling evidence other than the defendant.

6. The defence witnesses give evidence and are cross-examined by the prosecution; the defendant does not have to give evidence personally but the judge may comment on the failure to do so in his summing-up to the jury.

7. The prosecutor makes a closing speech to the jury pointing out the strengths of the prosecution case.

8. The defence makes a closing speech to the jury pointing out the weaknesses of the prosecution case.

9. The judge sums up the case to the jury and directs them on any relevant law.

10. The jury retire to consider their verdict in private.

11. The jury's verdict is given in open court.

12. If the verdict is guilty the judge then sentences the accused; if the verdict is not guilty the accused is discharged. Normally, once a defendant is found not guilty he can never be tried for that offence again. However, the Criminal Justice Act 2003 removes this 'double jeopardy' rule for serious cases if 'new and compelling evidence' comes to light, so that a defendant can be tried a second time.

Examination Question

(a) Describe the process used to decide in which court a person should be tried.

(b) Scott has been charged with the theft of a laptop computer worth £800 and has pleaded not guilty to the charge.

Explain the factors which may determine the court in which Scott would be tried.

OCR G141 January 2007

Chapter 7

Criminal appeals

The appeal rights of the defendant and the prosecution are completely different. Originally only the defendant had a right of appeal, but in the last 20 years various rights have also been given to the prosecution.

7.1 Appeals from the Magistrates' Court

The appeal routes from the Magistrates' Courts are completely different to appeals from the Crown Court. The appeal route from the Magistrates' Court will depend on whether the appeal is only on a point of law, or whether it is for other reasons. The two appeal routes are to the Crown Court, or to the Queen's Bench Divisional Court.

7.1.1 Appeals to the Crown Court

This is the normal route of appeal and is only available to the defence. If the defendant pleaded guilty at the Magistrates' Court, then he can only appeal against sentence. If the defendant pleaded not guilty and was convicted, then the appeal can be against conviction and/or sentence. In both cases the defendant has an automatic right to appeal and does not need to get leave (permission) to appeal.

At the Crown Court the case is completely re-heard by a judge and two magistrates. They can come to the same decision as the magistrates and confirm the conviction, or they can decide that the case is not proved and reverse the decision. In some cases it is possible for them to vary the decision and find the defendant guilty of a lesser offence.

Where the appeal is against sentence, the Crown Court can confirm the sentence or they can increase or decrease it. However, any increase can only be up to the magistrates' maximum powers for the case.

Over the last few years there have been about 12,000 appeals to the Crown Court each year, and judicial statistics published by the Ministry of Justice show that the appeal is allowed in approximately one quarter of cases, while the magistrates' order is varied in about another quarter. This means that about half of those who appeal have some success.

If it becomes apparent that there is a point of law to be decided, then the Crown Court can decide that point of law, but there is the possibility of a further appeal by way of a case stated appeal being made to the Queen's Bench Divisional Court (see section 7.1.2). A diagram setting out the appeal routes from the Magistrates' Court is shown in Figure 7.1.

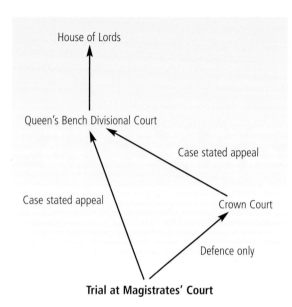

House of Lords

Queen's Bench Divisional Court

Case stated appeal

Case stated appeal

Crown Court

Defence only

Trial at Magistrates' Court

Figure 7.1 Appeal routes from the Magistrates' Court

7.1.2 Case stated appeals

These are appeals on a point of law which go to the Queen's Bench Divisional Court. Both the prosecution and the defence can use this appeal route and it can be direct from the Magistrates' Court, or following an appeal to the Crown Court. The magistrates (or the Crown Court) are asked to state the case by setting out their findings of fact and their decision. The appeal is then argued on the basis of what the law is on those facts; no witnesses are called. The appeal is heard by a panel of two or three High Court Judges from the Queen's Bench Division, though in some cases a judge from the Court of Appeal may form part of the panel.

This route is only used by the defendant against a conviction, or by the prosecution against an acquittal. It cannot be used to challenge the sentence. The appeal is because they claim the magistrates came to the wrong decision by making a mistake about the law. The Divisional Court may confirm, vary or reverse the decision or remit (send back) the case to the Magistrates' Court for the magistrates to implement the decision on the law.

There are only about 100 appeals by way of case stated made each year.

Further appeal to the House of Lords

From the decision of the Queen's Bench Divisional Court there is a possibility of a further appeal to the House of Lords. Such an appeal can only be made if:

1. the Divisional Court certifies that a point of law of general public importance is involved
2. the Divisional Court or the House of Lords gives leave (permission) to appeal because the point is one which ought to be considered by the House of Lords.

An example of a case which followed this appeal route was *C v DPP* (1994). This case concerned the legal point about the presumption of criminal responsibility of children from the age of 10 up to their fourteenth birthday. Until this case, it had been accepted that a child of this age could only be convicted if the prosecution proved that the child knew he was doing wrong. The Divisional Court held that times had changed and that children were more mature and the rule was not needed. They decided that children of this age were presumed to know the difference between right and wrong, and that the prosecution did not need to prove 'mischievous discretion'.

The case was then appealed to the House of Lords who overruled the Divisional Court, holding that the law was still that a child of this age was presumed not to know he was doing wrong, and therefore not to have the necessary intention for any criminal offence. A child of this age could only be convicted if the prosecution disproved this presumption by bringing evidence to show that the child was aware that what he was doing was seriously wrong. The House of Lords ruling was on the basis that it was for Parliament to make such a major change to the law, not the courts. The courts were bound by precedent. Precedent is where a court has to follow a point of law decided previously (see Chapter 14).

7.2 Appeals from the Crown Court

7.2.1 Appeals by the defendant

The defendant has the possibility of appealing against conviction and/or sentence to the Court of Appeal (Criminal Division). So, at the end of any trial in which a defendant has been found guilty, his lawyer should advise him on the possibility of an appeal. This must be done verbally at the court, or in writing within 14 days of the trial. It is intended to make sure that each defendant has advice within the time limits for making an appeal. In order to appeal, a notice of appeal must be filed at the Court of Appeal (Criminal Division) within 28 days of conviction.

Leave to appeal

The rules on appeals are set out in the Criminal Appeal Act 1995 and in all cases the defendant must get leave to appeal from the Court of Appeal, or a certificate that the case is fit for appeal from the trial judge. The idea of having to get leave is that cases which are without merit are filtered out and the court's time saved.

The Criminal Appeal Act 1995

The Criminal Appeal Act 1995 simplified the grounds under which the court can allow an appeal. The Act states that the Court of Appeal:

> (a) shall allow an appeal against conviction if they think that the conviction is unsafe; and
>
> (b) shall dismiss such an appeal in any other case.

Since the European Convention on Human Rights has been incorporated into our law by the Human Rights Act 1998, the Court of Appeal has taken a broad approach to the meaning of 'unsafe'. In particular, a conviction has been held to be 'unsafe' where the defendant has been denied a fair trial.

The Criminal Justice and Immigration Bill 2007 proposes to amend the grounds for appeal. It will add a provision that 'a conviction is not unsafe if the Court of Appeal are satisfied that the appellant is guilty of the offence'. This proposed change has been criticised, as the Court of Appeal will not have heard the evidence at the original trial. It is a review court and not the trial court.

New evidence

Any new evidence must appear to be capable of belief and would afford a ground for an appeal. This has to be considered together with whether it would have been admissible at the trial and why it was not produced at that trial.

Court of Appeal's powers

The Court of Appeal can allow a defendant's appeal and quash the conviction. Alternatively, it can vary the conviction to that of a lesser offence of which the jury could have convicted the defendant.

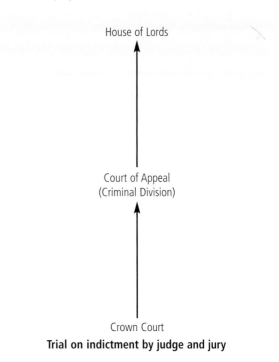

Figure 7.2 Appeal routes from the Crown Court

As far as sentencing is concerned, the court can decrease, but not increase, it on the defendant's appeal. Where the appeal is not successful, the court can decide to dismiss the appeal.

The Court of Appeal also has the power to order that there should be a re-trial of the case in front of a new jury. The power was given to it in 1988, but initially was not often used; for example, in 1989 only one re-trial was ordered. However, its use has increased, with between 50 and 70 re-trials being ordered each year.

7.2.2 Appeals by the prosecution

Originally the prosecution had no right to appeal against either the verdict or sentence passed in the Crown Court. Gradually, however, some limited rights of appeal have been given to them by Parliament.

Against a judge's ruling

If the trial judge gives a ruling on a point of law which effectively stops the case against the defendant, the prosecution now have the right to appeal against that ruling. This right was given by the Criminal Justice Act 2003. It makes sure that an error of law by the judge does not lead to an acquittal.

Against acquittal

There are only two limited situations in which the prosecution can appeal against an acquittal by a jury.

1. Where the acquittal was the result of the jury or witnesses being 'nobbled', ie where some jurors are bribed or threatened by associates of the defendant. In these circumstances, provided there has been an actual conviction for jury 'nobbling', the Criminal Procedure and Investigations Act 1996 allows an application to be made to the High Court for an order quashing the acquittal. Once the acquittal is quashed, the prosecution could then start new proceedings for the same offence. As yet, this power has never been used.

2. Where there is new and compelling evidence of the acquitted person's guilt and it is in the public interest for the defendant to be retried.

This power is given by the Criminal Justice Act 2003 and it is only available for some 30 serious offences, including murder, manslaughter, rape and terrorism offences. It is known as 'double jeopardy', since the defendant is being tried twice for the same offence.

The DPP has to consent to the re-opening of investigations in the case. Once the evidence has been found, then the prosecution have to apply to the Court of Appeal for the original acquittal to be quashed.

This power has been used in cases where new techniques of DNA testing now show that a defendant who was acquitted is in fact the offender. The first case in which this power was used is shown in the following article.

Man admits murder in first UK double jeopardy case

Fifteen years after he was cleared of murder, the first person in Britain to face a retrial under new double jeopardy rules admitted today that he killed his victim.

Billy Dunlop, 43, pleaded guilty to murdering pizza delivery girl Julie Hogg, 22, in Billingham, Teeside, when he appeared at the Old Bailey today.

Dunlop stood trial twice in 1991 for her murder but each time a jury failed to reach a verdict. He was formally acquitted under the convention that the prosecution do not ask for a third trial in such circumstances.

But in April last year the double jeopardy rule – which prevented a defendant who had been acquitted from being tried again for the same offence – was changed under the Criminal Justice Act 2003.

The following November the Director of Public Prosecutions announced the legal process to re-try Dunlop had begun. The case was sent to the Court of Appeal where his acquittal was quashed.

Taken from an article in the *Daily Mail*,
11 September 2006

Key facts

Party	Court which hears appeal	Reason for appealing	Relevant Act of Parliament
Defence	Court of Appeal	against sentence and/or conviction need leave to appeal	Criminal Appeal Act 1995 conviction 'unsafe'
Defence	Further appeal to House of Lords	on point of law of general public importance need leave to appeal	
Prosecution	Court of Appeal	against a judge's ruling on a point of law	Criminal Justice Act 2003
Prosecution	High Court	asking for order to quash acquittal because of interference with witness or jury	Criminal Procedure and Investigations Act 1996
Prosecution	Court of Appeal	to have acquittal quashed because of new and compelling evidence	Criminal Justice Act 2003
Prosecution	Court of Appeal	Attorney-General's reference on a point of law: does not affect acquittal	Criminal Justice Act 1972
Prosecution	Court of Appeal	Attorney-General against lenient sentence	Criminal Justice Act 1988
Prosecution	Further appeal to House of Lords	on point of law of general public importance need leave to appeal	

Figure 7.3 Key facts chart on appeal rights from the Crown Court

Referring a point of law

The prosecution have a special referral right in cases where the defendant is acquitted. This is under s 36 of the Criminal Justice Act 1972 which allows the Attorney-General to refer a point of law to the Court of Appeal, in order to get a ruling on the law. The decision by the Court of Appeal on that point of law does not affect the acquittal but it creates a precedent for any future case involving the same point of law.

Against sentence

Under s 36 of the Criminal Justice Act 1988 the Attorney-General can apply for leave to refer an unduly lenient sentence to the Court of Appeal for re-sentencing. This power was initially available for indictable cases only, but was extended in 1994 to many triable either way offences, provided that the trial of the case took place at a Crown Court. This power is used successfully in a number of cases each year. There has recently been an increase in the number of such referrals.

One case which was referred in 2004 was that of Luan Plakici, who had been found guilty of kidnapping, procuring girls for sex and living off prostitution. He had brought young girls into Britain from Eastern Europe and then forced them to work as prostitutes. At his trial he was sentenced to ten years' imprisonment. On the Attorney-General's reference, the Court of Appeal increased this to 23 years' imprisonment.

Another case in 2007, was of a 14-year-old schoolboy who set fire to a school in West Yorkshire and caused £3 million worth of damage. His original sentence was a supervision order. The Court of Appeal held that this was 'unduly lenient' and changed the sentence to a four-year detention order.

7.2.3 Appeals to the House of Lords

Both the prosecution and the defence may appeal from the Court of Appeal to the House of Lords, but it is necessary to have the case certified as involving a point of law of general public importance, and to get leave to appeal, either from the House of Lords or from the Court of Appeal. There are very few criminal appeals heard by the House of Lords. In 2003 there were 220 petitions for leave to appeal considered, but leave was granted in only seven of these.

7.2.4 References to the European Court of Justice

Where a point of European law is involved in a case it is possible for any court to make a reference to the European Court of Justice under Art 234 of the Treaty of Rome (see Chapter 18). However, this is a fairly rare occurrence in criminal cases, as most of the criminal law is purely 'domestic' and not affected by European Union law.

7.3 The Criminal Cases Review Commission

Before 1997 there was no independent body to review possible miscarriages of justice. If the defendant's appeal failed, then there was little that he could do. The Home Secretary did have the power to review cases, but this was not sufficiently independent from the Government. In fact, the Home Secretary only used this power in a small number of cases.

To provide a better system for investigating possible miscarriages of justice, the Criminal Cases Review Commission was set up by the Criminal Appeal Act 1995.

The Commission has the power to investigate possible miscarriages of justice (including summary offences) and to refer cases back to the courts. In addition the Court of Appeal may direct the Commission to investigate and report to the court on any matter which comes before it in an appeal if it feels an investigation is likely to help the court resolve the appeal.

The members of the Commission are appointed by the Queen – at least one-third are legally qualified and at least two-thirds have relevant experience of the criminal justice system. They have about 60 support staff, treble the number previously used in the Home Office for such work. However, most of the re-investigation work is done by the police. This is felt to be unsatisfactory as it does not really make such a re-investigation independent, although it is true to say that many of the past miscarriages of justice have come to light as the result of investigation by other police forces.

Work

The Criminal Cases Review Commission took over the investigation of miscarriages of justice at the beginning of April 1997.

The main bulk of cases it investigates are brought to its attention by defendants themselves or by defendants' families, though some cases have been referred by the Court of Appeal and others have been identified by the Commission itself. Some of the first cases it investigated were alleged miscarriages of justice from over 40 years ago, such as the case of Derek Bentley. Bentley was hanged for murder in 1953, while his co-defendant, Craig, who actually fired the fatal shot, was not hanged due to his youth. Over the years there have been many attempts to have the case re-opened but it was not until the Criminal Cases Review Commission took over the investigation that the case was referred back to the Court of Appeal. In July 1998 the Court of Appeal held that the summing-up of the judge at the trial had not been fair and it quashed the conviction.

Referrals to the Court of Appeal

By the end of 2007 the Criminal Cases Review Commission had received over 10,000 applications. The Commission had referred 375 cases to the Court of Appeal – 337 of these had been heard and the convictions quashed in 235 cases.

Recent cases included that of Sally Clark who, in 2003, had her conviction for murdering her two babies quashed after the scientific evidence was shown to be flawed. In 2004, Sion Jenkins' conviction for the murder of his foster daughter was quashed, also because of flawed scientific evidence.

 Internet Research

Check the website for the Criminal Cases Review Commission (**www.ccrc.gov.uk**) and find out:

1. How many cases has the Commission now dealt with?
2. How many cases has it referred to the Court of Appeal?
3. In how many cases has the defendant had his conviction quashed?

Chapter 8

Sentencing

8.1 The role of the courts

Whenever a person pleads guilty, or is found guilty of an offence, the role of the court is to decide what sentence should be imposed on the offender. Judges and magistrates have a fairly wide discretion as to the sentence they select in each case, although they are subject to certain restrictions. Magistrates can only impose a maximum of six months' imprisonment for one offence (12 months' for two) and a maximum fine of £5,000. The Criminal Justice Act 2003 has provision for these sentencing powers to increase to 12 months for one offence and 15 months for two or more offences. Judges in the Crown Court have no such limits; they can impose up to life imprisonment for some crimes and there is no maximum figure for fines. Figure 8.1 shows the percentages of different sentences imposed in Magistrates' Courts and at the Crown Court in 2005. The differing percentages of offenders given an immediate custodial sentence stresses that the Crown Court is dealing with more serious offences.

8.1.1 Restrictions on the courts' powers

However, there are other restrictions, both in the Magistrates' Court and the Crown Court. Each crime has a maximum penalty for that type of offence set by Parliament – for example, the crime of theft has a fixed maximum of seven years' imprisonment, so that no matter how much has been stolen, the judge can never send an offender to prison for longer that this. Some offences have a maximum sentence of life imprisonment: these

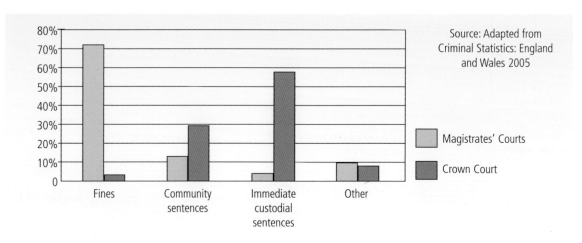

Figure 8.1 Sentencing in the Magistrates' Courts and Crown Court

include manslaughter and rape. In such cases the judge has complete discretion when sentencing; the offender may be sent to prison for life or given a shorter prison sentence, or a non-custodial sentence may even be thought appropriate. Murder is the exception as it carries a mandatory life sentence; in other words, the judge has to pass life imprisonment: there is no other sentence available.

8.2 Aims of sentencing

When judges or magistrates pass a sentence they will not only look at the sentences available, they will also have to decide what they are trying to achieve by the punishment they give. Section 142 of the Criminal Justice Act 2003 sets out the purposes of sentencing for those aged 18 and over saying that a court must have regard to:

- the punishment of offenders
- the reduction of crime (including its reduction by deterrence)
- the reform and rehabilitation of offenders
- the protection of the public and
- the making of reparation by offenders to persons affected by their offences.

Punishment is often referred to as retribution. In addition to the purposes of sentencing given in the 2003 Act, denunciation of crime is also recognised as an aim of sentencing. Each of the aims will now be examined in turn.

8.2.1 Retribution/punishment

Retribution is based on the idea of punishment because the offender deserves punishment for his or her acts. It does not seek to reduce crime or alter the offender's future behaviour. This idea was expressed in the nineteenth century by Kant in *The Metaphysical Elements of Justice* when he wrote:

> Judicial punishment can never be used merely as a means to promote some other good for the criminal himself or

for civil society, but instead it must in all cases be imposed on him only on the ground that he has committed a crime.

Retribution is therefore concerned only with the offence that was committed and making sure that the punishment inflicted is in proportion to that offence.

The crudest form of retribution can be seen in the old saying 'an eye for an eye and a tooth for a tooth and a life for a life'. This was one of the factors used to justify the death penalty for the offence of murder. In America, at least one judge has been known to put this theory into practice in other offences, by giving victims of burglary the right to go, with a law officer, to the home of the burglar and take items up to the approximate value of those stolen from them. In other crimes it is not so easy to see how this principle can operate to produce an exact match between crime and punishment.

Tariff sentences

Retribution, today, is based more on the idea that each offence should have a certain tariff or level of sentencing. The Sentencing Guidelines Council produces guidelines for this. For example for robbery the Council has set tariffs for adult offenders. These are shown in Figure 8.2.

8.2.2 Deterrence

This can be individual deterrence or general deterrence. Individual deterrence is intended to ensure that the offender does not re-offend, through fear of future punishment. General deterrence is aimed at preventing other potential offenders from committing crimes. Both are aimed at reducing future levels of crime.

Individual deterrence

There are several penalties that can be imposed with the aim of deterring the individual offender from committing similar crimes in the future.

Type/nature of activity	Starting point	Sentencing range
The offence includes the threat or use of minimal force and removal of property	12 months custody	Up to 3 years custody
A weapon is produced and used to threaten, and/or force is used which results in injury to the victim	4 years custody	2-7 years custody
The victim is caused serious physical injury by the use of significant force and/or use of a weapon	8 years custody	7-12 years custody

Figure 8.2 Sentencing Council's Guidelines on robbery

These include a prison sentence, a suspended sentence or a heavy fine. However, prison does not appear to deter as about 55 per cent of adult prisoners re-offend within two years of release. With young offenders, custodial sentences have even less of a deterrent effect. Over 70 per cent of young offenders given a custodial sentence re-offend within two years.

Critics of the theory of deterrence point out that it assumes that an offender will stop to consider what the consequences of his action will be. In fact most crimes are committed on the spur of the moment, and many are committed by offenders who are under the influence of drugs or alcohol. These offenders are unlikely to stop and consider the possible consequences of their actions.

It is also pointed out that fear of being caught is more of a deterrent and that while crime detection rates are low, the threat of an unpleasant penalty, if caught, seems too remote. Fear of detection has been shown to be a powerful deterrent by the success rate of closed circuit televisions used for surveying areas. In one scheme on London's District Line of the underground system there was an 83 per cent reduction in crime in the first full year that surveillance cameras were used.

General deterrence

The value of this is even more doubtful as potential offenders are rarely deterred by severe sentences passed on others. However, the courts do occasionally resort to making an example of an offender in order to warn other potential offenders of the type of punishment they face.

General deterrence also relies on publicity so that potential offenders are aware of the level of punishment they can expect. Deterrent sentences will, therefore, be even less effective in cases of drug smuggling by foreign nationals. Yet this is one of the crimes in which the courts seem tempted to resort to the hope that a severe sentence passed on one (or more) offender, will somehow deter other potential offenders.

General deterrence is in direct conflict with the principle of retribution, since it involves sentencing an offender to a longer term than is deserved for the specific offence. It is probably the least effective and least fair principle of sentencing.

8.2.3 Reform/rehabilitation

Under this the main aim of the penalty is to reform the offender and rehabilitate him or her into society. It is a forward-looking aim, with the hope that the offender's behaviour will be altered by the penalty imposed, so that he or she will not offend in the future (it aims to reduce crime in this way). This principle of sentencing came to the fore in the second half of the twentieth century with the development of community sentences.

As the abuse of drugs is the cause of many offences, there are also requirements – drug testing and treatment orders – aimed at trying to rehabilitate drug abusers.

Reformation is a very important element in the sentencing philosophy for young offenders, but it is also used for some adult offenders. The court will be given information about the defendant's background, usually through a pre-sentence report prepared by the probation service. Where relevant, the court will consider other factors, such as school reports, job prospects, or medical problems.

Individualised sentences

Where the court considers rehabilitation, the sentence used is an individualised one aimed at the needs of the offender. This is in direct contrast to the concept of tariff-sentences seen in the aim of retribution. One of the criticisms of this approach is, therefore, that it leads to inconsistency in sentencing. Offenders who have committed exactly the same type of offence may be given different sentences because the emphasis is on the individual offender. Another criticism is that it tends to discriminate against the underprivileged. Offenders from poor home backgrounds are less likely to be seen as possible candidates for reform.

8.2.4 Protection of the public

The public need to be protected from dangerous offenders. For this reason life imprisonment or a long term of imprisonment are given to those who commit murder or other violent or serious sexual offences.

Under the Criminal Justice Act 2003 a defendant can be sentenced to imprisonment for public protection. This is given where the court is of the opinion that there is a significant risk to members of the public of serious harm being caused by the defendant in the future.

Extended sentences can also be given where it is thought necessary to protect the public. This adds an extra period to the defendant's sentence during which he is freed on licence.

For less serious offences there are other ways in which the public can be protected. For example, dangerous drivers are disqualified from driving. Another method is to include an exclusion order as a requirement in a community order. This will ban the offender from going to places where he is most likely to commit an offence. The use of such a banning order is shown in *R v Winkler* (2004).

In this case the defendant committed an affray in Manchester when attending a football match in which Oldham Athletic, the team he supported, was playing. The judge banned the defendant from going into Oldham town centre on home match days and also banned him from approaching within half a mile of any football stadium. Both bans were for a period of six years.

Another method of protecting the public is to impose a curfew order on the offender ordering him to remain at home for certain times of the day or night. The curfew can be monitored by an electronic tag, which should trigger an alarm if the offender leaves his home address during a curfew period.

8.2.5 Reparation

This is aimed at compensating the victim of the crime usually by ordering the offender to pay a sum of money to the victim or to make restitution, for example by returning stolen property to its rightful owner. The idea that criminals should pay compensation to the victims of their crimes is one that goes back to before the Norman Conquest to the Anglo-Saxon courts. In England today, the courts are required to consider ordering compensation to the victim of a crime, in addition to any other penalty they may think appropriate. Under s 130 of the Powers of Criminal Courts (Sentencing) Act 2000 courts are under a duty to give reasons if they do not make a compensation order. There are also projects to bring offenders and victims together, so that the offenders may make direct reparation.

The concept of restitution also includes making reparation to society as a whole. This can be seen mainly in the use of an unpaid work requirement

Key facts

Theory	Aim of theory	Suitable punishment
Retribution/ Punishment	Punishment imposed only on ground that an offence has been committed	● Tariff sentences ● Sentence must be proportionate to the crime
Deterrence	Individual – the offender is deterred through fear of further punishment General – potential offenders warned as to likely punishment	● Prison sentence ● Heavy fine ● Long sentence as an example to others
Rehabilitation	Reform offender's behaviour	● Individualised sentence ● Community order
Protection of the public	Offender is made incapable of committing further crime Society is protected from crime	● Long prison sentences ● Tagging ● Banning orders
Reparation	Repayment/reparation to victim or to community	● Compensation order ● Unpaid work ● Reparation schemes
Denunciation	Society expressing its disapproval Reinforces moral boundaries	● Reflects blameworthiness of the offence

Figure 8.3 Key facts chart on aims of sentencing

where offenders are required to do so many hours work on a community project under the supervision of the probation service.

8.2.6 Denunciation

This is society expressing its disapproval of criminal activity. A sentence should indicate both to the offender and to other people that society condemns certain types of behaviour. It shows people that justice is being done. Lord Denning when giving written evidence to the Royal Commission on Capital Punishment put it in this way:

> Punishment is the way in which society expresses its denunciation of wrong doing: and in order to maintain respect for the law it is essential that the punishment inflicted for grave crimes should adequately reflect the revulsion felt by the great majority of citizens for them.

Denunciation also reinforces the moral boundaries of acceptable conduct and can mould society's views on the criminality of particular conduct – for example, drink driving is now viewed by the majority of people as unacceptable behaviour. This is largely because of the changes in the law and the increasingly severe sentences that are imposed. By sending offenders to prison, banning them from driving and imposing heavy fines, society's opinion of drink driving has been changed.

Activity

Read the following article and answer the questions following it.

Tougher jail terms DO deter criminals, admits Home Office

A Home Office report has concluded that stiffer prison sentences deter crime . . . the study found that convicts jailed for less than a year are almost 50 per cent more likely to commit a fresh crime within two years of their release than those locked up for between one and four years.

And they are twice as likely to break the law as those jailed for at least four years.

The report is embarrassing for the Government. Only this month [May 2007], Lord Falconer, newly-created Justice Secretary, announced that tens of thousands of burglars and other thieves would receive community punishments instead of jail sentences under plans to ease chronic prison overcrowding.

In March [2007] the Prime Minister signalled that there should be greater emphasis on rehabilitating offenders, tougher community sentences and crime prevention . . .

Figures show that 70 per cent of convicts jailed for under 12 months re-offended within two years, compared with 49 per cent of those convicted to between one and four years and 36 per cent of those serving at least four years.

The report said prisoners released from longer sentences were less likely to re-offend because they were older, had time to be rehabilitated and had been convicted of more serious "one-off" offences.

Taken from an article by Ian Drury in the *Daily Mail*, 19 May 2007

Questions

1. What sentencing aim does this article suggest that stiffer prison sentences promotes?
2. What sentencing aim did the Prime Minister want emphasised?
3. What sentencing aim does the Home Office Report say had an effect on longer term prisoners?
4. Name and explain two other sentencing aims.

8.3 Sentencing practice in the courts

The court will usually consider both the offence and the background of the offender, as well as the aims of sentencing. In order to do this the court must know details of the offence, so, where the defendant pleads guilty, the prosecution will outline the facts of the case. As seen in section 6.1.2, the defendant is asked if he agrees with those facts and, if not, a Newton hearing will be held for the facts to be established. This is important as the details of the offence can affect the sentence. Where the defendant has pleaded not guilty and been convicted after a trial, the court will have heard full information about the case during the trial.

8.3.1 Factors surrounding the offence

In looking at the offence, the most important point to establish is how serious was it, of its type? This is now set out in s 143(1) of the

Criminal Justice Act 2003 which states that:

> In considering the seriousness of the offence, the court must consider the offender's culpability in committing the offence and any harm which the offence caused, or was intended to cause or might reasonably foreseeably have caused.

The Act goes on to give certain factors which are considered as aggravating factors making an offence more serious. These are:

* previous convictions for offences of a similar nature or relevant to the present offence
* the fact that the defendant was on bail when he committed the offence
* racial or religious hostility being involved in the offence
* hostility to disability or sexual orientation being involved in the offence.

Other points the courts will want to know may include, for example in a case of theft, how much was stolen, and was the defendant in a position of trust? In a case of assault the court will need to know what injuries were inflicted and whether the assault was premeditated or was the victim particularly vulnerable (perhaps elderly).

Where the offender was in a position of trust and abused that trust, then the offence will be considered as being more serious and meriting a longer than usual sentence.

Where several defendants are convicted of committing a crime jointly, the court will want to know if any of them played a greater part than the others, and who was involved in planning it. The sentences that each receives will reflect the part they played in the offence.

8.3.2 Reduction in sentence for a guilty plea

There can be a reduction in sentence for a guilty plea, particularly where made early in the proceedings. The Sentencing Guidelines Council

has suggested that the reduction for a guilty plea at the first reasonable opportunity should attract a reduction of up to one-third, whereas a plea of guilty after the trial has started would only be given a one-tenth reduction. The amount of reduction is on a sliding scale, as shown in Figure 8.4.

Figure 8.4 Reduction in sentence for a guilty plea

The concept of reducing the level of sentence imposed on a defendant just because he has pleaded guilty has caused controversy. Many people believe that if someone has 'done the crime, they should do the time'. However, in its draft guidelines, the Sentencing Guidelines Council gave its reasons for allowing discounts in sentences for guilty pleas by stating:

> A reduction in sentence is appropriate because a guilty plea avoids the need for a trial, shortens the gap between charge and sentence, saves considerable cost, and, in the case of an early plea, saves victims and witnesses from the concern about having to give evidence.

After publicity about cases where defendants had had their sentences reduced because they pleaded guilty, the Government asked the Sentencing Guidelines Council to look at the issue again. The Council's revised guidelines, published in 2007, state that where the prosecution evidence is overwhelming (ie the evidence against the defendant is exceptionally strong) the reduction for pleading guilty should be less. The recommended reduction when a plea of guilty is made at the first reasonable opportunity in such a case is 20 per cent.

8.3.3 The offender's background

Previous convictions

As far as the offender is concerned, the court will want to know whether he has any previous convictions. The court may also take into account the failure of an offender to respond to previous sentences, in deciding the seriousness of the current offence. The past record of the offender will also determine whether he has to receive a minimum sentence or an automatic life sentence for certain offences.

Another important factor is whether the offender was on bail when he committed the offence. If this is the case, the court must treat that fact as an aggravating factor.

Pre-sentence reports

These are prepared by the probation service. The court does not have to (but usually will) consider such a report before deciding to impose a custodial sentence, though for very serious offences such a report may not be relevant. Where the court is considering a community sentence, they are likely to have a report before they decide on the sentence. The report will give information about the defendant's background and suitability, or otherwise, for a community-based sentence. The defendant's background may be important in showing both why the offender committed a crime, and indicate if he is likely to respond to a community-based penalty.

Medical reports

Where the offender has medical or psychiatric problems, the court will usually ask for a report to be prepared by an appropriate doctor. Medical conditions may be important factors in deciding the appropriate way of dealing with the offender; the courts have special powers where the defendant is suffering from mental illness. The treatment of mentally ill defendants is considered further in section 8.6.

The financial situation of the offender

Where the court considers that a fine is a suitable penalty, it must inquire into the financial circumstances of the offender, and take this into account when setting the level of the fine.

8.3.4 Sentencing Guidelines Council

In 2003 the Sentencing Guidelines Council was set up under the Criminal Justice Act 2003. This Council can decide to issue guidelines on any aspect of sentencing. Also, if the Secretary of State or the Sentencing Advisory Panel makes a proposal to the Council that there should be guidelines for a particular offence or aspect of sentencing, then the Council must make guidelines on that point.

When the Sentencing Guidelines Council decides to make guidelines, it must have regard to:

- the need for consistency in sentencing
- the sentences imposed by courts for offences of the relevant category
- the cost of different sentences and their relative effectiveness in preventing re-offending
- the need to promote public confidence in the criminal justice system
- the views of the Sentencing Advisory Panel.

The Sentencing Guidelines Council has issued guidelines for sentencing for various types of offences. These guidelines include:

- overarching principles for seriousness factors in offences
- overarching principles on sentencing in domestic violence cases
- specific guidance on sentencing for robbery
- specific guidance for sentences in cases of manslaughter where there was provocation.

Degree of provocation	Sentence range	Starting point
Low	10 years to life	12 years' custody
Substantial	4–9 years	8 years' custody
High	if custody is absolutely necessary, up to 4 years	3 years' custody

Figure 8.5 Sentencing guidelines on manslaughter through provocation

For this last category the Council stresses that:

- sentences for public protection *must* be considered in all cases of manslaughter and
- the degree of provocation is a critical factor in deciding the sentence.

The guidelines for this are shown in Figure 8.5.

8.4 Powers of the courts

As already indicated, the courts have several different types of sentences available to them. There are four main categories: custodial sentences, community sentences, fines and discharges. The courts also have the power to make additional orders such as compensation orders, and, in motoring offences, have other powers such as disqualification from driving.

8.4.1 Custodial sentences

A custodial sentence is the most serious punishment that a court can impose. Custodial sentences range from a few weeks to life imprisonment. They include:

- mandatory and discretionary life sentences
- fixed-term sentences
- custody plus (short-term sentence)
- suspended sentences.

Custodial sentences are meant to be used only for serious offences. Section 152 of the Criminal Justice Act 2003 says that the court must not pass a custodial sentence unless it is of the opinion that the offence (or combination of offences):

 was so serious that neither a fine alone nor a community sentence can be justified.

The age of the offender is also important as young offenders should only be given a custodial sentence as a last resort. Where a young offender is given a custodial sentence they are always held in separate units from adults.

The court must state its reason for imposing a custodial sentence, and in the case of the Magistrates' Court, that reason must be written on the warrant of commitment and entered in the court register.

In the guidelines on suggested 'entry points' published by the Magistrates' Association, a custodial sentence is advised for offences such as assaulting a police officer in the execution of his duty, and burglary of a residential property.

Mandatory life sentences

For murder, the only sentence a judge can impose is a life sentence. However, the judge is allowed to state the minimum number of years' imprisonment that the offender must serve before being eligible for release on licence. This minimum term is now governed by the Criminal Justice Act 2003. This gives judges clear starting points for the minimum period to be ordered. The starting points range from a full-life term down to 12 years. A whole-life term should be set where the offence falls into one of the following categories:

Inside Winchester prison

- the murder of two or more persons, where each murder involves a substantial degree of premeditation or planning or the abduction of the victim or sexual or sadistic conduct
- the murder of a child if involving the abduction of the child or sexual or sadistic motivation
- a murder done for the purpose of advancing a political, religious or ideological cause or
- a murder by an offender previously convicted of murder.

Cases which have a starting point of 30 years include where the murder is of a police or prison officer in the course of his duty, or a murder using a firearm or explosive or the sexual or sadistic murder of an adult or a murder that is racially or religiously aggravated. For any offence of murder which is not specifically given a starting point of a whole-life term or 30 years, a starting point of 15 years is given. Where the offender was under the age of 18 at the time of the offence this period is 12 years. Once the judge has decided on the starting point, any aggravating or mitigating factors must then be considered.

Aggravating factors which can increase the minimum term ordered by the judge include the fact that the victim was particularly vulnerable because of age or disability, or any mental or physical suffering inflicted on the victim before death. Mitigating factors include the fact that the offender had an intention to cause grievous bodily harm rather than an intention to kill, a lack of premeditation or the fact that the offender acted to some extent in self-defence (though not sufficient to give him a defence). Where there are mitigating factors the judge can set a minimum term of less than any of the starting points.

A sentence of life imprisonment also has normally to be imposed where an offender over the age of 18 is convicted of a second serious sexual or violent offence. The judge can set an appropriate minimum time to be served in prison. Where there are 'exceptional circumstances' the judge does not have to impose a life sentence.

Discretionary life sentences

For other serious offences such as manslaughter, rape and robbery the maximum sentence is life imprisonment, but the judge does not have to impose it. The judge has discretion in sentencing and can give any lesser sentence where appropriate. This can even be a fine or a discharge.

Fixed-term sentences

For other crimes, the length of the sentence will depend on several factors, including the maximum sentence available for the particular crime, the seriousness of the crime and the defendant's previous record. Imprisonment for a set number of months or years is called a 'fixed-term' sentence.

Prisoners do not serve the whole of the sentence passed by the court. Anyone sent to prison is automatically released after they have served half of the sentence. Only offenders aged 21 and over can be given a sentence of imprisonment.

Home Detention Curfew

The Crime and Disorder Act 1998 allows early release from prison on condition that a curfew condition is included. The curfew is enforced by electronic tagging. The period of curfew is increased with the length of sentence. There is no automatic right to be released on curfew; each prisoner is assessed to see if he or she is suitable. If a Home Detention Curfew order is not made, then the prisoner must serve half the sentence before release on licence.

The reason for introducing such Home Detention Curfews is to encourage recently released prisoners to structure their lives more effectively as well as prevent re-offending. Also by releasing prisoners early in this way the prison population is reduced.

Extended sentences

Section 85 of the Powers of Criminal Courts (Sentencing) Act 2000 gives the sentencing court power to pass an extended sentence for a sexual or violent offence. This means that the offender is given a custodial sentence plus a further period (the 'extension period') during which the offender

is at liberty on licence. The extension period cannot exceed 10 years for a sexual offence or five years for a violent offence.

The idea behind this sentence is to have greater control over sexual offenders when they leave prison. Such offenders are also required to register with the police so that it is known where they are living.

Minimum sentences

There is a minimum sentence of seven years for anyone aged 18 or over who is convicted on three separate occasions of dealing in Class A drugs. There is also a minimum sentence of three years for those convicted of burglary of a residential building for a third time. In both these cases judges can impose a lesser sentence if there are exceptional circumstances.

Prison population

A problem is that prisons in England and Wales are overcrowded. There has been a big increase in the number of people in prison and there are not enough prison places. Figure 8.6 shows the increase in the prison population between 1951 and 2006.

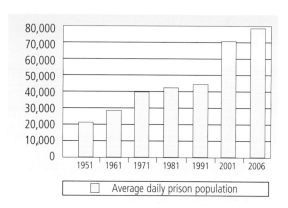

Figure 8.6 Average daily prison population for England and Wales 1951–2006

The Government has forecast that the prison population is likely to rise to 93,000 by 2009.

Internet Research

Look up the current prison population on the Internet. It can be found at
www.hmprisonservice.gov.uk

Suspended prison sentences

An adult offender may be given a suspended prison sentence of up to two years (six months maximum in the Magistrates' Court). This means that the sentence does not take effect immediately. The court will fix a time during which the sentence is suspended; this can be for any period up to two years. If, during this time, the offender does not commit any further offences, the prison sentence will not be served. However, if the offender does

Activity

Read the following extract from an article in the *New Law Journal* and answer the questions below.

Taking responsibility

Fifty-eight per cent of all prisoners and three in four young offenders are re-convicted within two years of release, *write Finola Farrant and Joe Levenson.* Why is this and what can be done?

Prisoners have many of the characteristics of social exclusion:

- 26 per cent have spent time in care as a child;
- 47 per cent of women in prison have no educational qualifications;
- 66 per cent of men in prison do not have a job at the time of their conviction; and
- eight per cent of female prisoners have previously been admitted to a psychiatric hospital . . .

The Prison Reform Trust recently published

Barred Citizens: Volunteering and Active Citizenship by Prisoners, which examined and identified the benefits of volunteering and active citizenship by prisoners. Volunteering can offer a means of improving the employment prospects of prisoners by providing work experience, improving skills and confidence and enabling prisoners to gain a work reference . . .

Prisoners currently face great difficulties finding employment after release because of low educational attainment, health problems, a lack of suitable housing and obsolete skills. Ex-prisoners also frequently face discrimination from employers . . .

Volunteering, especially when it involves undertaking community placements, allows prisoners to build or maintain links with the outside world.

Taken from 'Taking Responsibility' by Finola Farrant and Joe Levenson, *New Law Journal*, LexisNexis Butterworths, 6 August 2002

Questions

1. What percentage of prisoners re-offend within two years of release?

2. What problems do many of those who are convicted have prior to their conviction?

3. What problems are faced by prisoners when they finish their sentence?

4. What solution does the article suggest for some of these problems?

5. Suggest other ways in which offenders could be prepared to reintegrate into society.

commit another offence within the period of suspension, then the prison sentence is 'activated' and the offender will serve that sentence together with any sentence for the new offence.

A suspended sentence should only be given where the offence is so serious that an immediate custodial sentence would have been appropriate, but there are exceptional circumstances in the case that justify suspending the sentence.

The suspended sentence can be combined with any of the requirements used in a community order (see section 8.4.2). If the offender fails to meet the requirements the suspended sentence may be 'activated'. This means that the offender will be made to serve the term of imprisonment. Prior to the Criminal Justice Act 2003, a suspended sentence could only be combined with a fine or a compensation order, leaving the offender unsupervised. As a result, a suspended sentence was seen as a 'soft option' and rarely used by the courts.

8.4.2 Community orders

The Criminal Justice Act 2003 created one community order under which the court can combine any requirements they think are necessary. These requirements are listed below. The sentencers can 'mix and match' requirements allowing them to fit the restrictions and rehabilitation to the offender's needs. The sentence is available for offenders aged 16 and over. The full list of requirements available to the courts is set out in s 177 of the Criminal Justice Act 2003. This states:

177(1) Where a person aged 16 or over is convicted of an offence, the court by or before which he is convicted may make an order imposing on him any one or more of the following requirements:

(a) an unpaid work requirement

(b) an activity requirement

(c) a programme requirement

(d) a prohibited activity requirement

(e) a curfew requirement

(f) an exclusion requirement

(g) a residence requirement

(h) a mental health treatment requirement

(i) a drug rehabilitation requirement

(j) an alcohol treatment requirement

(k) a supervision requirement, and

(l) in the case where the offender is aged under 25, an attendance centre requirement.

Each of these is defined within the Criminal Justice Act 2003. Most are self-explanatory from their name, such as drug rehabilitation and alcohol treatment. Much crime is linked to drug and alcohol abuse and the idea behind these two requirements is to tackle the causes of crime, and hopefully prevent further offences. Mental health treatment is also aimed at the cause of the offender's behaviour. The main other requirements are explained briefly below.

Unpaid work requirement

This requires the offender to work for between 40 and 300 hours on a suitable project organised by the probation service. The exact number of hours will be fixed by the court, and those hours are then usually worked in eight-hour sessions, often at weekends. The type of work involved will vary, depending on what schemes the local probation service have running. The offender may be required to paint school buildings, help build a play centre or work on conservation projects. When Eric Cantona, the French footballer, was found guilty of assaulting a football fan, the court ordered that he help at coaching sessions for young footballers.

One criticism is that the number of hours is not enough – other countries which run similar schemes can impose much longer hours. However, re-offending rates are lower than for other community sentences. NB The lower limit of 40 hours may be reduced to 20 hours.

This is the government's latest idea for a community sentence.

Prohibited activity requirement

This requirement allows a wide variety of activities to be prohibited. The idea is to try to prevent the defendant from committing another crime of the type he has just been convicted of. Often the defendant is forbidden to go into a certain area where he has caused trouble. In some cases the defendant has been banned from wearing a 'hoodie'. In 2006, a defendant who was found guilty of criminal damage was banned from carrying paint, dye, ink or marker pens.

Curfew requirement

Under this, an offender can be ordered to remain at a fixed address for between 2 and 12 hours in any 24-hour period. This order can last for up to six months and may be enforced by electronic tagging (where suitable). Courts can only make such an order if there is an arrangement for monitoring curfews in their area. Such monitoring can be done by spot-checks, with security firms sending someone to make sure that the offender is at home or offenders may be electronically tagged. There are also pilot schemes on using

satellite technology to track those who are tagged.

The cost of tagging is quite expensive, being estimated at £675 per offender per month. However, this does compare favourably with the cost of keeping an offender in prison as the estimated cost of this is £1,555 per offender per month.

Initially tagging appeared to be a successful method of preventing reoffending. However, a report in 2007 showed that 58 per cent of offenders broke the terms of their tagging order. More than a quarter committed further offences while tagged.

Exclusion requirement

Offenders are ordered not to go to certain places. The order can specify different places for different periods or days. This is intended to keep offenders away from areas where they are most likely to commit crime. For example, a persistent shoplifter could be banned from certain shopping areas. The order can be for up to two years for offenders 16 and over, and a maximum of three months for those under 16.

Supervision requirement

For this requirement the offender is placed under the supervision of a probation officer for a period of up to three years. During the period of supervision the offender must attend appointments with the supervising officer or with any other person decided by the supervising officer.

The Criminal Justice Act 2003 states that a supervision requirement may be imposed for the purpose of 'promoting the offender's rehabilitation'.

8.4.3 Fines

This is the most common way of disposing of a case in the Magistrates' Court where the maximum fine is £5,000 for an individual offender. The magistrate can impose a fine of up to £20,000 on businesses who have committed offences under certain regulations, such as health and safety at work. In the Crown Court only a small percentage of offenders are dealt with by way of a fine.

8.4.4 Discharges

These may be either a conditional discharge or an absolute discharge. A conditional discharge means that the court discharges an offender on the condition that no further offence is committed during a set period of up to three years. It is intended to be used where it is thought that punishment is not necessary. If an offender re-offends within the time limit, the court can then impose another sentence in place of the conditional discharge, as well as imposing a penalty for the new offence. Conditional discharges are widely used by Magistrates' Courts for first-time minor offenders.

An absolute discharge means that, effectively,

Activity

Look at the bar chart on the opening page of this chapter which shows the types of sentence used in the Magistrates' and the Crown Courts and answer the following questions.

1. What type of sentence are offenders most likely to be given at the Crown Court?
2. What type of sentence are offenders most likely to be given at the Magistrates' Courts?
3. Why do you think the sentences used most frequently are different for the two courts?
4. Which two types of sentence show the biggest difference in percentages given at the Crown Court and at the Magistrates' Courts?
5. Why do you think the percentages for these two types of sentence are different in the Magistrates' Court and the Crown Court?

no penalty is imposed. Such a penalty is likely to be used where an offender is technically guilty but morally blameless. An example could be where the tax disc on a vehicle has fallen to the floor – it is technically not being displayed and an offence has been committed. So, in the unlikely situation of someone being prosecuted for this, the magistrates, who would have to impose some penalty, would most probably decide that an absolute discharge was appropriate.

8.4.5 Disqualification from driving

Where a defendant is charged with a driving offence, the courts may also have the power to disqualify that person from driving for a certain period of time. The length of the disqualification will depend on the seriousness of the driving offence. Usually the courts will impose a fine as well as disqualification. For a first-time drink-driving offence the courts have to disqualify the defendant for a minimum of 12 months, unless there are very exceptional reasons not to disqualify. If an offender has a previous drink-drive conviction, then the minimum is usually three years' disqualification.

The courts can use this power to disqualify in any other crime where the offender has used a vehicle to commit an offence. For example, a defendant who drives a car in order to do a burglary could be disqualified from driving, but this power is not often used.

8.4.6 Other powers available to the courts

The courts have other powers which are aimed at compensating victims and/or making sure that the defendant does not benefit from his or her crimes.

Compensation orders and restitution orders

Courts can make an order that the defendant pay a sum of money to his victim in compensation.

They are encouraged to use this order by the fact that they must give reasons if they do not make a compensation order in any case in which they have the power to do so. In the Magistrates' Court the maximum amount of compensation is £5,000.

If the defendant still has the property he obtained from the victim, then the courts can make an order that the property is returned. This is called a restitution order.

Deprivation and forfeiture orders

A court can order an offender to be deprived of property he has used to commit an offence. For example, a person convicted of drink-driving could be ordered to lose his car. There is special power to order forfeiture in drug-related cases. The Proceeds of Crime Act 1995 also gives the courts powers to take from criminals all profits from crime for up to six years before conviction.

Deferred sentences

Where the judge has a good reason to believe that the offender's circumstances are about to change, the sentence may be deferred for up to six months. This is to see if the change makes a difference to the defendant's behaviour. A sentence should only be deferred where the change in circumstances is such that punishment will not be necessary, or a lesser penalty be more suitable as a result of the change. The offender has to consent to sentence being deferred.

8.5 Young offenders

This term includes all offenders under the age of 21. However, there are considerable variations in the different sentences available for those under 18, under 16, under 14 and under 12. The main aim in sentencing young offenders is reformation and rehabilitation. As already seen in Chapter 6, offenders under 18-years-old are normally dealt with in the Youth Court.

8.5.1 Available sentences
Young Offenders' Institutions

Offenders aged 18 to 20 can be sent to a Young Offenders' Institution as a custodial sentence. The minimum sentence is 21 days and the maximum is the maximum allowed for the particular offence. If the offender becomes 21 years old while serving the sentence, he will be transferred to an adult prison.

Detention and training orders

The Crime and Disorder Act 1998 created a custodial sentence, called a detention and training order, for young offenders. The sentence must be for a specified period with a minimum of four months and a maximum of 24 months. In between these, the order can be for six months, eight months, 10 months, 12 months or 18 months. No other length of time can be given.

A detention and training order can be passed on offenders from the age of 12 to the age of 21, but for those under the age of 15 this order can only be made if they are persistent offenders.

Detention for serious crimes

For very serious offences, the courts have additional power to order that the offender be detained for longer periods. For 10- to 13-year-olds this power is only available where the crime committed carries a maximum sentence of at least 14 years' imprisonment for adults. For 14- to 17-year-olds, it is also available for causing death by dangerous driving, or for causing death by careless driving while under the influence of drink or drugs. The length of detention imposed on the young offender cannot be more than the maximum sentence available for an adult.

Detention at Her Majesty's Pleasure

Any offender aged 10–17 who is convicted of murder must be ordered to be detained during Her Majesty's Pleasure. This is an indeterminate sentence which allows the offender to be released when suitable. The judge in the case can recommend a minimum number of years that should be served before release is considered, and the Lord Chief Justice will then set the tariff.

If an offender reaches 21 while still serving a sentence he will be transferred to an adult prison.

Community orders

These can only be given to young offenders aged 16 and over. The same requirements as for adults can be imposed. These include an unpaid work requirement, an activity requirement, a prohibited activity requirement and a curfew requirement (see section 8.4.2 for full list). The exception to the age limit is that a curfew order can be imposed on offenders from the age of 10 upwards.

Attendance Centre Orders

This type of order is only for those under 25, and is available for all young offenders from the age of 10 upwards. It involves attendance at a special centre for two or three hours a week – up to a maximum of 36 hours for 16- to 24-year-olds, and 24 hours for 10- to 15-year-olds. The minimum number of hours is usually 12, but can be less for offenders under the age of 14. The centres used to be run by the police but are now under the supervision of the probation service; they are usually held on Saturday afternoons and will include organised leisure activities and training. An Attendance Centre Order cannot be made if the offender has served a period of detention previously.

Supervision Orders

Those under 18 can be placed under the supervision of one of the following:

- the local social services
- a probation officer

Key facts

Types of sentence	Age limitations
Custodial sentences	• Prison only for 21+ • Young Offenders' Institution 18 to 20-year-olds • Detention and training order for 12 to 17-year-olds • Powers of detention for 10 to 17-year-olds in serious cases
Community sentences	• May 'mix and match' different requirements to suit different offenders' needs for 16+ • Curfew requirements and exclusion requirements are also available for 10+ • Attendance centres for 10 to 24-year-olds • Supervision Orders for 10 to 17-year-olds • Action Plan Orders for 10 to 17-year-olds
Fines	• Over-18s: Magistrates' Court, maximum £5,000 (Crown Court, no limit) • 14–17: maximum £1,000 • 10–13: maximum £250
Discharges	• Conditional discharge – 10+ • Absolute discharge – 10+
Other powers	• Disqualification from driving – 10+ • Compensation orders – 10+ • Reparation orders – 10–17

Figure 8.7 Key facts chart on sentencing powers of the courts

- a member of a Youth Offending Team.

This can be for a period of up to three years.

Action Plan Orders

Section 69 of the Crime and Disorder Act 1998 created a new community order called an Action Plan Order which the courts can impose on offenders under the age of 18. In the White Paper *No More Excuses*, the Government said it was intended to be 'a short intensive programme of community intervention combining punishment, rehabilitation and reparation to change offending behaviour and prevent further crime'.

The order places the offender under supervision and also sets out requirements the offender has to comply with in respect to his actions and whereabouts during a period of three months.

These requirements can be any of the following:

- to participate in set activities
- to present himself to a specified person at set times and places
- to attend at an attendance centre
- to stay away from certain places
- to comply with arrangements for his education
- to make reparation.

Fines

The maximum amount of a fine varies with the age of the offender: 10- to 13-year-olds can only be fined a maximum of £250, while for 14- to 17-year-olds the maximum is £1,000. Those aged 18 and over are subject to the normal maximum of the Magistrates' Court of £5,000.

Reparation Orders

A Reparation Order may be imposed on offenders under the age of 18. This order cannot be made in combination with a custodial sentence, Community Service Order, a combination order, a Supervision Order or an Action Plan Order.

An order will require the offender to make reparation as specified in the order:

- to a person or persons who were victims of the offence or were otherwise affected by it or
- to the community at large.

The order is for a maximum of 24 hours' work and the reparation order must be completed under supervision within three months of its imposition. An order for direct reparation to a victim can only be made with that person's consent.

Discharges

These may be used for an offender of any age, and are commonly used for first-time young offenders who have committed minor crimes.

However, the courts cannot conditionally discharge an offender in the following circumstances:

- where a child or young offender who is convicted of an offence has been warned within the previous two years, unless there are exceptional circumstances which must be explained in open court
- where the offender is in breach of an anti-social behaviour order
- where the offender is in breach of a sex offender order.

Reprimands and warnings

These are not sentences passed by a court, but methods by which the police can deal with offenders without bringing the case to court. For either a reprimand or warning to be given there must be evidence that a child or young person has committed an offence and admits it. In addition, the police must be satisfied that it would not be in the public interest for the offender to be prosecuted. A reprimand or warning can only be given if the offender has never been convicted of any offence.

There is a limit to the number of times and the occasions on which an offender can be 'cautioned'. The first step is the reprimand. This can only be given if the child or young person has not been previously reprimanded or warned. Even then it should not be used where the constable considers the offence to be so serious as to require a warning.

An offender may be warned only if he has not been warned before or if an earlier warning was more than two years before. When warned the child or young offender must be referred to a Youth Offending Team. This team assesses the case and, unless it considers it inappropriate to do so, arranges for the offender to participate in a rehabilitation scheme.

8.5.2 Parental responsibility

If the parents agree, they can be bound over to keep their child under control for a set period of up to one year. If the child commits an offence during this period the parents will forfeit a sum of money up to a maximum of £1,000. If a parent unreasonably refuses to be bound over, the court has the power to fine that parent instead. Parents can also be bound over to ensure that a young offender complies with a community sentence.

Where an offender under 16 years old is fined or ordered to pay compensation, the court must require the offender's parents to pay, and the financial situation of the parent is taken into account in deciding the amount of the order.

Parenting orders

This is intended to offer training and support to parents to help change their children's offending behaviour. In this way it is more practical than the existing provisions which merely make a parent responsible for their child's offending behaviour. Under such an order a parent can be required to attend counselling or guidance sessions for up to three months on a maximum basis of once a week.

In addition, the parent may be required to comply with conditions imposed by the courts; for example, escort the child to school or ensure that a responsible adult is present in the home in the evening to supervise the child. A court may make a parenting order where:

- the court makes a child safety order
- the court makes an anti-social behaviour order

(or sex offender order) in respect of a child
- a child or young person is convicted of an offence
- a parent is convicted of an offence relating to truancy under the Education Act 1996.

An order should only be made if it is desirable in the interests of preventing the conduct which gave rise to the order. Where a person under the age of 16 is convicted of an offence, the court should make a parenting order unless it is satisfied that it is not desirable in the interests of preventing the conduct which gave rise to the order. In this case the court must state in open court that it is not satisfied it is desirable and explain why not.

8.5.3 Youth Offending Teams

The Crime and Disorder Act 1998 made it the duty of each local authority to establish one or

Activity

Suggest a suitable sentence for the following offenders and explain what the aim of the sentence would be.

1. Kevin, aged 22, has been found guilty by the magistrates of two charges of criminal damage. The amount of damage involved is estimated at £600. He is single, unemployed and has no previous convictions.
2. Melanie, aged 15, appeared before the local youth court and admitted shoplifting on five occasions. She also admitted two offences of taking and driving a car without the owner's consent. She has appeared before the youth court on two previous occasions for similar offences.
3. Andrew, aged 26, has been found guilty at the Crown Court of an assault causing grievous bodily harm. He committed this offence while on bail charged with another offence of violence.

more Youth Offending Teams (YOTs) in their area. The main idea in establishing these teams is to build on co-operation between agencies involved, especially social services and the probation service. These teams are to co-ordinate the provision of youth justice services in the area.

A YOT must include a probation officer, a local authority social worker, a police officer, a representative of the local health authority and a person nominated by the chief education officer. Any other appropriate person may also be invited to join the team.

The role of YOTs is highlighted by the fact that, under s 66 of the Crime and Disorder Act 1998, any offender who is warned must be referred to the local YOT. Youth courts may also refer offenders to the YOT.

8.6 Mentally ill offenders

The law recognises that, so far as possible, mentally ill offenders should not be punished but should receive treatment. Where an offence has been committed by an offender who is mentally ill, the courts have a wider range of powers available to them. In addition to the ordinary sentences which can be given, there are special provisions aimed at treating such offenders in a suitable way.

The main additional powers available to the courts are to: give the offender a community sentence, with a requirement that he or she attends for treatment; make a hospital order or to make a restriction order under s 41 of the Mental Health Act 1983.

A community order requiring the offender to have treatment will be made where the court is satisfied that the mental condition is treatable, and that there is no need to make a hospital order. A hospital order will be made if the condition makes it appropriate that the offender should stay in hospital for treatment.

However, there are some cases in which the protection of the public is a key element. Under s 41 of the Mental Health Act 1983 offenders with severe mental problems, who are considered to be a danger to the community, can be sent to a secure hospital such as Broadmoor. Magistrates' Courts cannot make such an order; it can only be made by a Crown Court. The order can be that the offender be detained for a set period or, where necessary, for an indefinite period. If an offender is ordered to be detained for an indefinite period, the hospital can only discharge him with the permission of the Home Secretary or the Mental Health Review Tribunal.

Examination Questions

(a) Describe the sentences available for adult offenders.

(b) Discuss the advantages and disadvantages of custodial sentences.

Specimen paper, OCR

Chapter 9

The judiciary

When speaking of judges as a group, they are referred to as the 'judiciary'. There are many different levels of judges, but their basic function is the same. Their main role is to make decisions in respect of disputes. This they must do in a fair, unbiased way, applying the law and the legal rules of England and Wales.

The judiciary is divided into what are known as 'superior' judges (those in the High Court and above) and 'inferior' judges (those in the lower courts). This distinction affects training, work and, in particular, the terms on which they hold office. So it is important to start by understanding which judges sit in which court.

9.1 Types of judges

9.1.1 Superior judges

Superior judges are those in the House of Lords, the Court of Appeal and the High Court. They are:

- the Lords of Appeal in Ordinary – this is the correct title for the Law Lords who sit in the House of Lords
- the Lord Justices of Appeal in the Court of Appeal
- High Court Judges (also known as puisne (pronounced 'pew-nay') judges) who sit in the three divisions of the High Court: judges in the Queen's Bench Division of the High Court also sit to hear serious cases in the Crown Court.

The head of the judiciary is the Lord Chief Justice. As well as being head of the whole judiciary, this judge is also head of the Criminal Division of the Court of Appeal.

There are also senior judges who head the Civil Division of the Court of Appeal and the divisions of the High Court. These are:

- the Master of the Rolls who is head of the Civil Division of the Court of Appeal
- the President of the Queen's Bench Division of the High Court
- the Chancellor of the High Court who is head of the Chancery Division
- the President of the Family Division of the High Court.

The parade of judges and silks on the first day of the legal year

9.1.2 Inferior judges

The inferior judges include:

- Circuit Judges, who sit in both the Crown Court and the County Court
- Recorders, who are part-time judges who usually sit in the Crown Court, though a few may hear cases in the County Court
- District Judges, who hear small claims and other matters in the County Court
- District Judges (Magistrates' Courts), who sit in Magistrates' Courts in London and other major towns and cities
- chairmen of tribunals.

9.2 Qualifications

The relevant qualifications for the different judicial posts are set out in the Courts and Legal Services Act 1990. This Act bases qualifications on the relevant certificate of advocacy. This means that the candidate must have qualified to have the right to present cases in court. The Act also provides for promotion from one level of judicial post to the next. Before this Act was passed only barristers who had practised at the Bar for at least ten years could become High Court Judges or above.

Now, to become a judge at any level, it is necessary to have qualified as either a barrister or a solicitor. However, it is no longer essential to have practised. The Courts and Legal Services Act provides that academic lawyers can be appointed as judges as well as those who have practised as a barrister or a solicitor. Also, since 1994, barristers and solicitors working in the civil service and Crown Prosecution Service have been eligible to become judges. These changes have all helped to widen the pool of potential candidates for judgeships.

The qualifications for each level of judge are set out below.

9.2.1 Law Lords

These are appointed from those who hold high judicial office, for example as a judge in the Court

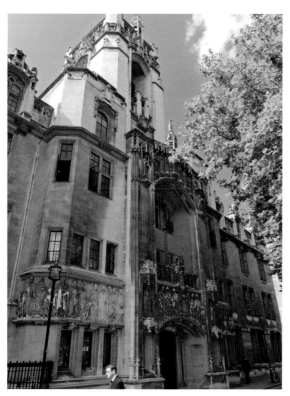

Middlesex Guildhall, which is to be the home of the new Supreme Court

of Appeal, or from those who have been qualified to appear in the Supreme Court for at least 15 years. The House of Lords is the final appellate court for Scotland and Northern Ireland as well. This means judges can also be appointed from those who have practised as an advocate in Scotland for at least 15 years or as a member of the Bar in Northern Ireland for at least 15 years or held high judicial office in their own legal system. There are twelve Lords of Appeal in Ordinary. This is the correct title of the Law Lords. They sit on the Appellate Committee of the House of Lords.

All judgments by the Law Lords are put on the website for Parliament (www.parliament.uk).

Note that the Constitutional Reform Act 2005 has provision for the Appellate Committee of the House of Lords to be abolished and replaced by an independent Supreme Court. This is likely to occur in 2009.

9.2.2 Lords Justices of Appeal

These must have held a High Court qualification for at least ten years or be an existing High Court Judge. In practice nearly all Lords Justices of Appeal have been appointed from existing High Court Judges. Up to 2006 all Lords Justices of Appeal had been qualified as barristers, but in 2007, the first solicitor Lord Justice of Appeal was appointed.

9.2.3 High Court Judges

In order to be eligible to be appointed as a High Court Judge it is necessary either to have had the right to practise in the High Court for at least ten years or to have been a Circuit Judge for at least two years. Prior to the Courts and Legal Services Act 1990 only those who had practised as a barrister for at least ten years were eligible. The present qualification routes give solicitors the chance to become High Court Judges. This can be either by promotion from a Circuit judgeship or by holding a certificate of advocacy for ten years. So far there have been only two solicitors appointed to the High Court. The first was in 1993 and the second in 2000. This second solicitor judge (Sir Lawrence Collins) has since been promoted to the Court of Appeal.

9.2.4 Circuit Judges

There are different routes to becoming a Circuit Judge. The candidate can either have had rights of audience for at least ten years in either the Crown Court or the County Court or have been a Recorder. This route via being a Recorder has existed since 1971 and allows solicitors who have not got the required certificate of advocacy a route into the judiciary. About 17 per cent of Circuit Judges are solicitors. The Courts and Legal Services Act 1990 also allows for promotion after being a District Judge, stipendiary magistrate or chairman of an employment tribunal for at least three years. These proposals widened the pool of potential judges and are starting to lead to a better cross-section among the judges.

9.2.5 Recorders

This is a part-time post. The applicant must have been qualified as a barrister or solicitor for at least ten years. Usually an applicant is appointed as a recorder in training first and then after two or three years can apply to be appointed as a Recorder. Recorders sit as a judge for 20 days in the year; the rest of the time they continue in their private practice as a solicitor or barrister or with their academic work. The appointment is for five years and most Recorders work in the Crown Court, though it is also possible for them to sit in the County Court.

9.2.6 District Judges

These need a seven-year general qualification. This means they can be appointed from either barristers or solicitors, but in practice the vast majority of District Judges are solicitors. They work in the County Court and are concerned only with civil cases.

9.2.7 District Judges (Magistrates' Courts)

These also need a seven-year general qualification. This means they can be appointed from either barristers or solicitors. They work only in major Magistrates' Courts.

9.3 Selection

9.3.1 History

Until 2005, the Lord Chancellor was the key figure in the selection of superior judges. The Lord Chancellor's Department would keep information on all possible candidates. These files would contain confidential information and opinions from existing judges on the suitability of each person. The contents of these files were secret.

When there was a vacancy for a judicial position in the House of Lords, the Court of Appeal or the High Court, the Lord Chancellor would consider the information in these files and decide which person he thought was the best for the post. That person would then be invited to become a judge.

Not surprisingly, this system of selection was seen as secretive. It was also felt that it favoured white males, as there were few women in the higher ranks of the judiciary.

Matters improved for High Court judgeships as, from 1998, vacancies were advertised and any qualified person could apply. However, even then, the Lord Chancellor continued to invite people to become judges, rather than appoint solely from those who applied.

The major role of the Lord Chancellor in appointment was very controversial, as the Lord Chancellor is a political appointment. It was thought that the appointment of judges should be independent from any political influence. So the method of appointment was changed by the Constitutional Reform Act 2005 and a Judicial Appointments Commission created to deal with selection of judges.

9.3.2 The Judicial Appointments Commission

Virtually all judges are now selected by the Judicial Appointments Commission. This was created under the Constitutional Reform Act 2005 and started work in April 2006. The Commission is responsible for selecting between about 500 and 700 people for appointment to judicial posts each year.

There are 15 members of this Commission. There must be:

- 6 lay members
- 5 judges – 3 of these from the Court of Appeal or High Court plus 1 Circuit Judge and 1 District Judge or equivalent
- 1 barrister
- 1 solicitor
- 1 magistrate
- 1 tribunal member.

The key features of the new process for appointing judges are:

- appointments are made solely on merit
- the Commission is entirely responsible for assessing the merit of the candidates and selecting candidates for appointment
- no candidate can be appointed unless recommended by the Commission
- the Commission must consult with the Lord Chief Justice and another judge of equivalent experience before recommending a candidate for appointment
- the Lord Chancellor has limited powers in relation to each recommendation for appointment. He can reject a candidate once or ask the Commission to reconsider once but he must give reasons in writing for this.

The power of the Lord Chancellor to reject a candidate or ask the Commission to reconsider has been criticised. In July 2007 the Government issued a Green Paper considering whether the Lord Chancellor should continue to have any role in the selection of superior judges, or whether some other system should be used.

Judicial qualities

The Commission has listed five qualities that are desirable for a good judge. These are:

- intellectual capacity
- personal qualities including integrity, independence of mind, sound judgement, decisiveness, objectivity and willingness to learn
- ability to understand and deal fairly
- authority and communication skills
- efficiency.

The process

Positions are advertised widely in newspapers, legal journals and also online. To encourage a wide range of candidates to apply, the Commission runs roadshows and other outreach events designed to communicate and explain the appointments system to potential applicants.

All candidates have to fill in an application form. Candidates are also asked to nominate between three and six referees. In addition, the Commission has published a list of people whom it may consult about candidates. These include existing judges.

For lower-level posts, applicants will also be asked to write an essay or do a case study.

The Commission will then select the best candidates to be interviewed. The interview process may include role play or taking part in a formal, structured discussion. After the interviews, the final selections will be made and recommended to the Lord Chancellor for appointment.

In 2006, the first vacancies for High Court judgeships were advertised through this system. There were 129 applicants, but only 18 of these were women and all the applicants were white.

More information can be found on the Judicial Appointments Commission's website at www.judicialappointments.gov.uk.

 Internet Research

Look at the Commission's website to see if any judicial posts are currently being advertised.

9.3.3 The Law Lords

The appointment of judges for the House of Lords is not dealt with by the Judicial Appointments Commission. This is because the Appellate Committee of the House of Lords is to be abolished and replaced by a new Supreme Court.

The system for selecting judges for the House of Lords is that the Lord Chancellor draws up a short list in order of preference. The Prime Minister then selects from this list and nominates that person to be appointed by the Queen. In virtually every case the first choice candidate of the Lord Chancellor will be the one who is appointed. However, it is known that when Mrs Thatcher was Prime Minister, she on at least one occasion vetoed the first choice and nominated the second choice.

9.3.4 Judges of the new Supreme Court

When the Supreme Court is established, probably in 2009, all existing Law Lords will automatically become judges in this court. Judges for new appointments after that will be selected according to the method set out in Part 3 of the Constitutional Reform Act 2005. This states that when there is a vacancy, the Lord Chancellor must convene a Supreme Court selection commission.

This commission must include the President and the Deputy President of the Supreme Court and one member of the Judicial Appointments Commission. As the Supreme Court is also the final court of appeal for Scotland and Northern Ireland, the commission must also include a member of the Judicial Appointments Board for Scotland and the Northern Ireland Judicial Appointments Commission.

The commission will decide the selection process to be used. It will then use that process to select a candidate and report that selection to the Lord Chancellor.

Under s 29 of the Constitutional Reform Act 2005, the Lord Chancellor can reject that candidate or ask the commission to reconsider. This can only be done if the Lord Chancellor is of the opinion that the person selected is not suitable for the office or that there is evidence that the person is not the best candidate on merit. The Lord Chancellor must give his reasons for rejecting a candidate or asking the commission to reconsider in writing.

Once the Lord Chancellor has accepted the commission's nomination, he then notifies the Prime Minister and the Prime Minister must recommend to the Queen that she appoints that person. The Prime Minister will not be able to recommend another person for appointment. This will prevent the situation where Mrs Thatcher, on one occasion, refused to nominate the first-choice candidate, from ever happening again.

9.4 Appointment

Once a candidate has been selected and that selection accepted by the Lord Chancellor, then the appointment is made by the Queen for all judicial posts from District Judges up to the House of Lords.

9.5 Judicial roles

The work that a judge does depends on the level of court in which he works.

9.5.1 Law Lords

Judges in the House of Lords hear about 70 cases each year. These are appeals. They can be in civil or criminal cases. However, there are always far more civil appeals each year. A case can only be appealed to the House of Lords if there is a point of law involved. Often civil cases involve complicated and technical areas of law such as planning law or tax law.

The Law Lords usually sit as a panel of five judges to hear a case. However, for some very important cases, they can sit as a panel of seven judges. This happened in the case of *Pepper v Hart* (1993) on the use of *Hansard* in statutory interpretation (see Chapter 17).

Any decision the House of Lords makes on a point of law becomes a precedent for all lower courts to follow (see Chapter 14).

9.5.2 Lords Justices of Appeal

There are some 37 Lords Justices of Appeal. They sit in both the civil and criminal divisions of the Court of Appeal, so they deal with both civil and criminal cases. Their workload is much heavier than that of the House of Lords.

On the criminal side, they will hear over 7,000 applications for leave to appeal against sentence or conviction. These are dealt with by one judge. Only about a quarter of these get leave to appeal, so the full court then has about 1,800 criminal appeals to hear. In addition, they hear over 3,000 civil appeals. These may be appeals against the finding of liability or an appeal about the remedy awarded, eg the amount of money given as damages.

Court of Appeal Judges usually sit as a panel of three to hear cases. On rare occasions in important cases, there may be a panel of five. Decisions by the Court of Appeal on points of law become precedents which lower courts must follow (see Chapter 14).

Because the workload of the Court of Appeal is so large, High Court Judges are often used to form part of the panel. This means there may be one Lord Justice of Appeal sitting with two High Court Judges.

In law reports Court of Appeal Judges are referred to as 'Lord Justice' or 'Lady Justice', but when their judgments are being quoted it is usually abbreviated to the surname, followed by 'LJ', for example 'Arden LJ'.

9.5.3 High Court Judges

Each judge in the High Court will be assigned to one of the Divisions. There are 72 judges in the Queen's Bench Division, 17 in the Chancery Division and 18 in the Family Division.

There are also Deputy High Court Judges who sit to help with the workload.

The main function of High Court Judges is to try cases. These are cases at first instance because it is the first time the case has been heard by a court. They will hear evidence from witnesses,

decide what the law is and make the decision as to which side has won the case. If the claim is for damages (an amount of money) the judge decides how much should be awarded to the winning claimant. The type of work dealt with by each Division is more fully described in Chapter 2. When hearing first instance cases, judges sit on their own. In some rare cases there may be a jury.

High Court Judges also hear some appeals. These are mainly from civil cases tried in the County Court. The judges in the Queen's Bench Division also hear criminal appeals from the Magistrates' Courts by a special case stated method. These are appeals on law only. When sitting to hear appeals, there will be a panel of two or three judges.

Judges from the Queen's Bench Division also sit to hear criminal trials in the Crown Court. When they do this, they sit with a jury. The jury decide the facts and the judge decides the law. Where a defendant pleads guilty or is found guilty by a jury, the judge then has to decide on the sentence.

In law reports High Court Judges are referred to as 'Mr Justice' or 'Mrs Justice', but when their judgments are being quoted it is usually abbreviated to the surname, followed by 'J', for example 'Dobbs J'.

9.5.4 Inferior judges

Circuit Judges sit in the County Court to hear civil cases and also in the Crown Court to try criminal cases. In civil cases they sit on their own (it is very rare to have a jury in a civil case in the County

 Internet Research

Look up law reports on the Internet. Try **www.bailii.org**.

TRY TO FIND:

1. A law report in which there was a female judge.

2. A report of the Court of Appeal in which at least one of the judges is only of High Court level.

3. A report from the High Court in which the judge sitting is only a Deputy High Court Judge.

Key facts

Court	Judges	Qualifications	Role
House of Lords	Lords of Appeal in Ordinary Also known as Law Lords	15-year Supreme Court qualification *or* have held high judicial office	Hear appeals on points of law Civil and criminal cases
Court of Appeal	Lords Justices of Appeal	10-year Supreme Court qualification *or* be an existing High Court Judge	Hear appeals Criminal cases against conviction and/or sentence Civil cases on the finding and/or the amount awarded
High Court	High Court Judges Also know as puisne judges	10-year Supreme Court qualification *or* be a Circuit Judge for 2 years	Sit in one of the 3 Divisions Hear first-instance cases and decide liability and remedy Some appeal work
Crown Court	High Court Judges Circuit Judges Recorders	See above 10-year Crown Court or County Court qualification *or* be a Recorder or District Judge for 2 years 10-year Crown Court or County Court qualification	Try cases with a jury Decide the law Pass sentence on guilty defendants
County Court	Circuit Judges District Judges	See above 7-year general qualification	Civil cases – decide liability and remedy District Judges hear small claims
Magistrates' Courts	District Judges (Magistrates' Courts)	7-year general qualification	Criminal cases – decide law and verdict Pass sentence on guilty defendants Some family work

Figure 9.1 Key facts chart on judges

Court). They decide the law and the facts. They make the decision on who has won the case.

In criminal cases they sit with a jury. The jury decide the facts and the judge decides the law. Where a defendant pleads guilty or is found guilty by a jury, the judge then has to decide on the sentence.

Recorders are part-time judges who are appointed for a period of five years. They are used mainly in the Crown Court to try criminal cases, but some sit in the County Court to help with civil cases.

District Judges sit in the County Court mainly to deal with small claims cases (under £5,000) but can also hear other cases for larger amounts.

District Judges (Magistrates' Courts) sit and try criminal cases in the Magistrates' Courts. They sit on their own and decide facts and law. When a defendant pleads guilty or is found guilty, they also have to decide on the sentence.

They may also sit to hear family cases, but this will usually be with two lay magistrates.

9.6 Training

The training of judges is carried out by the Judicial Studies Board. Most of the training is focused at the lower end of the judicial scale, being aimed at Recorders. Once a lawyer has been appointed as a Recorder in training, they go on a one-week course run by the Judicial Studies Board, and then shadow an experienced judge for a week. After this they will sit to hear cases, though there will be one-day courses available from time to time, especially on the effect of new legislation.

Critics point out that the training is very short, and that even if all the people involved are experienced lawyers this does not mean that they have any experience of doing such tasks as summing-up to the jury or sentencing. There is also the fact that some Recorders will not have practised in the criminal courts as lawyers, so their expertise is limited and a one-week course is a very short training period.

There is no compulsory training given to new High Court Judges, although they are invited to attend the courses run by the Judicial Studies Board. The attitude of the judiciary to training has changed considerably over the last 20 years. Training used to be seen as insulting to lawyers who had spent all their working lives in the courts building up expertise in their field. It was also seen as a threat to judicial independence. However, the need for training is now fully accepted.

Human awareness training

In 1993 the Judicial Studies Board recommended that training should include racial awareness courses. This was accepted by the Lord Chancellor. All Circuit Judges and Recorders now have to attend a course designed to make them aware of what might be unintentionally discriminatory or offensive, such as asking a non-

Christian for their Christian name. The Board has also introduced training in human awareness, covering gender awareness, and disability issues. The training explores the perceptions of unrepresented parties, witnesses, jurors, victims and their families, and tries to make judges more aware of other people's viewpoints.

Legal research

Another problem that exists is the lack of research facilities for judges at all levels – this is especially true of the appellate courts, where the cases are likely to involve complex legal points. The judges in the Court of Appeal have only four days a month for legal reading, and, unlike many foreign courts, there are no lawyers attached to the court to research the law. In the European Court of Justice there are Advocates-General who are independent lawyers working for the court, whose task is to research legal points and present their findings.

9.6.1 Should there be a 'career' judiciary?

In many continental countries becoming a judge is a career choice made by students once they have their basic legal qualifications. They will usually not practise as a lawyer first, but instead are trained as judges. Once they have qualified as a judge they will sit in junior posts and then hope to be promoted up the judicial ladder. This has two distinct advantages over the system in use in this country:

- The average age of judges is much lower, especially in the bottom ranks. In this country an assistant Recorder will normally be in their late thirties or early forties when appointed, and the average age for appointment to the High Court Bench tends to be late forties/early fifties.
- Judges have had far more training in the specific skills they need as judges.

The disadvantage of the continental system is that

judges may be seen as too closely linked to the Government as they are civil servants. In this country, judges are generally considered as independent from the Government. This point of judicial independence is explored more fully in section 9.10.

9.7 Tenure

It is important that judges should be impartial in their decisions. In particular, it is important that the Government cannot force a judge to resign if that judge makes a decision with which the Government of the day disagrees. In this country, judges are reasonably secure from political interference.

9.7.1 Security of tenure of superior judges

Superior judges have security of tenure in that they cannot be dismissed by the Government. This right originated in the Act of Settlement 1700 which allowed them to hold office while of good behaviour. (Before 1700, the Monarch could dismiss judges at will.) The same provision is now contained in the Supreme Court Act 1981 for High Court Judges and Lords Justices of Appeal, and in the Appellate Jurisdiction Act 1876 for the Law Lords. As a result, they can only be removed by the Monarch following a petition presented to him or her by both Houses of Parliament. This gives superior judges protection from political whims and allows them to be independent in their judgments.

This power to remove a superior judge has never been used for an English judge, though it was used in 1830 to remove an Irish judge, Jonah Barrington, who had misappropriated £700 from court funds.

The Lord Chancellor can, however, after consulting with senior judges, declare vacant the office of any judge who (through ill-health) is incapable of carrying out his work and of taking the decision to resign. This power was first introduced in the Administration of Justice Act

1973 and is now contained in the Supreme Court Act 1981.

In fact, what has happened on two occasions in the past is that pressure has been put on unsatisfactory High Court Judges to resign. The first of these was in 1959 when the Lord Chancellor asked Mr Justice Hallett to resign; the second in 1998 when Mr Justice Harman resigned after criticisms by the Court of Appeal.

9.7.2 Tenure of inferior judges

These do not have the same security of tenure of office as superior judges since the Lord Chancellor has the power to dismiss inferior judges for incapacity or misbehaviour. A criminal conviction for dishonesty would obviously be regarded as misbehaviour and would lead to the dismissal of the judge concerned. This has happened only once, in the case of Bruce Campbell, a Circuit Judge, who was convicted of evading Customs duty on cigarettes and whisky. The Lord Chancellor has also indicated that drunken driving would probably be seen as misbehaviour, as would racial or sexual harassment.

Under the Constitutional Reform Act 2005, the Lord Chancellor must comply with set procedures before he can remove any judge from office.

In addition, under the Constitutional Reform Act 2005, the Lord Chief Justice has the power to suspend a person from judicial office if they are subject to criminal proceedings or have been convicted. The Lord Chief Justice can only exercise this power if the Lord Chancellor agrees, and must use set procedures.

Any judge who is suspended or disciplined in any other way can make a complaint to an Ombudsman if the procedures have not been carried out correctly and fairly.

9.7.3 Retirement

Since the Judicial Pensions and Retirement Act 1993 all judges now have to retire at the age of 70, though there are some situations in which

Key facts

Judges	Court/s	Tenure
Lords of Appeal in Ordinary (Law Lords)	House of Lords	'whilst of good behaviour' (Appellate Jurisdiction Act 1876, s 6)
Lords Justices of Appeal	Court of Appeal	'whilst of good behaviour' (Supreme Court Act 1981, s 11(3))
High Court Judges (puisne judges)	High Court / Crown Court for serious cases	'whilst of good behaviour' (Supreme Court Act 1981, s 11(3))
Circuit Judges	Crown Court / County Court	Can be dismissed by Lord Chancellor for incapacity or misbehaviour (Courts Act 1971, s 17(4))
District Judges	County Court / Magistrates' Court	Can be dismissed by the Lord Chancellor
Recorders	Crown Court / Some may sit in County Court	Appointed for period of five years; Lord Chancellor can decide not to re-appoint

Figure 9.2 Key facts chart on judges and their tenure

authorisation can be given for a judge to continue beyond that age. Prior to this Act judges in the High Court and above could remain sitting as judges until they were 75. All inferior judges now also retire at 70.

9.8 Composition of the Bench

One of the main criticisms of the Bench is that it is dominated by elderly, white, upper-class males. There are very few women judges, and even fewer judges from ethnic minorities. So far as the age of judges is concerned, it is unusual for any judge to be appointed under the age of 40, with superior judges usually being well above this age.

9.8.1 Women in the judiciary

The number of women in judicial posts is very small, although there has been an improvement in recent years. During the 1990s there was an increase in the number of women appointed to

the High Court. The first woman judge in the Queen's Bench Division was appointed in 1992, and the first in the Chancery Division in 1993.

The first woman in the Court of Appeal was appointed in 1988. This was Lady Butler-Sloss. The legal system was so unused to women in the higher levels of the judiciary that when she was appointed she had to be addressed in court as 'My Lord', and in law reports her title was written as 'Lord Butler-Sloss'! It was not until the Courts Act 2003 that the official title of women judges in the Court of Appeal became 'Lady Justice of Appeal'.

It was not until 1999 that a second woman was appointed to the Court of Appeal, and a third in 2000. In February 2001 the first all-female Court of Appeal panel sat. The first, and so far only, woman judge in the House of Lords was appointed in 2004.

In 2007 the total number of women judges in the High Court was still only ten out of over 100 judges, with only three women out of 37 judges in the Court of Appeal.

Activity

Read the following newspaper article and answer the questions below.

Do you fancy being a High Court judge? Forget the whisper over a drink at your Inn of Court or the traditional 'tap on the shoulder'. Dust off your CV and send in an application. And then prepare yourself for an 'interview' with a selection panel. This is the new world of appointing judges . . .

The selection process will be undertaken by the Judicial Appointments Commission, the independent body set up under the Constitutional Reform Act in 2005 to take over responsibility for selecting judges from the Lord Chancellor's officials.

There has been advertising for High Court judges before – but they were selected on paper. This time, the candidates will undergo a face-to-face discussion – and that, with references and their own application form, will combine to inform the selection.

Baroness Usha Prashar, who is chairman of the 15 lay and judicial commissioners and 105 staff, will now be responsible for 500 to 700 appointments a year, including the High Court . . .

The aim she says is for a much more transparent process that will encourage a greater diversity of candidates. 'Up to now the process was perceived to be very secretive and not very open. There was a view that it was those who you knew who counted – and that probably deterred a lot of people who felt they would not get a fair deal. This will be objective and transparent and hopefully that will encourage more people to apply.'

Taken from an article by Frances Gibb in *The Times*, 31 October 2006

Questions

1. Who was responsible for appointing judges under the old system?

2. Who is responsible for appointing judges now?

3. Describe the problems with the old system of appointing judges.

4. Describe how the new system operates.

5. Explain whether you think that the new system will encourage a wider range of applicants for judgeships.

Lower down the judicial ladder, there are slightly more women being appointed than in the past. In 2007, 12 per cent of Circuit Judges and 15 per cent of Recorders were female. The highest percentages of women were for District Judges (23 per cent).

9.8.2 Ethnic minorities

In 2004 the first ethnic minority judge was appointed to the High Court. Even at the lower levels, ethnic minorities are still poorly represented. In 2007 only 1.5 per cent of Circuit Judges and 4.5 per cent of Recorders were from an ethnic minority. These percentages have not changed much over the past five years. It will be interesting to see if the new appointments system leads to greater diversity.

9.8.3 Educational and social background

At the higher levels judges tend to come from the upper levels of society, with many having been educated at public school and nearly all attending Oxford or Cambridge University. A survey by the magazine *Labour Research* found that of the 85 judges appointed from 1997 to mid-1999, 73 per cent had been to public school and 79 per cent to Oxbridge. Judges (especially superior judges) will have spent at least 20 years working as barristers and mixing with a small group of like-minded people. As a result, judges are seen as out of touch with society. Occasionally the media report actions or comments which appear to support this view, for example where a judge said of an eight-year-old rape victim that she was 'no angel'. Since 1995, training in human awareness has been given to prevent such offensive remarks. Lord Taylor, a former Lord Chief Justice, who was one of the few senior judges who had attended a State school, pointed out that judges live in the real world and do ordinary things like shopping in supermarkets.

 Internet Research

Look up the judicial website **www.judiciary.gov.uk**.

1. Look up the names of the judges in the House of Lords. Choose any two and look at their biographies. Find out the following matters:

   (a) Which school did they go to?
   (b) At which university did they get their degree?
   (c) When did they first become a judge?
   (d) When did they become a judge in the House of Lords?

2. Find out how many woman judges there are in the Court of Appeal.

3. Find out how many ethnic minority judges there are in the High Court.

9.9 Theory of the separation of powers

The theory of separation of powers was first put forward by Montesquieu, a French political theorist, in the eighteenth century. The theory states that there are three primary functions of the State and that the only way to safeguard the liberty of citizens is by keeping these three functions separate. These functions are:

- legislative
- executive
- judiciary.

As the power of each is exercised by independent and separate bodies, each can keep a check on the others and thus limit the amount of power wielded by any one group. Ideally, this theory requires that individuals should not be members of more than one 'arm of the state'.

Some countries, for example the USA, have a written constitution which embodies this theory. In the United Kingdom we have no such written constitution, but even so the three organs of State are roughly separated. There is some overlap, especially in the fact that the Lord Chancellor is involved in all three functions of the State. However, the Lord Chancellor's role in relation to the judiciary is now much reduced.

The three arms of the State identified by Montesquieu are:

1. **The legislature**
   This is the law-making arm of the State and in our system this is Parliament.

2. **The executive** or the body administering the law
   Under the British political system this is the Government of the day which forms the Cabinet.

3. **The judiciary** who apply the law
   In other words, the judges.

There is an overlap between the executive and the legislature, in that the Ministers forming the Government also sit in Parliament and are active in the law-making process. With the exception of the Lord Chancellor, there is very little overlap between the judiciary and the other two arms of the State. This is important because it allows the judiciary to act as a check and ensure that the executive does not overstep its constitutional powers. This is in accordance with Montesquieu's theory. However, it is open to debate whether the judiciary is truly independent from the other organs of government.

9.10 Independence of the judiciary

As already stated, an independent judiciary is seen as important in protecting the liberty of the individual from abuse of power by the executive. Judges in the English system can be thought of as being independent in a number of ways.

9.10.1 Independence from the legislature

Judges are generally not involved in the law-making functions of Parliament. Full-time judges are not allowed to be members of the House of Commons. The rule is not as strict for part-time judges so that Recorders and Assistant Recorders can be Members of Parliament. However, judges can be members of the House of Lords in its legislative function, as the Law Lords are life peers and can take part in debates on new laws. In addition, any judge who is also a peer may sit in the House of Lords.

There is a convention that the Law Lords will not take part in very political debates, but over recent years there have been instances where they have entered into controversial areas of law-making.

Under the Constitutional Reform Act 2005 there is provision to abolish the Judicial Committee of the House of Lords. Instead there will be a new Supreme Court as the final court of appeal. The first judges will be the existing Law Lords. This Supreme Court will be separate from

Parliament and the judges will not have the right to sit in Parliament in the House of Lords. This reform will be brought in when the new Supreme Court building is ready. This is likely to be in 2009.

9.10.2 Independence from the executive

Superior judges cannot be dismissed by the Government and in this way they can truly be said to be independent of the Government. They can make decisions which may displease the Government, without the threat of dismissal. The extent to which judges are prepared to challenge or support the Government is considered in section 9.10.4. Judicial independence is now guaranteed under s 3 of the Constitutional Reform Act 2005. This states that the Lord Chancellor, other Ministers in the Government and anyone with responsibility for matters relating to the judiciary or the administration of justice must uphold the continued independence of the judiciary.

The section also specifically states that the Lord Chancellor and other Ministers must not seek to influence particular judicial decisions.

Ministry of Justice

In 2007 a Ministry of Justice was created to bring together all the key elements of the justice system under one ministry. Previously two ministries, the Department for Constitutional Affairs and the Home Office, had had responsibility for separate parts of the justice system.

The Ministry of Justice has responsibility for:

- the civil courts
- the criminal courts
- the judiciary
- legal aid and funding of cases
- prisons
- the probation service
- sentencing.

There are fears that the budget of the new department will not be sufficient for all this and that prisons will take a large part of the budget.

This could result in there not being enough money for the courts service.

Judges are also worried about the effect of the change on their independence. The Minister for Justice is also the Lord Chancellor. As the Minister for Justice is a key role in the executive, it is difficult to see how he can also maintain the independence of the judiciary.

9.10.3 Freedom from pressure

There are several ways in which judges are protected from outside pressure when exercising their judicial functions.

1. They are given a certain degree of financial independence, as judicial salaries are paid out of the consolidated fund so that payment is made without the need for Parliament's authorisation. This does not completely protect them from parliamentary interference with the terms on which they hold office. As already seen, changes can be made to retirement ages and qualifying periods for pensions.
2. Judges have immunity from being sued for actions taken or decisions made in the course of their judicial duties. This was confirmed in *Sirros v Moore* (1975) and is a key factor in ensuring judicial independence in decision-making.
3. As already noted, the security of tenure of the superior judges protects them from the threat of removal.

9.10.4 Independence from political bias

This is the area in which there is most dispute over how independent the judiciary are. Writers, such as Professor Griffith, have pointed out that judges are too pro-establishment and conservative with a small 'c'.

Pro-Government decisions

Griffith cited cases such as the 'GCHQ case' in showing that judges tend to support the establishment. This case, *Council of Civil Service*

Unions v Minister for the Civil Service (1984), concerned the Minister for the Conservative Government withdrawing the right to trade union membership from civil servants working at the intelligence headquarters in Cheltenham. The House of Lords upheld the Minister's right, and the decision was seen as anti-trade union.

Anti-Government decisions

There is, however, evidence that judges are not as pro-establishment as sometimes thought. Lord Taylor, when giving the Dimbleby Lecture in 1992, pointed out that this could be seen in the case of the Greenham Common women who had camped by an RAF base in protest against nuclear missiles. In *DPP v Hutchinson* (1990) some of the women were prosecuted under a bylaw for being on Ministry of Defence property unlawfully. The case went all the way to the House of Lords, where the Law Lords ruled in the women's favour, holding that the Minister had exceeded his powers in framing the bylaw so as to prevent access to common land.

Human rights

More recently, the courts have upheld challenges by asylum seekers and by those held under the Anti-Terrorism, Crime and Security Act 2001. In *R (on the application of Q) v Secretary of State for the Home Department* (2003) Collins J in the High Court declared that the Home Secretary's power to refuse to provide assistance to asylum seekers who had not immediately, on their entry to this country, declared their intention to claim asylum was unlawful. The Court of Appeal upheld this decision, although they did suggest how the relevant Act could be made compatible with human rights.

In *A and another v Secretary of State for the Home Department* (2004) the House of Lords declared that the Anti-Terrorism, Crime and Security Act 2001 was incompatible with the Convention. The Act allowed foreign nationals to be detained indefinitely without trial where there was suspicion that they were involved in terrorist activity. The

Lords held that this breached both Art 5 (the right to liberty) and Art 14 (no discrimination on basis of nationality). This decision forced the Government to change the law.

With the Human Rights Act 1998 incorporating the European Convention on Human Rights, judges can declare that an Act is incompatible with the Convention. This puts pressure on the Government to change the law.

The courts also have a duty to interpret laws in a way which is compatible with the Convention.

So, while it is true that judges are still predominantly white, male, middle-class and elderly, it is possible to argue that they are no longer so out of touch with the 'real world', and that they are increasingly prepared to challenge the establishment.

9.10.5 Independence from case

Judges must not try any case where they have any interest in the issue involved. The Pinochet case in 1998 reinforced this rule. In that case the House of Lords judges heard an appeal by the former head of the state of Chile. There was a claim to extradite him to Chile to face possible trial for crimes involving torture and deaths which had occurred there while he was head of state.

Amnesty International, the human rights movement, had been granted leave to participate in the case. After the House of Lords ruled that Pinochet could be extradited, it was discovered that one of the judges, Lord Hoffmann, was an unpaid director of Amnesty International Charitable Trust. Pinochet's lawyers asked for the decision to be set aside and to have the case re-heard by a completely independent panel of judges.

The Law Lords decided that their original decision could not be allowed to stand. Judges had to be seen to be completely unbiased. The fact that Lord Hoffmann was connected with Amnesty meant that he might be considered not to be completely impartial. The case was retried with a new panel of judges.

Human rights

The test for bias has been influenced by the European Convention on Human Rights. In *Re Medicaments (no 2), Director General of Fair Trading v Proprietary Association of Great Britain* (2001) the Court of Appeal followed decisions of the European Court of Human Rights. The court said that the test was an objective one of whether the circumstances were such as to lead a fair-minded and informed observer to conclude that there was a real possibility of bias. This is the test now used in our courts.

Examination Questions

(a) Describe the qualification, selection and training of judges.

(b) Discuss the way in which judicial independence is maintained.

OCR Specimen paper

Chapter 10

The legal profession

I n England and Wales there are two types of lawyers (barristers and solicitors), jointly referred to as 'the legal profession'. Most countries do not have this clear-cut division among lawyers: a person will qualify simply as a lawyer, although, after qualifying, it will be possible for them to specialise as an advocate, or in a particular area of law. This type of system is also seen in this country in the medical profession, where all those wishing to become doctors take the same general qualifications. After they have qualified, some doctors will go on to specialise in different fields, perhaps as surgeons, and will take further qualifications in their chosen field.

In England, not only are the professions separate, but there is no common training for lawyers, although there have been increasing calls for this. As far back as 1971 the Ormrod Committee was in favour of a common education for all prospective lawyers. In 1994 the Lord Chancellor's advisory committee on legal education, under Lord Steyn, recommended that, instead of having separate training for barristers and solicitors, 'the two branches of the profession should have joint training. All those qualifying would then work for six months or a year at a solicitors', with those who wished to become barristers going on to do extra training at the Bar. Yet despite these recommendations, the training of the two professions remains separate.

10.1 Solicitors

There are over 100,000 solicitors practising in England and Wales and they are controlled by their own professional body: the Law Society.

10.1.1 Training

To become a solicitor it is usual to have a law degree, although those with a degree in a subject other than law can do an extra year's training in core legal subjects, and take the Common Professional Examination or Graduate Diploma in Law. The next stage is the one-year Legal Practice Course. This is much more practically based than the previous Law Society Finals course and includes training in skills such as client-interviewing, negotiation, advocacy, drafting documents and legal research. There is also an emphasis on business management, for example keeping accounts.

Training contract

Even when this course has been passed, the student is still not a qualified solicitor. He must next obtain a training contract under which he works in a solicitors' firm for two years, getting practical experience. This training period can also be undertaken in certain other legal organisations such as the Crown Prosecution Service, or the legal department of a local authority. During this two-year training contract the trainee will be paid, though not at the same rate as a fully qualified solicitor, and will do his own work, supervised by a solicitor. He will also have to complete a 20-day Professional Skills Course which builds on the skills learned on the LPC. At the end of the time, the trainee will be admitted as a solicitor by the Law Society and his name will be added to the roll (or list) of solicitors. Even after qualifying, solicitors have to attend continuing education courses to keep their knowledge up to date.

Non-graduate route

There is also a route under which non-graduates can qualify as solicitors by first becoming legal executives. This route is only open to mature candidates and takes longer than the graduate route. The three routes to becoming a solicitor are shown in Figure 10.1.

Criticisms of the training process

There are several criticisms of the training process.

1. The first of these is a financial problem, in that students will usually have to pay the fees of the Legal Practice Course (about £7,000) and support themselves during this year. This problem has arisen because, as the LPC is a post-graduate course, students must pay all the cost. The result of this policy is that students from poor families cannot afford to take the course and are therefore prevented from becoming solicitors, even though they may have obtained a good law degree. Other students may take out bank loans, so that although they qualify, they start the training period with a large debt. In order to overcome this problem a few universities have started offering four-year degree courses, combining a law qualification and a practical course, so students pay only the university fees. This financial problem is also one faced by prospective barristers. The problem has increased since universities started charging £3,000 a year from 2006.

2. A point common to solicitors and barristers is that non-law graduates do only one year of formal law for the Graduate Diploma in Law. The Ormrod Committee, which reported on legal education in 1971, thought that the main entry route should be via a law degree, but in practice 25 per cent of solicitors will not have taken a law degree. One critic posed the question of whether the public would be satisfied with doctors who have only studied

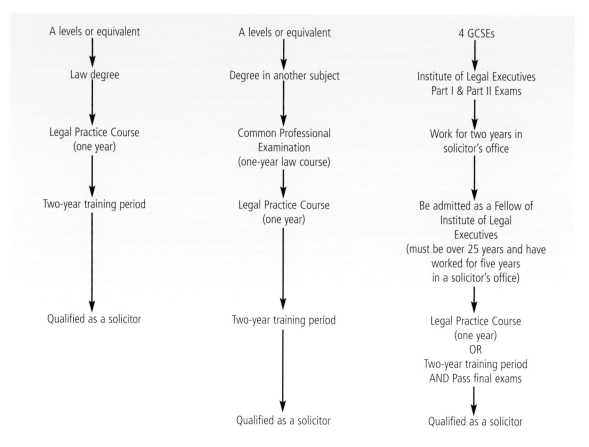

Figure 10.1 Training routes to become a solicitor

medicine for one year, concentrating on only six subjects. Yet this is precisely what is occurring in the legal profession.

3. A third problem is one of over-supply, so that students who have passed the LPC are unable to obtain a training contract. However, this problem is not as bad as it was in the 1990s.

10.1.2 Solicitors' work

The majority of those who succeed in qualifying as a solicitor will then work in private practice in a solicitors' firm. However, there are other careers available, and some newly-qualified solicitors may go on to work in the Crown Prosecution Service or for a Local Authority or Government Department. Others will become legal advisers in commercial or industrial businesses.

A solicitor in private practice may work as a sole practitioner or in a partnership. There are about 9,000 firms of solicitors, ranging from the small 'high street' practice to the big city firms. The number of partners is not limited, and some of the biggest firms will have over a hundred partners as well as employing assistant solicitors.

The type of work done by a solicitor will largely depend on the type of firm in which he is working. A small high street firm will probably be a general practice advising clients on a whole range of topics such as consumer problems, housing and business matters and family problems. A solicitor working in such a practice is likely to spend some of his time interviewing clients in his office and negotiating on their behalf, and a large amount of time dealing with paperwork. This will include:

- writing letters on behalf of clients
- drafting contracts, leases or other legal documents
- drawing up wills
- dealing with conveyancing (the legal side of buying and selling flats, houses, office buildings and land).

The solicitor may also, if he wishes, act for some of his clients in court. Standing up in court and putting the client's case, and questioning witnesses is known as advocacy. Some solicitors will specialise in this and spend much of their time in court.

Specialising

Although some solicitors may be general practitioners handling a variety of work it is not unusual, even in small firms, for a solicitor to specialise in one particular field. The firm itself may only handle certain types of cases (perhaps only civil actions) and not do any criminal cases, or a firm may specialise in matrimonial cases.

Even within the firm the solicitors are likely to have their own field of expertise. In large firms there will be an even greater degree of specialisation with departments dealing with one aspect of the law. The large city firms usually concentrate on business and commercial law. Amounts earned by solicitors are as varied as the types of firm, with the top earners in big firms on £500,000 or more, while at the bottom end of the scale some sole practitioners will earn less than £30,000.

Conveyancing

Prior to 1985 solicitors had a monopoly on conveyancing: this meant that only solicitors could deal with the legal side of transferring houses and other buildings and land. This was changed by the Administration of Justice Act 1985 which allowed people other than solicitors to become licensed conveyancers. As a result of the increased competition in this area, solicitors had to reduce their fees, but even so they lost a large proportion of the work. This led to a demand for wider rights of advocacy.

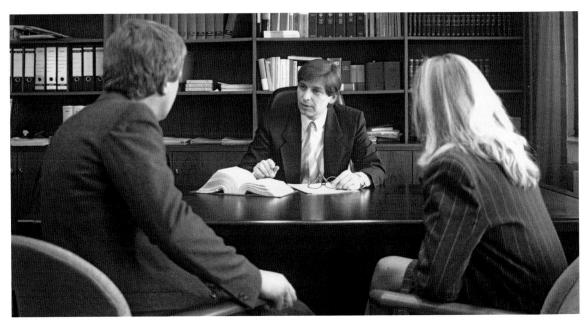

A solicitor interviewing clients

Original rights	To present cases in County Court and Magistrates' Court, also at Crown Court on committal for sentence or appeal from Magistrates' Court
Practice Direction 1986	Following *Abse v Smith*, allowed to make statement in High Court in cases in which terms had been agreed
Courts and Legal Services Act 1990	Solicitors allowed to apply for certificate of advocacy to conduct cases in the higher courts. Must have experience of advocacy, take course and pass examinations
Access to Justice Act 1999	Solicitors to have full rights of audience

Figure 10.2 Key facts chart on solicitors' rights of audience

Rights of advocacy

All solicitors have always been able to act as advocates in the Magistrates' Courts and the County Courts, but their rights of audience in the higher courts used to be very limited. Normally a solicitor could only act as advocate in the Crown Court on a committal for sentence, or on an appeal from the Magistrates' Court, and then only if he or another solicitor in the firm had been the advocate in the original case in the Magistrates' Court.

Until 1986, solicitors had no rights of audience in open court in the High Court, though they could deal with preliminary matters in preparation for a case. This lack of rights of audience was emphasised in *Abse v Smith* (1986) in which two Members of Parliament were contesting a libel action. They came to an agreed settlement, but the solicitor for one of them was refused permission by the judge to read out the terms of that settlement in open court. Following this decision the Lord Chancellor and the senior judges in each division of the High Court issued a Practice Direction, allowing solicitors to appear in the High Court to make a statement in a case that has been settled.

Certificate of advocacy

The first major alteration to solicitors' rights of audience came in the Courts and Legal Services Act 1990. Under this Act, a solicitor in private practice had the right to apply for a certificate of advocacy which enabled him to appear in the higher courts. Such a certificate was granted if the solicitor already had experience of advocacy in the Magistrates' Court and the County Court, took a short training course and passed examinations on the rules of evidence. The first certificates were granted in 1994 and by 2007 about 3,000 solicitors had qualified to be advocates in the higher courts.

Solicitors with an advocacy qualification are also eligible to be appointed as Queen's Counsel (see section 10.2.3) and also to be appointed to higher judicial posts.

The Access to Justice Act 1999 (s 36) provides that all solicitors will eventually be given full rights of audience. However, new training requirements to allow solicitors to obtain these rights have not yet been brought in.

Multi-discipline partnerships

Section 66 of the Courts and Legal Services Act 1990 allows solicitors to form partnerships with other professions, for example accountants. This would give clients a wider range of expertise and advice in a 'one-stop shop'. However, the Law Society and the Bar Council have rules which prohibit the creation of multi-discipline partnerships, so that, as yet, 'one-stop shops' are not allowed by the professional bodies governing solicitors and barristers. However, this will change under the Legal Services Act 2007 (see section 10.3).

10.1.3 Complaints against solicitors

A solicitor deals directly with clients and enters into a contract with them. This means that if the client does not pay, the solicitor has the right to sue for his fees. It also means that the client can sue his solicitor for breach of contract if the solicitor fails to do the work.

A client can also sue the solicitor for negligence in and out of court work. This happened in *Griffiths v Dawson* (1993) where solicitors for the plaintiff had failed to make the correct application in divorce proceedings against her husband. As a result the plaintiff lost financially and the solicitors were ordered to pay her £21,000 in compensation.

Other people affected by the solicitor's negligence may also have the right to sue in certain circumstances. An example of this was the case of *White v Jones* (1995) where a father wanted to make a will leaving each of his daughters £9,000. He wrote to his solicitors, instructing them to draw up a will to include this. The solicitors received this letter on 17th July 1986 but had done nothing about it by the time the father died on 14th September 1986. As a result, the daughters did not inherit any money and they successfully sued the solicitor for the £9,000 they had each lost.

Negligent advocacy

It used to be held that a solicitor presenting a case in court could not be sued for negligence. However, in *Hall v Simons* (2000), the House of Lords decided that advocates can be liable for negligence.

Complaints procedure

There have been problems with the complaints procedure operated by the Law Society. One of the main concerns has been that the Law Society's main roles are to regulate the solicitors' profession and to represent solicitors. By operating its own complaints procedure, there was a conflict between the interest of the solicitor and the interest of the client who was complaining.

The other problem for those complaining about poor service by a solicitor was that the complaints bodies run by the Law Society have themselves been frequently criticised for delays and inefficiency.

In 2004 the Law Society created a new complaints procedure. This was the Consumer Complaints Service. This new body is still not as efficient as it should be. The Legal Service Ombudsman's report for 2006–07 found that only 68 per cent of investigations were handled satisfactorily. However, this was an improvement from 62 per cent in 2004–05. The Legal Service Ombudsman pointed out that 'the overall performance is well short of where a modern consumer-focused organisation should be'.

Future reforms

The Legal Services Act 2007 has provision for the creation of the Office for Legal Complaints. This will be completely independent of the Law Society and any other sector of the legal profession. The Office will have a non-lawyer as Chairman and the majority of members must also be non-lawyers. This Office will deal with complaints against solicitors and also all other sectors of the legal profession (see section 10.3.2).

The Legal Service Complaints Commissioner

The Legal Service Complaints Commissioner has the right to investigate the handling of complaints and to make recommendations about the arrangements for dealing with complaints. He can also impose targets for handling complaints and, if these are not met, fine the professional body concerned.

In 2006 the Legal Services Complaints Commissioner fined the Law Society £250,000 for submitting an inadequate complaints-handling plan for the coming year.

The Legal Services Ombudsman

Under the Courts and Legal Services Act 1990, the post of Legal Services Ombudsman was created to examine complaints against solicitors, and also barristers and licensed conveyancers, where the professions' own regulatory bodies did not provide a satisfactory answer. Under the Access to Justice Act 1999 the Ombudsman has power to order that the solicitor concerned should pay compensation or that the Law Society itself should compensate the client.

10.2 Barristers

There are about 12,000 barristers in independent practice in England and Wales. Collectively, barristers are referred to as 'the Bar' and they are controlled by their own professional body – the General Council of the Bar. All barristers must also be a member of one of the four Inns of Court (Lincoln's Inn, Inner Temple, Middle Temple and Gray's Inn), all of which are situated near the Royal Courts of Justice in London.

10.2.1 Training

Entry to the Bar is normally degree-based, though there is a non-degree route for mature entrants, under which a small number of students qualify. As with solicitors, graduate students without a law degree can take the one-year course for the Common Professional Examination or Graduate Diploma in Law in the core subjects, in order to go on to qualify as a barrister. All student barristers have to pass the Bar Vocational Course which emphasises the practical skills of drafting pleadings for use in court, negotiation and advocacy.

All student barristers must join one of the four Inns of Court and used to have to dine there

A barrister in robes

12 times before being called to the Bar. Students may now attend in a different way, for example a weekend residential course. This helps students on courses outside London as travelling costs are lower. The idea behind the rule requiring all trainee barristers to dine was that they met senior barristers and judges and absorbed the traditions of the profession. In practice, few barristers dine at their Inns and students are unlikely to meet anyone except other students.

Once a student has passed the Bar Vocational Course, he is then 'called to the Bar'. This means that they are officially qualified as a barrister. However, there is still a practical stage to their training which must be completed. This is called 'pupillage'.

Pupillage

After the student has passed the Bar Vocational Course there is 'on-the-job' training where the trainee barrister becomes a pupil to a qualified barrister. This effectively involves 'work shadowing' that barrister, and can be with the same barrister for 12 months or with two different pupil masters for six months each. There is also a requirement that they take part in a programme of continuing education organised by the Bar Council. After the first six months of pupillage, barristers are eligible to appear in court and may conduct their own cases. During pupillage trainee barristers are paid a small salary – usually about half the amount paid to trainee solicitors.

The various training routes are shown in Figure 10.3.

10.2.2 Barristers' work

Barristers practising at the Bar are self-employed, but usually work from a set of chambers where they can share administrative expenses with other barristers. Most sets of chambers are fairly small, comprising about 15–20 barristers. They will employ a clerk as a practice administrator –

booking in cases and negotiating fees – and they will have other support staff. One of the problems facing newly qualified barristers is the difficulty of finding a tenancy in chambers. Many will do a third six-month pupillage and then 'squat' as an unofficial tenant before obtaining a place. The rule on having to practise from chambers has been relaxed, so that it is technically possible for barristers to practise from home. However, despite the fact that a tenancy in chambers is not essential, it is still viewed as the way to allow a barrister to build a successful practice.

The majority of barristers will concentrate on advocacy, although there are some who specialise in areas such as tax and company law, and who rarely appear in court. Barristers have rights of audience in all courts in England and Wales. Even those who specialise in advocacy will do a certain amount of paperwork, writing opinions on cases, giving advice and drafting documents for use in court.

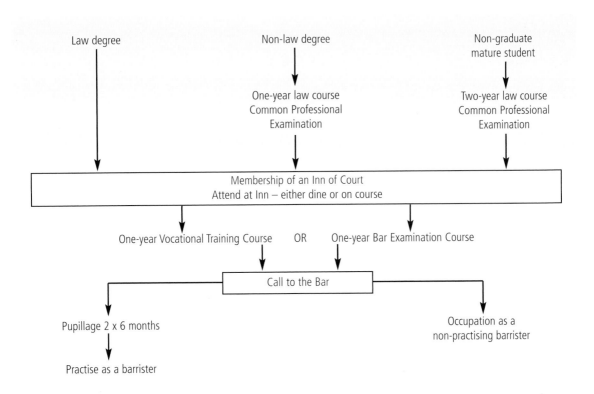

Figure 10.3 Training routes to becoming a barrister

Key facts

	Solicitors	Barristers
Training	Degree, if not in law then must do Common Professional Examination or Graduate Diploma in Law	
	Legal Practice Course Training contract	Bar Vocational Course Must join one of the 4 Inns of Court Pupillage
Role	Private practice in solicitors' firm Wide variety of work Contracts, leases, wills, conveyancing etc Direct access by clients	Self-employed in chambers Mostly court work Also write opinions and draft documents Since 2004 direct access by clients in civil cases
	May be employed in CPS, CDS, local authority etc or private commercial business	
Advocacy	Automatic rights in Magistrates' Courts and County Court Advocacy certificate for higher courts (Courts and Legal Services Act 1990) Plans for full rights (Access to Justice Act 1999)	Full rights in all courts
Queen's Counsel	Selection is now by an independent QC selection panel Applicants will be judged on 7 competencies Applicants give referees and are interviewed by 2 members of the panel	
Supervision	Law Society Office for the Supervision of Solicitors – criticised for inefficiency	Bar Council Lay Complaints Commissioner + Professional Conduct and Complaints Committee Complaints system working well with a high level of satisfaction
	Legal Services Ombudsman Legal Services Complaints Commissioner	

Figure 10.4 Key facts chart comparing solicitors and barristers

Direct access

Originally it was necessary for anybody who wished to instruct a barrister to go to a solicitor first. The solicitor would then brief the barrister. This was thought to create unnecessary expense for clients, as it meant they had to use two lawyers instead of one. As a result of criticism the Bar first of all started to operate a system called Bar Direct under which certain professionals such as accountants and surveyors could brief a barrister direct without using a solicitor. This was extended to other professionals and organisations. Then in September 2004 the Bar granted direct access to anyone (business or individual) for civil cases. It is no longer necessary to go to a solicitor in order to instruct a barrister for civil cases. However, direct access is still not allowed for criminal cases or family work.

Cab rank rule

Normally barristers operate what is known as the 'cab rank rule', under which they cannot turn down a case if it is on the area of law they deal with and they are free to take the case. However, where clients approach a barrister direct, the 'cab rank rule' does not apply. Barristers can turn down a case which would require investigation or support services which they cannot provide.

Employed barristers

The employed Bar, which includes those barristers working for the Crown Prosecution Service, have full rights of audience. They can appear in the Magistrates' Court, the Crown Court, High Court or appellate courts.

10.2.3 Queen's Counsel

After at least 10 years as a barrister or as a solicitor with an advocacy qualification, it is possible to apply to become a Queen's Counsel (QC). About 10 per cent of the Bar are Queen's Counsel and it is known as 'taking silk'. QCs usually take on more complicated and high-profile cases than junior barristers (all barristers who are not Queen's Counsel are known as 'juniors'), and they can command higher fees for their recognised expertise. Often a QC will have a junior barrister to assist with the case.

Until 2004 Queen's Council were appointed by the Lord Chancellor. However, the Lord Chancellor's criteria for selecting QCs have been criticised as being too secretive. There was also the fact that fewer than 10 per cent of QCs are women and only a very few are from ethnic minorities. In turn, this has an effect on the composition of the judiciary since senior judges are usually chosen from the ranks of Queen's Counsel. The position of women and ethnic minorities in the legal profession is considered in more detail in section 10.5.

This led to a change in the method of appointment.

New appointment system

Selection of who should become a QC is now made by an independent selection panel. Lawyers apply to become QCs. They have to pay a fee of £2,500. Applicants provide references (these can include references from clients) and are interviewed by members of the panel. The panel then recommends those who should be appointed to the Lord Chancellor.

The first appointments of QCs under the new system were made in 2006; 443 applied and 175 were appointed. Of these, 33 were women, 10 ethnic minority and four solicitors.

The most notable fact is the number of women who were successful – but this may only reflect the fact that there are more women in the profession.

10.2.4 Complaints against barristers

Where a barrister receives a brief from a solicitor, he does not enter into a contract with his client and so cannot sue if their fees are not paid. Similarly, the client cannot sue for breach of contract. However, they can be sued for negligence. In *Saif Ali v Sydney Mitchell and Co* (1980) it was held that a barrister could be sued for negligence in respect of written advice and opinions. In that case a barrister had given the wrong advice about who to sue, with the result that the claimant was too late to start proceedings against the right person.

In *Hall (a firm) v Simons* (2000) the House of Lords held that lawyers could also be liable for negligence in the conduct of advocacy in court. This decision overruled the earlier case of *Rondel v Worsley* (1969) in which barristers were held not to be liable because their first duty was to the courts and they must be 'free to do their duty fearlessly and independently'.

The Law Lords in *Hall (a firm) v Simons* felt that in light of modern conditions it was no longer in the public interest that advocates should have immunity from being sued for negligence. They pointed out that doctors could be sued and they had a duty to an ethical code of practice and might have difficult decisions to make when treating patients. There was no reason why advocates should not be liable in the same way.

They also pointed out that allowing advocates to be sued for negligence would not be likely to lead to the whole case being re-argued. If an action against an advocate was merely an excuse to get the whole issue litigated again, the matter would almost certainly be struck out as an abuse of process.

Bar Standards Board

Complaints against barristers are handled by the Bar Standards Board. If there was poor service, the Board can order the barrister to pay

Activity

Read the following article and answer the questions below.

Talent, not cash, should open the door to the Bar

The ancient buildings, paved courtyards and well-tended lawns of the Inns of Court shout privilege. But is the privilege of being a barrister one that anyone can attain – regardless of social background or wealth?

Concerns that it is now harder to enter the Bar have grown along with the costs of university and Bar training. Nearly one in three students arrive with debts of £20,000. The one-year vocational course can add another £15,000 – and non-law graduates have to fund an extra year on top of that.

But the barrier is not just financial. Geoffrey Vos, QC, whose father was a Bermondsey leather merchant, identifies other hurdles: lack of contacts or knowledge about the profession;

its intimidating environment; the scramble to find a pupillage, or training place; and then the challenge of securing a seat in chambers. Finally, there is uncertainty of success or earning power.

The profession's entry profile is far more diverse that it was. But then what? Getting in is just the first hurdle. Perceived obstacles once inside can be a further deterrent. At the top the profession is still mostly male, white and privileged: 73 per cent of barristers in eight top commercial chambers went to private schools. At law firms, the proportion of women partners over ten years has risen slowly from 16.55 per cent to 23.2 per cent now. Women in the higher levels of the profession are nowhere near beginning to reflect the level of women entering the profession.

Adapted from an article by Frances Gibb in The Times, 3 April 2007

Questions

1. The article mentions the Inns of Court. Name the four Inns of Court.

2. Briefly describe what the Bar Vocational Course consists of.

3. Why do non-law graduates have to do an extra year?

4. What financial barriers are there to becoming a barrister?

5. What other barriers are there to becoming a barrister?

6. In which area have the legal professions become more diverse?

7. What are the problems at the higher levels of the legal professions?

@ Internet Research

The article on the previous page states that the profession's entry is far more diverse than it was.

Try to find out what the current figures are for entrants to the legal professions. Try the websites for the Law Society and the Bar: **www.lawsociety.org.uk** and **www.barcouncil.org.uk**.

compensation of up to £15,000 to the client. The complaints process is overseen by an independent Lay Complaints Commissioner.

Senate of the Inns of Court

Barristers can be disciplined by the Senate of the Inns of Court if they fail to maintain the standards set out in their Code of Conduct. In extreme cases the Senate can disbar a barrister from practising.

Legal Services Ombudsman

As set out earlier in section 10.1.3, there has been a Legal Services Ombudsman since 1991, whose work involves investigating complaints about all the legal professions. There are comparatively few complaints against barristers and the Ombudsman has found that the Bar Council usually handles about 90 per cent of complaints satisfactorily.

10.3 Legal Services Act 2007

10.3.1 Background

In 2001 a report by the Office of Fair Trading recommended that unjustified restrictions on competition in the legal profession should be removed.

In 2004 the Clementi Report into the legal profession was published (*Review of the Regulatory*

Framework for the Legal Services in England and Wales – Final Report). The main recommendations were that:

- there should be a new complaints body which is independent of the professions
- there should be a legal services board as regulator over all the legal professional bodies
- Legal Disciplinary Practices (LDPs) should be permitted where there are barristers, solicitors and non-lawyers working together in the same practice
- non-lawyers would be allowed to own and manage LDPs, but there would be safeguards to make sure that they were 'fit to own' such a practice.

10.3.2 The Legal Services Act

This Act was passed by Parliament in the autumn of 2007. It starts by setting out regulatory objectives for legal services. These are:

(a) supporting the constitutional principle of the rule of law

(b) improving access to justice

(c) protecting and promoting the interests of consumers

(d) promoting competition in the provision of services

(e) encouraging a strong, diverse and effective legal profession

(f) increasing public understanding of the citizen's legal rights and duties

(g) promoting and maintaining adherence to the professional principles.

Legal Services Board

The Act provides for the creation of the Legal Services Board. The role of the Board is to have independent oversight regulation of the legal profession. It will consist of a Chairman and 7 to 10 members appointed by the Secretary of State. The first Chairman must be a non-lawyer and the majority of members must also be non-lawyers.

The Home Affairs Committee reported on the Bill when it was in draft form. The committee was concerned that the Lord Chancellor was involved in the appointment of the Chairman and members of the Board. It felt that this prevented the Board from being independent of the Government. The final Act provides that the Lord Chancellor has to consult the Lord Chief Justice on appointments.

Complaints about legal services

The Act has provision for establishing the Office for Legal Complaints to handle all complaints in respect of the legal profession. The Office will have a Chairman and between six and eight members. The Chairman must be a non-lawyer and the majority of members must also be non-lawyers.

The location of this Office is to be in the West Midlands and staff will be drawn largely from the Law Society's Consumer Complaints Service. This is the organisation that has been frequently criticised for its inefficient handling of complaints.

The Bar is concerned that its complaints handling will become less efficient under the new system.

Alternative Business Structures (ABS)

Until 2008 there were restrictions on the types of business structures in the legal profession. The main restrictions were:

- barristers and solicitors could not operate from the same business
- lawyers were not allowed to enter into partnership with non-lawyers
- on non-lawyers being involved in the ownership or management of legal businesses
- legal practices could not operate as companies.

So, generally, barristers and solicitors could not work together, nor could lawyers and non-lawyers work together in legal businesses. The Legal Services Act changes this by allowing:

- legal businesses to include lawyers and non-lawyers

- legal businesses to include barristers and solicitors
- non-lawyers to own legal businesses
- legal businesses to operate as companies.

From 2008 solicitors will be allowed to form Legal Disciplinary Practices (LDPs). In these up to 25 per cent of partners can be non-lawyers.

From 2011 Alternative Business Structures (ABSs) will be allowed. These have to be given a licence in order to operate. Access to justice must be considered when such a licence is applied for. This is to prevent commercial businesses choosing only the most profitable areas of law and possibly leaving an area without lawyers to do the less profitable types of law.

 Internet Research

Look up the Legal Services Act 2007 on **www.opsi.gov.uk**. At the start of the Act there is an index of contents. Use this to find which part of the Act deals with:

(a) The Legal Services Board

(b) Alternative Business Structures

(c) Legal complaints.

10.4 Fusion

A major debate used to be whether the two professions should be merged into one profession. The advantages of fusion were thought to be:

- reduced costs, as only one lawyer would be needed instead of a solicitor and a barrister
- less duplication of work because only one person would be doing the work, instead of a solicitor preparing the case and then passing it on to a barrister
- more continuity, as the same person could deal with the case from start to finish.

The disadvantages of fusion were seen as:

- a decrease in the specialist skills of advocacy
- loss of the independent Bar and the lack of availability of advice from independent specialists at the Bar
- less objectivity in consideration of a case; at the moment the barrister provides a second opinion
- loss of the 'cab rank rule' under which barristers have to accept any case offered to them (except when they are already booked on another case for the same day). This principle allows anyone to get representation, even if their case is unpopular or unlikely to win.

The argument for fusion is no longer so important since the changes made by the Courts and Legal Services Act 1990 and the Access to Justice Act 1999 mean that barristers and solicitors can take a case from start to finish. Under the Access to Justice Act, barristers have the right to do litigation (ie the preliminary work in starting a case) which has in the past always been done by solicitors. At the same time, solicitors have wider rights of advocacy and may represent clients in all courts.

The changes made by the Legal Services Act 2007 mean that there is even less need for the professions to be fused. Barristers and solicitors can work together in the same legal business.

10.5 Women and ethnic minorities in the legal profession

The legal profession has an image of being white male-dominated. Both women and ethnic minorities are under-represented in the higher levels of the legal professions.

Women

Women are forming an increasing number of the entrants to the professions. They now make up

over half of new solicitors and half of new entrants to the Bar. As a result of the increasing numbers of women studying law, there are now greater numbers of women in both professions: 30 per cent of members of the Bar and 42 per cent of solicitors are female. Despite this there are very few women at the higher levels in either profession. For example, at the Bar only about 10 per cent of QCs are women. Women solicitors tend to be in junior positions as assistant solicitors or junior partners.

One of the reasons put forward to explain this is that the increase in entrants is a fairly recent phenomenon. Twenty years ago there were comparatively few women going into the legal professions, and so it is not so surprising that there are correspondingly fewer women in senior positions.

In the solicitors' profession about 23 per cent of partners are women. This figure is increasing, but a survey in 2001 found that many women solicitors did not want to become partners.

Women also tend to earn less than their male counterparts, even when they do achieve higher status, especially in the solicitors' ranks. Women solicitors do not earn the same level of salary as male solicitors. Even the starting salaries of women are lower. The gap becomes bigger the higher up the profession, with men earning on average £15,000 more per year than women.

Ethnic minorities

Ethnic minorities are also increasing in both legal professions. About 10 per cent of solicitors and barristers in practice are from ethnic minorities. As with women, they are more likely to be in junior positions. An interesting fact is that ethnic minority lawyers are better represented in the Crown Prosecution Service, making up about 15 per cent of lawyers there.

There are also some increases at higher levels in the legal profession. For example, the new procedure for appointing QCs appears to have encouraged ethnic minority lawyers to apply. In

2006, when the first appointments were made under the new system, 10 of the new QCs were from ethnic minorities. This was about 6 per cent of total appointments.

This trend is important as it means there is likely to be an increase in judges appointed from ethnic minorities in future.

Examination Questions

(a) Describe the training of barristers and solicitors.

(b) Discuss the disadvantages of the current system of training barristers and solicitors.

OCR G141 June 2007

Chapter 11

Magistrates

There is a tradition of using lay people, ie people who are not legally qualified, in the decision-making process in our courts. Today this applies particularly to the Magistrates' Courts and the Crown Court. However, in the past lay people were also frequently used to decide civil cases in the High Court and the County Court, and there are still some cases in which a jury can be used in the civil courts. There are also lay people with expertise in a particular field who sit as part of a panel as lay assessors. This occurs in the Patents Court and the Admiralty Court in the High Court as well as in tribunals (especially employment tribunals and social security appeals tribunals).

11.1 Lay magistrates

There are about 29,000 lay magistrates sitting as part-time judges in the Magistrates' Courts; another name for lay magistrates is Justices of the Peace. They sit to hear cases as a bench of two or three magistrates. The size of panel has been limited to a maximum of three, although before 1996 there could be up to seven magistrates sitting together to hear a case. A single lay magistrate sitting on his or her own has very limited powers. They can, however, issue search warrants and warrants for arrest and conduct Early Administrative Hearings.

There are also District Judges (Magistrates' Courts) who work in Magistrates' Courts. These are not lay people but are qualified lawyers who can sit on their own to hear any of the cases that come before the court. Under s 16(3) of the

Justices of the Peace Act 1979 they have the same powers as a bench of lay magistrates. Since the duties of these District Judges are the same as those of lay magistrates and since the history of the two is linked, details of District Judges (formerly known as stipendiary magistrates) are also included in this chapter.

11.1.1 History of the magistracy

The office of Justice of the Peace is very old, dating back to the twelfth century at least. In 1195 Richard I appointed 'keepers of the peace'. By the mid-thirteenth century the judicial side of their position had developed and by 1361 the title Justice of the Peace was being used. Over the years they were also given many administrative duties, for example being responsible for the poor law, highways and bridges, and weights and measures. In the nineteenth century, elected local authorities took over most of these duties, though some remnants remain especially in the licensing powers of the Magistrates' Courts.

The poor quality of the local Justices of the Peace in London and the absence of an adequate police force became a matter of concern towards the end of the eighteenth century. This led to seven public offices with paid magistrates being set up in 1792. This was the origin of the modern stipendiary magistrate. Until 1839 they were in charge of the police as well as hearing cases in court. Outside London, the first appointment of a paid magistrate was in Manchester in 1813. In 1835 the Municipal Corporations Act gave a general power for boroughs to request the appointment of a stipendiary magistrate. At the beginning a paid magistrate did not have to have any particular qualifications, but from 1839 they could only be appointed from barristers. Solicitors did not become eligible to be appointed as stipendiary magistrates until 1949.

11.2 Qualifications

11.2.1 Lay magistrates

Lay magistrates do not have to have any qualifications in law. There are, however, some requirements as to their character. In 1998, the Lord Chancellor set out six key qualities which candidates should have. These are:

- good character
- understanding and communication
- social awareness
- maturity and sound temperament
- sound judgement
- commitment and reliability.

They must have certain 'judicial' qualities – it is particularly important that they are able to assimilate factual information and make a reasoned decision upon it. They must also be able to take account of the reasoning of others and work as a team.

There are also formal requirements as to age

and residence: lay magistrates must be aged between 18 and 65 on appointment. It is rare that a person under 27 will be considered as it is felt they do not have enough experience.

However, since the age for appointment was reduced to 18 in 2003 there is an increased likelihood that young magistrates will be appointed if they are suitable. In 2004 there were at least two appointments of young magistrates. These were of one aged 21 in Shropshire and another aged 23 in West Yorkshire.

11.2.2 Area

Up to 2003 it was necessary for lay magistrates to live within 15 miles of the commission area for the court which they sat in. In 2003 the Courts Act abolished commission areas. Instead there is now one commission area for the whole of England and Wales. However, the country is divided into local justice areas. These areas are specified by the Lord Chancellor and lay magistrates are expected to live or work within or near to the local justice area to which they are allocated.

11.2.3 Commitment

The other requirement is that lay magistrates must be prepared to commit themselves to sitting at least 26 half days each year. It is thought that this level of commitment deters many people from becoming lay magistrates.

11.2.4 Restrictions on appointment

Some people are not eligible to be appointed. These include people with serious criminal convictions, though a conviction for a minor motoring offence will not automatically disqualify a candidate. Others who are disqualified include undischarged bankrupts, members of the forces and those whose work is incompatible with sitting as a magistrate, such as police officers and traffic wardens. Relatives of those working in the local criminal justice system are not likely to be appointed as it would not appear 'just' if, for example, the wife or husband of a local police officer were to sit to decide cases. In addition people whose hearing is impaired, or who by reason of infirmity cannot carry out all the duties of a Justice of the Peace cannot be appointed. Close relatives will not be appointed to the same bench.

Activity

1. Put the list of six key qualities in 11.2.1 into order, with the one that you think is most important first and the least important last.
2. Compare your list with those of two other people.
3. Explain what other qualities you think magistrates need.

11.2.5 District Judges

These were previously known as stipendiary magistrates. They must have a seven-year general qualification, that is a right of audience as an advocate, and are usually chosen from practising barristers or solicitors, or from others with relevant experience such as court clerks. They are only appointed to courts in London or other big cities such as Birmingham, Liverpool and Manchester. Before becoming a District Judge they will usually be an acting judge sitting part-time for two years to gain experience of sitting judicially, and to establish their suitability for full-time appointment.

11.3 Appointment

About 1,500 new lay magistrates are appointed each year. The appointments are made by the Lord Chancellor. In order to decide who to appoint, the Lord Chancellor relies on recommendations made to him by the local advisory committees – this method of appointment is much criticised.

11.3.1 Local advisory committees

The membership of the committees used to be secret but since 1993 all names must be published. The members tend to be current or ex-Justices of the Peace. About half the members have to retire in rotation every three years. The committees should have a maximum of 12 members and these should include a mixture of magistrates and non-magistrates.

Names of potential magistrates can be put forward by anyone. It is even possible for an interested person to ask that they themselves should be considered. Normally, names are put forward by groups such as the local political parties, trade unions and chambers of commerce. To try to encourage as wide a range of potential candidates as possible, committees have advertised for individuals to put themselves forward with advertisements being placed in local papers, or newspapers aimed at particular ethnic groups, and even on buses! For example, in Leeds, radio adverts have been used and people encouraged to come to open evenings at their local Magistrates' Court. This is in order to attract as wide a spectrum of potential candidates as possible. The intention is to create a panel representative of all aspects of society.

A balance of occupations is aimed at. The Lord Chancellor has set down 11 broad categories of occupations, and advisory committees are recommended that they should not have more than 15 per cent of the bench coming from any one category.

The advisory panels also have to bear in mind candidates' political allegiance. This is controversial but it is recognised as a way of trying to get a good balance of different social classes within the magistracy.

11.3.2 Interview panels

There is usually a two-stage interview process. At the first interview the panel tries to find out more about the candidate's personal attributes, in particular looking to see if they have the six key qualities required. The interview panel will also explore the candidate's attitudes on various criminal justice issues such as youth crime or drink-driving. The second interview is aimed at testing candidates' potential judicial aptitude and this is done by a discussion of at least two case studies which are typical of those heard regularly in Magistrates' Courts. The discussion might, for example, focus on the type of sentence which should be imposed on specific case facts.

The advisory committees will interview candidates and then submit names of those they think are suitable to the Lord Chancellor. He will then appoint new magistrates from this list. Once appointed, magistrates may continue to sit until the age of 70.

11.4 Composition of the Bench today

The traditional image of lay justices is that they are 'middle-class, middle-aged and middle-minded'. This image is to a certain extent true. Most magistrates are in the 45–65 age bracket. Magistrates under the age of 40 are still rare. The majority are supporters of the Conservative Party; this is so even in areas where there is a high Labour vote. A report, *The Judiciary in the Magistrates' Courts* (2002), found that lay magistrates:

- were drawn overwhelmingly from professional and managerial ranks and
- 40 per cent of them were retired from full-time employment.

However, in other respects the Bench is well balanced: 49 per cent of magistrates are women, as against 10 per cent of professional judges. Also, ethnic minorities are reasonably well represented in the magistracy. The National Strategy for the Recruitment of Lay Magistrates (2003) gave the statistics for ethnic minority lay magistrates as being 6 per cent of the total number of lay magistrates as against 7.9 per cent of the population as a whole. This compares very favourably to the professional judiciary where less

than 1 per cent are from ethnic minority backgrounds.

The relatively high level of ethnic minority magistrates is largely a result of campaigns to attract a wider range of candidates. Adverts are placed in national newspapers and also in TV guides and women's magazines. In an effort to encourage those from ethnic minorities to apply, adverts also appear in such publications as the *Caribbean Times*, the *Asian Times* and *Muslim News*. This has led to an increase in the number of ethnic minority appointments.

The Lord Chancellor has encouraged disabled people to apply to become magistrates. This has included appointing blind persons as lay magistrates.

 Internet Research

Look at the Magistrates' Association website at **www.magistrates-association.org.uk**. You can find out more about how to become a magistrate.

11.5 Magistrates' duties

They have a very wide workload which is mainly connected to criminal cases, although they also deal with some civil matters, especially family cases. They try 97 per cent of all criminal cases and deal with preliminary hearings in the remaining 3 per cent of criminal cases. This will involve Early Administrative Hearings, remand hearings, bail applications and committal proceedings. They also deal with civil matters which include the enforcing of debts owed to the utilities (gas, electricity and water), non-payment of the council tax and non-payment of television licences. In addition, they hear appeals from the refusal of a local authority to grant licences for the sale of alcohol and licences for betting and gaming establishments.

Youth Court

Specially nominated and trained justices form the Youth Court panel to hear criminal charges against young offenders aged 10–17 years old. These magistrates must be under 65 and a panel must usually include at least one man and one woman. There is also a special panel for the Family Court to hear family cases including orders for protection against violence, affiliation cases, adoption orders and proceedings under the Children Act 1989.

Appeals

Lay magistrates also sit at the Crown Court to hear appeals from the Magistrates' Court. In these cases the lay justices form a panel with a qualified judge.

11.6 Training of lay magistrates

The training of lay magistrates is supervised by the Magistrates' Committee of the Judicial Studies Board. This Committee has drawn up a syllabus of the topics which lay magistrates should cover in their training. However, because of the large numbers of lay magistrates, the actual training is carried out in local areas, sometimes through the clerk of the court, sometimes through weekend courses organised by universities with magistrates from the region attending.

Since 1998, magistrates' training has been monitored more closely. There were criticisms prior to then that, although magistrates were required to attend a certain number of hours' training, there was no assessment of how much they had understood. In 1998 the Magistrates New Training Initiative was introduced (MNTI 1). In 2004 this was refined by the Magistrates National Training Initiative (MNTI 2).

The framework of training is divided into four areas of competence, the first three of which are relevant to all lay magistrates. The fourth competence is for Chairmen of the Bench. The four areas of competence are:

1. Managing yourself – this focuses on some of the basic aspects of self-management in relation to preparing for court, conduct in court and ongoing learning.
2. Working as a member of a team – this focuses on the team aspect of decision-making in the Magistrates' Court.
3. Making judicial decisions – this focuses on impartial and structured decision-making.
4. Managing judicial decision-making – this is for the chairman's role and focuses on working with the legal adviser, managing the court and ensuring effective, impartial decision-making.

For delivering training there are Bench Training and Developmental Committees (BTDCs) and s 19(3) of the Courts Act 2003 sets out a statutory obligation on the Lord Chancellor to provide training and training materials.

11.6.1 Training of new magistrates

There is a syllabus for new magistrates which is divided into three parts. These are:

1. Initial introductory training: this covers such matters as understanding the organisation of the Bench and the administration of the court and the roles and responsibilities of those involved in the Magistrates' Court.
2. Core training: this provides the new magistrate with the opportunity to acquire and develop the key skills, knowledge and understanding required of a competent magistrate.
3. Activities: these will involve observations of court sittings and visits to establishments such as a prison or a probation office.

The training programme for new magistrates should normally follow the pattern set out in Figure 11.1.

Figure 11.1 New magistrates' training and appraisal pathway (taken from MNTI2 Handbook issued by the Judicial Studies Board)

11.6.2 Mentors

Each new magistrate keeps a Personal Development Log of their progress and has a mentor (an experienced magistrate) to assist them. The initial introductory training is covered before the new magistrate starts sitting in court. They will also take part in a structured court room observation of cases on at least three occasions. These should be arranged so that they see different aspects of the work and should include preliminary decisions such as bail, a short summary trial and sentencing.

11.6.3 Training sessions

These are organised and carried out at local level within the 42 court areas. Much of the training is delivered by Justices' Clerks. The Judicial Studies Board intends that most training should still be delivered locally. However, they take into account

the need to collaborate regionally and nationally where appropriate. In particular, the training of Youth and Family Panel Chairmen will be delivered nationally for areas which do not have enough such Chairmen requiring training to run an effective course locally.

11.6.4 Appraisal

During the first two years of the new magistrate sitting in court, between eight and eleven of the sessions will be mentored. In the same period the magistrate is also expected to attend about seven training sessions. After two years, or whenever it is felt that the magistrate is ready, there will be an appraisal of the magistrate to check if they have acquired the competencies.

Any magistrate who cannot show that they have achieved the competencies will be given extra training. If they still cannot achieve the competencies, then the matter is referred to the local advisory committee, who may recommend to the Lord Chancellor that the magistrate is removed from sitting.

This new scheme involves practical training 'on the job'. It also answers the criticisms of the old system where there was no check made on whether the magistrate had actually benefited from the training session they attended.

Those magistrates who chair the Bench are also appraised for this role, so that the quality of the chairing in court is improving.

11.7 Retirement and removal

The retirement age is 70, but when magistrates become 70 they do not officially retire – instead, their names are placed on the Supplemental List. This means that they can no longer sit in the Magistrates' Court. However, they can continue to carry out some administrative functions mainly connected with signing documents. Lay magistrates who move from the commission area to which they were appointed cannot continue as magistrates in that area. If they wish to continue as magistrates, their names will be placed on the Supplemental

List until there is a vacancy in their new area. Lay magistrates may, of course, resign from office at any time and many will resign before reaching 70.

11.7.1 Removal

Section 11 of the Courts Act 2003 gives the Lord Chancellor the power to remove a lay justice for the following reasons:

- on the ground of incapacity or misbehaviour
- on the ground of a persistent failure to meet such standards of competence as are prescribed by a direction given by the Lord Chancellor or
- if the Lord Chancellor is satisfied that the lay justice is declining or neglecting to take a proper part in the exercise of his functions as a Justice of the Peace.

Removal for misbehaviour usually occurs when a magistrate is convicted of a criminal offence. There are about 10 such removals each year. However, on occasions in the past there have been removals for such matters as taking part in a CND march or transvestite behaviour. There was considerable criticism of the Lord Chancellor's use of his power of removal in such circumstances and it is unlikely that such behaviour today would lead to removal from the Bench.

11.8 The magistrates' clerk

Every bench is assisted by a clerk. These are now also referred to as legal advisers. The senior clerk in each court has to be qualified as a barrister or solicitor for at least five years. The clerk's duty is to guide the magistrates on questions of law, practice and procedure. This is set out in s 28(3) of the Justices of the Peace Act 1979 which says:

> It is hereby declared that the functions of a justices' clerk include the giving to the justices . . . of advice about law, practice or procedure on questions arising in connection with the discharge of their functions.

Key facts

Qualifications	Live or work near court in which they sit Need common sense, integrity Disqualified for serious criminal record, bankruptcy or work that is incompatible
Appointment	By Lord Chancellor on the recommendation of local advisory committees
Training	Four basic competencies: Personal Development Log of progress Mentors and mentored sessions Attend about seven training sessions Appraisal
Composition	29,000 lay magistrates, 50.3 per cent men, 49.7 per cent women Over-representation of Conservative supporters Under-representation of young working class
Work	Summary trials Ancillary matters, eg issuing warrants, bail applications Youth court Family court Sit in Crown Court on appeal from Magistrates' Court

Figure 11.2 Key facts chart on lay magistrates

The clerk is not meant to assist in the decision-making and should not normally retire with the magistrates when they go to make their decision. In *R v Eccles Justices, ex parte Farrelly* (1992) the Queen's Bench Divisional Court quashed convictions because the clerk had apparently participated in the decision-making process.

Clerks deal with routine administrative matters and in May 1993 were given increased powers so that they can now issue warrants for arrest, extend police bail and adjourn criminal proceedings. The Crime and Disorder Act 1998 also gives clerks the powers to deal with Early Administrative Hearings.

11.9 Advantages of lay magistrates

11.9.1 Cross-section of society

Lay magistrates provide a wider cross-section on the Bench than would be possible with the use of professional judges. This is particularly true of women, with 49 per cent of magistrates being women compared with 10 per cent of professional judges. Also, ethnic minorities are reasonably well represented in the magistracy.

In 1999 the Lord Chancellor announced this campaign to attract a wider range of magistrates, but he pointed out that the magistracy was already very diverse:

> Magistrates come from a wide range of backgrounds and occupations. We have magistrates who are dinner ladies and scientists, bus drivers and teachers, plumbers and housewives. They have different faiths and come from different ethnic backgrounds, some have disabilities. All are serving their communities, ensuring that local justice is dispensed by local people. The magistracy should reflect the diversity of the community it serves.

Lay magistrates are more representative than District Judges in the Magistrates' Courts. In 2000 a report, *The Judiciary in the Magistrates' Courts*, pointed out that in comparison to lay magistrates, District Judges were:

- younger, but
- mostly white and male.

11.9.2 Local knowledge

Lay magistrates used to have to live within 15 miles of the area covered by the commission, in order that they would have local knowledge of particular problems in the area. Under the Courts Act 2003 there is no longer a formal requirement that they should live in or near the area in which they sit as a magistrate, although it is intended that normally magistrates will continue to sit in the local justice area in which they reside. However, if there is a good reason to do otherwise, for example where it is easier for the magistrate to sit in the area where he works, then this is allowed.

Even though lay magistrates live or work in the relevant justice area, it is sometimes argued that they do not have any real knowledge of the problems in the poorer areas. This is because most magistrates come from the professional and managerial classes and will live in the better areas. However, their main value is that they will have more awareness of local events, local patterns of crime and local opinions than a professional judge from another area.

Another problem is that during the last 10 years, some 125 Magistrates' Courts have been closed. This causes problems of access and attendance because in some areas people have long journeys to their 'local' court. It also means that the advantage of lay magistrates having local knowledge is being lost.

11.9.3 Cost

The use of unpaid lay magistrates is cheap. The report *The Judiciary in the Magistrates' Courts* (2000) found that at that time the cost of using lay magistrates was £52.10 per hour. As against this, the cost of using District Judges in the Magistrates' Courts was £61.78 an hour. When this is multiplied by the number of hours' work carried out by lay magistrates in the course of the year, it is obvious that the cost of replacing them with professional judges would be several millions of pounds. In addition, there would also be the problem of recruiting sufficient qualified lawyers.

The cost of a trial in the Magistrates' Court is also much cheaper than a trial in the Crown Court. This is partly because cases in the Crown Court are more complex and therefore likely to take longer. Even so, it is clear that the cost both to the Government and to defendants who pay for their own lawyer is much higher in the Crown Court.

11.9.4 Legal adviser

Since 1999, all newly appointed magistrates' clerks have to be legally qualified. In addition, existing clerks under the age of 40 in 1999 have to qualify within 10 years. This brings a higher level of legal skill to the Magistrates' Court. The availability of a legal adviser gives the magistrates access to any necessary legal advice on points that may arise in any case. This overcomes any criticism of the fact that lay magistrates are not themselves legally qualified. In addition, the training of lay magistrates is improving with the new training system and the strengthened role of the Judicial Studies Board in their training.

11.9.5 Few appeals

Comparatively few defendants appeal against the magistrates' decisions, and many of the appeals that are made are against sentence, not against the finding of guilt. In 2006 the *Judicial Statistics Annual Report* showed that only 12,992 appeals were made to the Crown Court from the Magistrates' Courts. Out of these, only 2,020 were allowed and in another 3,184 cases the Crown Court varied the decision/sentence. This was out

of a total workload of nearly 2 million defendants dealt with in the Magistrates' Courts.

There are also very few instances where an error of law is made. This is shown by the fact that there were only 100 appeals by way of case stated to the Queen's Bench Divisional Court. Of these appeals, 42 were allowed. From this it can be argued that despite the amateur status of lay magistrates, they do a remarkably good job.

11.10 Disadvantages of lay magistrates

11.10.1 Middle-aged, middle class

Lay magistrates are often perceived as being middle-aged and middle class. The report *The Judiciary in the Magistrates' Courts* (2000) showed that this was largely true. They found that 40 per cent of lay magistrates were retired and also that they were overwhelmingly from a professional or managerial background. However, as already discussed at section 11.9.1, lay magistrates are from a much wider range of backgrounds than professional judges.

11.10.2 Prosecution bias

It is often said that lay magistrates tend to be prosecution biased, believing the police too readily. One fact supporting this theory is that there is a lower acquittal rate in Magistrates' Courts than in the Crown Court. There is also the fact that they will see the same Crown Prosecution Service prosecutor or designated case worker frequently and this could affect their judgement. However, part of their training is aimed at eliminating this type of bias.

11.10.3 Inconsistency in sentencing

Magistrates in different areas often pass very different sentences for what appear to be similar offences. The Government's White Paper, *Justice for All*, set out differences found in the Criminal

Key facts

Advantages	Disadvantages
Cross-section of local people Good gender balance Improving ethnic balance Much better cross-section than District Judges	Not a true cross-section 40 per cent are retired people Majority are from professional or managerial background Older than District Judges
Live (or work) locally and so know the area and its problems	Unlikely to live in the poorer areas and so do not truly know the area's problems
Cheaper than using professional judges as they are only paid expenses Cheaper than sending cases to the Crown Court	
Improved training through MNTI2 and the increased role of Judicial Studies Board	There are inconsistencies in sentencing and decisions on bail
Have legal adviser for points of law	Not legally qualified
Very few appeals	

Figure 11.3 Key facts chart on advantages and disadvantages of using lay magistrates in the legal system

Statistics for 2001 when it gave these following examples:

- for burglary of dwellings, 20 per cent of offenders were sentenced to immediate custody in Teesside, compared with 41 per cent of offenders in Birmingham; 38 per cent of burglars at Cardiff Magistrates' Court received community sentences, compared with 66 per cent in Leicester
- for driving while disqualified, the percentage of offenders sentenced to custody ranged from 21 per cent in Neath Port Talbot [South Wales] to 77 per cent in Mid North Essex
- for receiving stolen goods, 3.5 per cent of offenders sentenced at Reading Magistrates' Court received custodial sentences compared with 48 per cent in Greenwich and Woolwich [South London] and 39 per cent at Camberwell Green [South London].

However, this has to be seen in context. Only 4 per cent of offenders dealt with by magistrates receive a prison sentence, so the problem may not be as severe as thought. Also, since these figures were compiled there has been a new edition of the *Magistrates' Association's Sentencing Guidelines*. It is thought that these are helping to promote common standards.

However, the 2004 statistics do not show any improvement. Magistrates in Sunderland discharged 36.4 per cent of all defendants, whereas only 9.2 per cent of defendants in Birmingham were discharged. In Newcastle, magistrates sentenced only 7.2 per cent of defendants to an immediate custodial sentence. In Hillingdon in West London, the magistrates sentenced 32 per cent of defendants to an immediate custodial sentence.

11.10.4 Reliance on the legal adviser

The lack of legal knowledge of the lay justices should be offset by the fact that a legally qualified clerk is available to give advice. However, this will not prevent inconsistencies in sentencing since the clerk is not allowed to help the magistrates decide on a sentence. In some courts it is felt that the magistrates rely too heavily on their clerk.

Examination Questions

(a) Describe the selection and training of lay magistrates.

(b) Discuss the advantages of using lay magistrates to make decisions in criminal matters.

OCR G141 June 2007

Chapter 12

Juries

12.1 History of the jury system

Juries have been used in the legal system for over 1,000 years. There is evidence that they were used even before the Norman Conquest. However, in 1215 when trial by ordeal was condemned by the Church and (in the same year) the Magna Carta included the recognition of a person's right to trial by 'the lawful judgment of his peers', juries became the usual method of trying criminal cases. Originally they were used for providing local knowledge and information, and acted more as witnesses than decision-makers. By the middle of the fifteenth century, juries had become independent assessors and assumed their modern role as deciders of fact.

12.1.1 Independence of the jury

The independence of the jury became even more firmly established following *Bushell's Case* (1670). In that case several jurors refused to convict Quaker activists of unlawful assembly. The trial judge would not accept the not guilty verdict, and ordered the jurors to resume their deliberations without food or drink. When the jurors persisted in their refusal to convict, the court fined them and committed them to prison until the fines were paid. On appeal, the Court of Common Pleas ordered the release of the jurors, holding that jurors could not be punished for their verdict. This established that the jury were the sole

arbiters of fact and the judge could not challenge their decision.

A more modern-day example demonstrating that judges must respect the independence of the jury is *R v McKenna* (1960). In that case the judge at the trial had threatened the jury that if they did not return a verdict within another 10 minutes they would be locked up all night. The jury then returned a verdict of guilty, but the defendant's conviction was quashed on appeal because of the judge's interference.

12.2 Modern-day use of the jury

Only a small percentage of cases is tried by jury today. However, juries are used in the following courts:

- Crown Court for criminal trials on indictment
- High Court, Queen's Bench Division (but only for certain types of cases)
- County Court (for similar cases to the Queen's Bench Division)
- Coroners' Courts (in some cases).

12.2.1 Juries in criminal cases

The most important use of juries today is in the Crown Court where they decide whether the defendant is guilty or not guilty. Jury trials, however, account for less than 1 per cent of all criminal trials. This is because 97 per cent of cases are dealt with in the Magistrates' Court and of the cases that go to the Crown Court, about two out of every three defendants will plead guilty. Also, some of the cases at the Crown Court, in which the defendant has entered a not guilty plea, will not go before a jury as the case will be discharged by the judge without any trial. This occurs where the Crown Prosecution Service withdraws the charges, possibly because a witness refuses to give evidence. A jury in the Crown Court has 12 members.

12.2.2 Juries in civil cases

Juries in civil cases are now only used in very limited circumstances, but where they are used they have a dual role. They decide whether the claimant has proved his case or not. Then, if they decide that the claimant has won the case, the jury also go on to decide the amount of damages that the defendant should pay to the claimant.

The rules for when juries may be used in civil cases are set out in s 69 of the Supreme Court Act 1981 for High Court cases, and s 66 of the County Courts Act 1984 for cases in that court. These Acts state that parties have the right to jury trial only in the following types of case:

- defamation, ie cases of libel and slander (this is the most frequent use of juries)
- false imprisonment
- malicious prosecution
- fraud.

All these cases involve character or reputation and it is for this reason that jury trial has been retained. Even for these cases a jury trial can be refused by the judge if the case involves complicated documents or accounts or scientific evidence and is therefore thought to be unsuitable for jury trial.

Where a jury is used in the High Court there will be 12 jurors. Very few cases use a jury, usually only about 10 cases a year.

Use of juries in personal injury cases

In other civil cases in the Queen's Bench Division of the High Court the parties can apply to a judge for trial by jury, but no case since 1966 has used a jury. This follows the case of *Ward v James* (1966) where the plaintiff was claiming for injuries caused in a road crash. In this case the Court of Appeal laid down guidelines for personal injury cases. These were:

- personal injury cases should normally be tried by a judge sitting alone, because such cases involve assessing compensatory damages which have to have regard to the conventional scales of damages
- there have to be exceptional circumstances before the court will allow a jury to be used in such a case.

The decision in *Ward v James* effectively stopped the use of juries for personal injury cases. The following cases show how the courts have proved very reluctant to let juries be used. In *Singh v London Underground* (1990) a request for a jury to try a personal injury case arising from the King's Cross Underground fire was refused. It was held that the case was unsuitable for jury trial because it involved such wide issues and technical points.

The case of *H v Ministry of Defence* (1991) further reinforced the rule in *Ward v James*; the defendant was a soldier who had received negligent medical treatment necessitating the amputation of part of his penis. He applied for jury trial, but it was held that jury trial for a personal injury claim would only be allowed in very exceptional circumstances and this case was not such a one. The court said that an example of when jury trial might be appropriate was where the injuries resulted from someone deliberately abusing their authority and there might well be a claim for exemplary damages.

County Court

Trial by jury in the County Court is very rare, but since 1991 with the changes in the jurisdiction (defamation actions can be transferred for trial to the County Court) there are occasionally cases in which a jury is used. Where a jury is used in the County Court there will be eight jurors.

Court	Type of case	Role	Number on jury
Crown Court	Serious criminal cases: eg murder, manslaughter, rape	Decide verdict 'Guilty' or 'Not guilty'	12
High Court	Defamation False imprisonment Malicious prosecution Any case alleging fraud	Decide liability If find for the claimant, also decide amount of damages	12
County Court	Defamation False imprisonment Malicious prosecution Any case alleging fraud	Decide liability If find for the claimant, also decide amount of damages	8
Coroners' Court	Deaths: ● In prison ● In policy custody ● Through an industrial accident ● Where health and safety of 　public is involved	Decide cause of death	7–11

Figure 12.1 Key facts chart on the use of juries

12.2.3 Coroners' Courts

In these courts a jury of between seven and 11 members may be used to enquire into deaths. A jury has to be used in four types of case; these are where there has been a death in:

● prison
● an industrial accident
● circumstances where the health and safety of the public is involved; for example the *Herald of Free Enterprise* disaster or the *Marchioness* tragedy on the Thames
● police custody or resulting from an injury caused by a police officer in the execution of his duty

Since 1977, a coroner is no longer obliged to summon a jury to decide cases involving road accidents or suspected homicide. He has a discretion as to whether a jury should be used in such cases. A recent case where a jury was used was the inquest into the death of Princess Diana.

12.3 Jury qualifications

12.3.1 Basic qualifications

The qualifications for jury service were revised in 1972 following the Morris Committee Report on jury service. Before this date there was a property qualification – in order to be a juror, it was necessary to be the owner or tenant of a dwelling. This restriction meant that women and young people who were less likely to own or rent property were prevented from serving on a jury. The Morris Committee thought that being a juror should be the counterpart of being a citizen. As a result, the qualifications for jury service were widened in the Criminal Justice Act 1972 and based on the right to vote. The present qualifications are set out in the Juries Act 1974 (as amended) so that to qualify for jury service a person must be:

- aged between 18 and 70
- registered as a parliamentary or local government elector
- ordinarily resident in the United Kingdom, the Channel Islands or the Isle of Man for at least five years since their thirteenth birthday.

However, certain people are not allowed to sit on a jury even though they are within these basic qualifications. These are people who are disqualified and those who are mentally disordered.

12.3.2 Disqualification

Some criminal convictions will disqualify a person from jury service. The type of sentence and the length of a prison sentence decide whether the person is disqualified and the period for which that disqualification lasts. Disqualified permanently from jury service are those who at any time have been sentenced to:

- imprisonment for life, detention for life or custody for life
- detention during Her Majesty's pleasure or during the pleasure of the Secretary of State
- imprisonment for public protection or detention for public protection
- an extended sentence
- a term of imprisonment of five years or more or a term of detention of five years or more.

Those in the following categories are disqualified for 10 years:

- at any time in the last 10 years served a sentence of imprisonment
- at any time in the last 10 years had a suspended sentence passed on them
- at any time in the last 10 years had a community order or other community sentence passed on them.

In addition, anyone who is currently on bail in criminal proceedings is disqualified from sitting as a juror.

If a disqualified person fails to disclose that fact

and turns up for jury service, they may be fined up to £5,000.

12.3.3 Mentally disordered persons

A 'mentally disordered person' is defined in the Criminal Justice Act 2003 as:

1. A person who suffers or has suffered from mental illness, psychopathic disorder, mental handicap or severe mental handicap and on account of that condition either:
   (a) is resident in a hospital or similar institution or
   (b) regularly attends for treatment by a medical practitioner.
2. A person for the time being under guardianship under s 7 of the Mental Health Act 1983.
3. A person who, under Part 7 of that Act, has been determined by a judge to be incapable of administering his property and affairs.

There are criticisms that this definition does not distinguish between those receiving treatment for mild depression from their GP and those sectioned under the Mental Health Act 1983. The definition of a 'mentally ill person' for the purposes of the Juries Act 1974 is likely to be amended in the future in answer to these criticisms.

12.3.4 Lack of capacity

A judge at the court may discharge a person from being a juror for lack of capacity to cope with the trial. This could be because the person does not understand English adequately or because of some disability which makes them unsuitable as a juror. This includes the blind, who would be unable to see plans and photographs produced in evidence. Section 9B(2) of the Juries Act 1974 makes it clear that the mere fact of a disability does not prevent someone from acting as a juror. The judge can only discharge the juror if he is satisfied that the disability means that that juror is not capable of acting effectively as a juror.

Deaf jurors

In June 1995 a deaf man was prevented from sitting on a jury at the Old Bailey despite wishing to serve and bringing with him a sign language interpreter. The judge pointed out that that would mean an extra person in the jury room and this was not allowed by law. He also said that the way in which witnesses gave evidence and the tone of their voice were important: 'a deaf juror may not be able to pick up these nuances and to properly judge their credibility'.

In November 1999 another deaf man challenged the ban on him sitting as a juror. The judge in this case felt that there was no practical reason why he should not sit, but the law only allowed the 12 jury members to be present in the jury room. It did not allow a 13th person – a sign-language interpreter – to be present. This made it impossible for the deaf man to be a juror.

12.3.5 The right to be excused from jury service

Prior to April 2004 people in certain essential occupations, such as doctors and pharmacists, had a right to be excused jury service if they did not want to do it. The Criminal Justice Act 2003 abolished this category. This means that doctors and other medical staff are no longer able to refuse to do jury service, though they can apply for a discretionary excusal.

Members of the forces

Full-time serving members of the forces may be excused from jury service if their commanding officer certifies that their absence from duty (because of jury service) would be prejudicial to the efficiency of the service.

12.3.6 Discretionary excusals

Anyone who has problems which make it very difficult for them to do their jury service may ask to be excused or for their period of service to be put back to a later date. The court has a discretion

to grant such an excusal but will only do so if there is a sufficiently good reason. Such reasons include being too ill to attend court or suffering from a disability that makes it impossible for the person to sit as a juror, or being a mother with a small baby. Other reasons could include business appointments that cannot be undertaken by anyone else, examinations or holidays that have been booked.

In these situations the court is most likely to defer jury service to a more convenient date, rather than excuse the person completely. This is stated in the current guidance for summoning officers which is aimed at preventing the high number of discretionary excusals. The guidance states that:

> The normal expectation is that everyone summoned for jury service will serve at the time for which they are summoned. It is recognised that there will be occasions where it is not reasonable for a person summoned to serve at the time for which they are summoned. In such circumstances the summoning officer should use his/her discretion to defer the individual to a time more appropriate. Only in extreme circumstances, should a person be excused from jury service.

If a person is not excused from jury service they must attend on the date set or they may be fined up to £1,000 for non-attendance.

12.3.7 Lawyers and police on juries

There used to be a category of people who were ineligible for jury service. This included judges and others who had been involved in the administration of justice within the previous 10 years. This category was abolished by the Criminal Justice Act 2003. This means that judges, lawyers, police, etc are now eligible to serve on juries. Many people feel that this could lead to bias or to a legally well-qualified juror influencing the rest of the jury.

In *R v Abdroikof, R v Green* and *R v Williamson* (2007) the House of Lords considered appeals where a police officer or prosecutor had been one of the jury members.

They held that the fact that one of the members of the jury was a police officer did not of itself make a trial unfair. However, a majority of three of the five judges held that in the situation where a police officer on the jury had worked in the same station as a police officer giving evidence for the prosecution in the trial, then there was the risk of bias. The test to be applied in such cases was:

> whether the fair-minded and informed observer, having considered the facts, would conclude that there was a real possibility that the tribunal was biased.

The House of Lords also quoted from the decision in *R v Sussex Justices, ex parte McCarthy* (1924) where the judge stated that justice must not only be done, but must be seen to be done.

The same three judges in a majority decision also held that the presence of a juror who was a local Crown Prosecutor in the Crown Prosecution Service meant that justice was clearly not being seen to be done. Lord Bingham stated:

> It is, in my opinion, clear that justice is not seen to be done if one discharging the very important neutral role of juror is a full-time, salaried, long-serving employee of the prosecutor.

Judges on jury service

In June 2004 (just two months after the rules on jury service changed) a judge from the Court of Appeal, Lord Justice Dyson, was summoned to attend as a juror. This prompted the Lord Chief Justice, Lord Woolf, to issue observations to judges who are called for jury service. These point out that:

- a judge serves on a jury as part of his duty as a private citizen

- excusal from jury service will only be granted in extreme circumstances
- deferral of jury service to a later date should be sought where a judge has judicial commitments which make it particularly inconvenient for him to do jury service at the time he was called to do so
- at court if a judge knows the presiding judge or other person in the case, he should raise this with the jury bailiff or a member of the court staff if he considers it could interfere with his responsibilities as a juror
- it is a matter of discretion for an individual judge sitting as a juror as to whether he discloses the fact of his judicial office to the other members of the jury
- judges must follow the directions given to the jury by the trial judge on the law and should avoid the temptation to correct guidance which they believe to be inaccurate as this is outside their role as a juror.

The point about letting the court know when someone involved in the case is personally known to the juror is also relevant to practising lawyers who are called for jury service. It was noticeable that when a Queen's Counsel was summoned for jury service at the Central Criminal Court (the Old Bailey) in the summer of 2004, he was prevented from sitting in each

Activity

Discuss whether you think the following people should sit on a jury:

1. A woman who was fined for shoplifting a month ago.
2. A man who was fined and disqualified from driving for taking cars without the consent of the owner.
3. A doctor who works in general practice.
4. A doctor who works in an accident and emergency unit of a busy city hospital.
5. A Circuit Judge who frequently tries cases in the Crown Court.

case that he was called for, on the grounds that he knew one or more people involved in each trial.

12.4 Selecting a jury

At each Crown Court there is an official who is responsible for summonsing enough jurors to try the cases that will be heard in each two-week period. This official will arrange for names to be selected at random from the electoral registers for the area which the court covers. This is done through a computer selection at a central office. It is necessary to summons more than 12 jurors as most courts have more than one court-room and it will not be known how many of those summonsed are disqualified – or will be excused. In fact, at the bigger courts up to 150 summonses may be sent out each fortnight.

Those summonsed must notify the court if there is any reason why they should not or cannot attend. All others are expected to attend for two weeks' jury service, though, of course, if the case they are trying goes on for more than two weeks they will have to stay until the trial is completed. Where it is known that a trial may be exceptionally long, such as a complicated fraud trial, potential jurors are asked if they will be able to serve for such a long period.

12.4.1 Vetting

Once the list of potential jurors is known, both the prosecution and the defence have the right to see that list. In some cases it may be decided that this pool of potential jurors should be 'vetted', ie checked for suitability. There are two types of vetting:

- routine police checks
- wider background checks.

Routine police checks

Routine police checks are made on prospective jurors to eliminate those disqualified. In *R v Crown Court at Sheffield, ex parte Brownlow* (1980)

the defendant was a police officer and the defence sought permission to vet the jury panel for convictions. The judge gave permission but the Court of Appeal, while holding that it had no power to interfere, said that vetting was 'unconstitutional' and a 'serious invasion of privacy' and not sanctioned by the Juries Act 1974.

However, in *R v Mason* (1980) where it was revealed that the Chief Constable for Northamptonshire had been allowing widespread use of unauthorised vetting of criminal records, the Court of Appeal approved of this type of vetting. Lawton LJ pointed out that, since it is a criminal offence to serve on a jury whilst disqualified, the police were only doing their normal duty of preventing crime by checking for criminal records. Furthermore, the court said that, if in the course of looking at criminal records convictions were revealed which did not disqualify, there was no reason why these should not be passed on to prosecuting counsel, so that this information could be used in deciding to stand by individual jurors (see section 12.4.3 for information on the right of stand by).

Juror's background

A wider check may be made on a juror's background and political affiliations. This practice was brought to light by the 'ABC' trial in 1978 where two journalists and a soldier were charged with collecting secret information. It was discovered that the jury had been vetted for their loyalty. The trial was stopped and a new trial ordered before a fresh jury. Following this, the Attorney-General published guidelines on when political vetting of jurors should take place. These guidelines state that:

(a) vetting should only be used in exceptional cases involving:

- national security where part of the evidence is likely to be given *in camera*
- terrorist cases.

(b) vetting can only be carried out with the Attorney-General's express permission.

Key facts

Court	Crown Court
Qualifications	18–70 age Registered to vote Resident in UK for at least five years since age 13
Disqualified	Sentenced to five years' or more imprisonment – disqualified for life Served a prison sentence OR suspended sentence OR a community order – disqualified for 10 years On bail – disqualified while on bail
Excusals	Members of the armed forces Discretionary – ill, business commitments, or other 'good reason'
Selection	A central office selects names from the lists of electors Summons sent to these people Must attend unless disqualified or excused
Vetting	May be checked for criminal record – *R v Mason* (1980) In cases of national security may be subject to a wider check on background subject to Attorney-General's guidelines
Challenges	Individual juror may be challenged for cause, eg knows defendant Whole panel may be challenged for biased selection – but no right to a multi-racial jury (*R v Ford* (1989)) Prosecution may 'stand by' any juror
Function	Decide verdict – 'Guilty' or 'Not guilty' Sole arbiters of fact but judge directs them on law
Verdict	Must try for a unanimous verdict BUT if cannot reach a unanimous verdict then a majority verdict can be accepted of 10:2 or 11:1

Figure 12.2 Key facts chart on the use of juries in criminal cases

12.4.2 Selection at court

The jurors are usually divided into groups of 15 and allocated to a court. At the start of a trial the court clerk will select 12 out of these 15 at random. If there are not enough jurors to hear all the cases scheduled for that day at the court, there is a special power to select anyone who is qualified to be a juror from people passing by in the streets or from local offices or businesses. This is called 'praying a talesman'. It is very unusual to use this power but it was used at Middlesex Crown Court in January 1992 when about half the

jury panel failed to turn up after the New Year's holiday and there were not sufficient jurors to try the cases.

12.4.3 Challenging

Once the court clerk has selected the panel of 12 jurors, these jurors come into the jury box to be sworn in as jurors. At this point, before the jury is sworn in, both the prosecution and defence have certain rights to challenge one or more of the jurors. There are two challenges which can be made and, in addition, the prosecution has a special right. These are:

- to the array
- for cause
- prosecution right to stand by jurors.

To the array

This right to challenge is given by s 5 of the Juries Act 1974 and it is a challenge to the whole jury on the basis that it has been chosen in an unrepresentative or biased way. This challenge was used successfully against the 'Romford' jury at the Old Bailey in 1993 when, out of a panel of 12 jurors, nine came from Romford, with two of them living within 20 doors of each other in the same street. In *R v Fraser* (1987) this method of challenging a jury was also used, as the defendant was of an ethnic minority background but all the jurors were white. The judge in that case agreed to empanel another jury. However, in *R v Ford* (1989) it was held that if the jury was chosen in a random manner then it could not be challenged simply because it was not multi-racial.

For cause

This involves challenging the right of an individual juror to sit on the jury. To be successful, the challenge must point out a valid reason why that juror should not serve on the jury. An obvious reason is that the juror is disqualified, but a challenge for cause can also be made if the juror knows or is related to a witness or defendant. If such people are not removed from the jury there is a risk that any subsequent conviction could be quashed.

This occurred in *R v Wilson* and *R v Sprason* (1995) where the wife of a prison officer was summoned for jury service. She had asked to be excused attendance on that ground, but this request had not been granted. She served on the jury which convicted the two defendants of robbery. Both defendants had been on remand at Exeter prison where her husband worked. The Court of Appeal said that justice must not only be done, it must be seen to be done and the

presence of Mrs Roberts on the jury prevented that, so that the convictions had to be quashed.

Prosecution right to stand by jurors

This is a right that only the prosecution can exercise. It allows the juror who has been stood by to be put to the end of the list of potential jurors, so that they will not be used on the jury unless there are not enough other jurors. The prosecution does not have to give a reason for 'standing by', but the Attorney-General's guidelines make it clear that this power should be used sparingly.

12.4.4 Criticisms of the selection of juries

Use of electoral register

The method of selecting jurors from the list of registered voters is open to criticism as it does not always give a representative sample of the population. It excludes some groups, such as the homeless who cannot register to vote. Also, not everyone who is eligible registers to vote. This is especially true of the young and those who change address frequently.

One of the debates has always been whether random selection produces juries which are reasonably representative of the local population. Studies done in the 1970s and 1980s found that juries in some areas were not truly representative in gender (fewer women), age (fewer young people) and race (under-representative of ethnic minorities).

However, a study, *Diversity and Fairness in the Jury System* published in 2007 and looking at juries in 2003 and 2005, found that juries are now representative in gender, age and race. The only under-representation found by the study was of lower classes and unemployed.

Disqualified jurors

Although some checks are carried out, many disqualified people fail to disclose this fact and sit on juries. One survey of Inner London juries

Activity

Read the following extract from *Diversity and Fairness in the Jury System* (2007) and answer the questions below.

The Criminal Justice Act 2003 removed ineligibility and the right of excusal from jury service for a number of groups (those aged 65–69, MPs, clergy, medical professionals and those in the administration of justice). But summoned jurors may still be disqualified or excused from jury service (due to age, residency, mental disability, criminal charges, language, medical or other reasons).

- The study found that the most significant factors predicating whether a summoned juror will serve or not are income and employment status, not ethnicity. Summoned jurors in the lower income brackets and those who are economically inactive are far less likely to serve than those in medium to high income brackets and those who are employed.
- In 2005, of all those who replied to their summonses, 64 per cent of jurors served, 9 per cent were disqualified or ineligible, 27 per cent were excused. Of those excused, most were for medical reasons that prevented serving (34 per cent) or child care (15 per cent) and work reasons (12 per cent). Fifteen per cent of all the summonses in the survey were either returned as undeliverable or not responded to, which occurred most often in areas of high residential mobility.
- The report established that most current thinking about who does and does not do jury service is based on myth, not reality.

Myth: Ethnic minorities are under-represented among those doing jury service.

Reality: Analysis showed that, in almost all courts (81 of the 84 surveyed), there was no significant difference between the proportion of black and ethnic minority jurors serving and the black and ethnic minority population levels in the local juror catchment area for each court.

Myth: Women and young people are under-represented among serving jurors, and the self-employed are virtually exempt for jury service.

Reality: The study establishes that jury pools at individual courts closely reflected the local population in terms of gender and age, and the self-employed are represented among serving jurors in direct proportion to their representation in the population.

Questions

1. What are the age limits for jury service?

2. What is the residency requirement to qualify for jury service?

3. What categories of people are disqualified from doing jury service?

4. What categories of people are less likely to serve on a jury?

5. What percentage failed to reply to their summons to do jury service?

6. For what types of reason were people excused from jury service?

7. What does the study show about the representative nature of juries?

estimated that one in every 24 jurors was disqualified. In one instance at Snaresbrook Crown Court, a man with 15 previous convictions sat as a juror in three cases and was the jury foreman in two of them. He later admitted that, as far as he was concerned, all defendants were not guilty unless they 'had been molesting kids'.

Excusals

If there are too many discretionary excusals it may lead to an unrepresentative jury. For this reason, wherever possible, jury service is deferred instead of excusing the juror from service.

Prosecution's right of 'stand by'

The prosecution's right of stand by was kept even when the defence's peremptory challenge was withdrawn. This might be seen as giving the prosecution an advantage in 'rigging' the jury, particularly when combined with vetting. However, even when a jury has been vetted, it does not always give the prosecution an advantage. This was seen in *Ponting's Case*, where the defendant was charged with an offence against the Official Secrets Acts and the jury was vetted. Despite the vetting the jury returned a not guilty verdict (see section 12.6.2 for further comment on this case).

12.5 The jury's role in criminal cases

The jury is used only at the Crown Court for cases where the defendant pleads not guilty. This means that a jury is used in about 20,000 cases each year.

12.5.1 Split function

The trial is presided over by a judge and the functions split between the judge and jury. The judge decides points of law and the jury decides the facts. At the end of the prosecution case, the judge has the power to direct the jury to acquit the defendant if he decides that, in law, the prosecution's evidence has not made out a case against the defendant. This is called a directed acquittal and occurs in about 10 per cent of cases.

Where the trial continues, the judge will sum up the case at the end, to the jury and direct them on any law involved. The jury retire to a private room and make the decision on the guilt or innocence of the accused in secret. Initially the jury must try to come to a unanimous verdict, ie one on which they are all agreed. The judge must accept the jury verdict, even if he does not agree with it. This long established principle goes back to *Bushell's Case* (1670). The jury do not give any reasons for their decision.

12.5.2 Majority verdicts

If, after at least two hours (longer where there are several defendants), the jury have not reached a verdict, the judge can call them back into the courtroom and direct them that he can now accept a majority verdict. Majority verdicts have been allowed since 1967. Where there is a full jury of 12, the verdict can be 10–2 or 11–1 either for guilty or for not guilty. If the jury has fallen below 12 for any reason (such as the death or illness of a juror during the trial) then only one can disagree with the verdict. That is, if there are 11 jurors, the verdict can be 10–1; if there are 10 jurors it can be 9–1. If there are only nine jurors the verdict must be unanimous. A jury cannot go below nine.

Majority verdicts were introduced because of the fear of jury 'nobbling', that is jurors being bribed or intimidated by associates of the defendant into voting for a not guilty verdict. When a jury had to be unanimous, only one member need be bribed to cause a 'stalemate' in which the jury were unable to reach a decision. It was also thought that the acquittal rates in jury trials were too high and majority decisions would result in more convictions.

Where the jury convict a defendant on a majority verdict, the foreman of the jury must announce the numbers both agreeing and disagreeing with the verdict in open court. This provision is aimed at making sure the jury have come to a legal majority, and not one, for example of eight to four, which is not allowed. However, in *R v Pigg* (1983), the Court of Appeal held that, provided the foreman announced the number who had agreed with the verdict, and that number was within the number allowed for a majority verdict, then the conviction was legal. It did not matter that the foreman had not also been asked how many disagreed with the verdict. About 20 per cent of convictions by juries each year are by majority verdict.

12.5.3 Secrecy

The jury discussion takes place in secret and there can be no inquiry into how the jury reached its verdict. This is because s 8 of the Contempt of Court Act 1981 makes disclosure of anything that happened in the jury room a contempt of court which is a criminal offence. It is a contempt 'to obtain, disclose or solicit any particulars of statements made, opinions expressed, arguments advanced or votes cast by members of a jury in the course of their deliberations in any legal proceedings'. The section was brought in because newspapers were paying jurors large sums of money for 'their story'. This is obviously not desirable, but the total ban on finding out what happens in the jury room means that it is difficult to discover whether jurors have understood the evidence in complex cases.

12.6 Advantages of jury trial

12.6.1 Public confidence

On the face of it, asking 12 strangers who have no legal knowledge and without any training to decide what may be complex and technical points is an absurd one. Yet the jury is considered as one of the fundamentals of a democratic society. The right to be tried by one's peers is a bastion of liberty against the State and has been supported by eminent judges. For example, Lord Devlin said juries are 'the lamp that shows that freedom

lives'. The tradition of trial by jury is very old and people seem to have confidence in the impartiality and fairness of a jury trial. This can be seen in the objection to withdrawing the right to jury trial from cases of 'minor' theft.

12.6.2 Jury equity

Since juries are not legal experts, are not bound to follow the precedent of past cases or even Acts of Parliament, and do not have to give reasons for their verdict, it is possible for them to decide cases on their idea of 'fairness'. This is sometimes referred to as 'jury equity'. Several cases have shown the importance of this, in particular *Ponting's Case* (1985) in which a civil servant was charged under the old wide-ranging s 2 of the Official Secrets Act 1911. He had leaked information on the sinking of the ship, The General Belgrano, in the Falklands War to a member of Parliament. At his trial he pleaded not guilty, claiming that his actions had been in the public interest. The jury refused to convict him even though the judge ruled there was no defence. The case also prompted the Government to reconsider the law and to amend s 2.

12.6.3 Open system of justice

The use of a jury is viewed as making the legal system more open. Justice is seen to be done as members of the public are involved in a key role and the whole process is public. It also helps to keep the law clearer as points have to be explained to the jury, enabling the defendant to understand the case more easily. Against this is the fact that the jury deliberate in private and that no one can inquire into what happened in the jury room. In addition, the jury do not have to give any reason for their verdict. When a judge gives a judgment he explains his reasoning and, if he has made an error, it is known and can be appealed against.

12.6.4 Secrecy of the jury room

This can be seen as an advantage, since the jury are free from pressure in their discussion. Jurors are protected from outside influences when deciding on the verdict. This allows juries to bring in verdicts that may be unpopular with the public as well as allowing jurors the freedom to ignore the strict letter of the law. It has been suggested that people would be less willing to serve on a jury if they knew that their discussions could be made public.

12.6.5 Impartiality

A jury should be impartial as they are not connected to anyone in the case. The process of random selection should result in a cross-section of society and this should also lead to an impartial jury, as they will have different prejudices and so should cancel out each others' biases. No one individual person is responsible for the decision. A jury is also not case hardened since they sit for only two weeks and are unlikely to try more than three or four cases in that time.

12.7 Disadvantages of jury trial

12.7.1 Perverse decisions

In section 12.6.2 we looked at the idea of jury equity. That is the fact that the jury can ignore an unjust law. However, in some circumstances this type of decision can be seen as a perverse decision and one which was not justified. Juries have refused to convict in other clear-cut cases such as *R v Randle and Pottle* (1991) where the defendants were charged with helping the spy George Blake to escape from prison. Their prosecution did not occur until 25 years after the escape, when they wrote about what they had done and the jury acquitted them, possibly as a protest over the time lapse between the offence and the prosecution.

Another case where the evidence was clear, yet the jury acquitted the defendants was *R v Kronlid and others* (1996). In this case, the defendants admitted they had caused £1.5 million damage to a plane. They pleaded not guilty on the basis that

they were preventing the plane from being sent to Indonesia where it would have been used in attacks against the people of East Timor. The jury acquitted them.

12.7.2 Secrecy

In section 12.6.4 we considered how the secrecy of the jury protects jurors from pressure. However, the secrecy of the jury room is also a disadvantage. This is because no reasons have to be given for the verdict, so there is no way of knowing if the jury did understand the case and come to the decision for the right reasons.

In *R v Mirza* (2004) the House of Lords ruled that it could not inquire into discussions in a jury room. Two separate cases were considered in the appeal. These were *R v Mirza* and *R v Connor and Rollock*.

In *Mirza* the defendant was a Pakistani who settled in the UK in 1988. He had an interpreter to help him in the trial and during the trial the jury sent notes asking why he needed an interpreter. He was convicted on a 10–2 majority. Six days after the jury verdict, one juror wrote to the defendant's counsel alleging that from the start of the trial there had been a 'theory' that the use of an interpreter was a 'ploy'. The juror also said that she had been shouted down when she objected and reminded her fellow jurors of the judge's directions.

In *Connor and Rollock* a juror wrote to the Crown Court stating that while many jurors thought it was one or other of the defendants who had committed the stabbing, they should convict both to 'teach them a lesson'. This was five days after the verdict but before sentence was passed. As in *Mirza*, there was a majority verdict of 10–2. The complaining juror said that, when she argued that the jury should consider which defendant was responsible, her co-jurors had refused to listen and remarked that if they did that they could be a week considering verdicts in the case.

The House of Lords held that s 8 of the Contempt of Court Act 1981 made it a contempt to disclose or obtain or solicit information about what had occurred in the jury room even for the purposes of an appeal. They also ruled that s 8 was compatible with Art 6 of the European Convention on Human Rights (the right to a fair trial). They pointed out that:

- confidentiality was essential to the proper functioning of the jury process
- there was merit in finality
- jurors had to be protected from harassment.

Exceptions

The only exception where an inquiry into jurors' conduct could be carried out was where the behaviour occurred outside the jury room as in *R v Young (Stephen)* (1995). In that case the defendant was charged with the murder of two people. The jury had to stay overnight in a hotel as they had not reached a verdict by the end of the first day of discussion. During this stay at the hotel some members of the jury held a seance using a ouija board to try to contact the dead victims and ask who had killed them. The next day the jury returned a verdict of guilty. When the fact that the ouija board had been used became known, the defendant appealed and the Court of Appeal quashed the verdict and ordered a re-trial of the case. The Court felt able to inquire into what had happened as it was in a hotel and not part of the jury discussions in the jury room.

Also, in *R v Karakaya* (2005) it was discovered that a juror had done an Internet search at home. He then brought the information into the jury room and it was available while the jury were discussing their verdict. The print-outs were discovered by the jury bailiff.

The Court of Appeal held that this contravened the fundamental rule that no evidence was to be introduced after the jury had retired to consider their verdict. The conviction was quashed as being unsafe.

12.7.3 Bias

However, although jurors have no direct interest in a case, and despite the fact that there are 12 of

them, they may still have prejudices which can affect the verdict. Some jurors may be biased against the police. In particular there is the worry that some jurors are racially prejudiced.

In *Sander v United Kingdom* (2000) the European Court of Human Rights ruled that there had been a breach of the right to a fair trial under Art 6 of the European Convention on Human Rights. In the case one juror had written a note to the judge during the trial raising concern over the fact that other jurors had been making openly racist remarks and jokes. The judge asked the jury to 'search their consciences'. The next day the judge received two letters, one signed by all the jurors in which they denied any racist attitudes and a second from one juror who admitted that he may have been the one making the jokes. Despite the discrepancies between these two letters, the judge allowed the case to continue with the same jury. The European Court of Human Rights held that in these circumstances the judge should have discharged the jury as there was an obvious risk of racial bias.

12.7.4 Media influence

Media coverage may influence jurors. This is especially true in high-profile cases, where there has been a lot of publicity about police investigations into a case. This occurred in the case *R v West* (1996) in which Rosemary West was convicted for the murders of ten young girls and women, including her own daughter. From the time the bodies were first discovered, the media coverage was intense. In addition, some newspapers had paid large sums of money to some of the witnesses in order to secure their story after the trial was completed. One of the grounds on which Rosemary West appealed against her conviction was that the media coverage had made it impossible for her to receive a fair trial. The Court of Appeal rejected the appeal, pointing out that otherwise it would mean that if 'allegations of murder were sufficiently horrendous so as to inevitably shock the nation, the accused could not be tried'. They also said that the trial judge had given adequate warning to the jury to consider only the evidence they heard in court.

Another case which highlighted media influence on the jury's decision was *R v Taylor and Taylor* (1993) in which two sisters were charged with murder. Some newspapers published a still from a video sequence which gave a false impression of what was happening. After the jury convicted the two defendants, the trial judge gave leave to appeal because of the possible influence this picture could have had on the jury's verdict and the Court of Appeal quashed the convictions.

12.7.5 Lack of understanding

There are worries that jurors may not understand the case which they are trying. This fear was partly borne out by a survey carried out in 1992 for the Runciman Commission, in which jurors were asked whether they thought they had been able to understand the evidence. Over half (56 per cent) of the jurors questioned thought that the jury as a whole had understood the evidence, with another two-fifths (41 per cent) believing that most of the jury had understood the case. However just under 10 per cent of jurors admitted that they had had difficulty.

It is worrying that in some cases a defendant's future is being decided by some members of the public who do not understand the case. For example, in one case at Snaresbrook Crown Court, the jury after they had retired to consider their verdict sent a note to the judge asking what they had to do! The judge discharged that jury from the case.

Recent research

Research into jury trials in Australia has revealed that some jurors did not know what verdict had been given in the case they had just tried. The research was into 32 trials about child abuse. It involved aspects such as how jurors thought the child witness had been treated in the case.

The jurors were given a questionnaire immediately after the verdict had been given. 277 jurors took part. The first question asked 'What was the verdict in this case?'. Only in a quarter of the trials did all the jurors give the correct answer. In the other cases at least one juror gave an incorrect version of the verdict. In one case four jurors said that the accused had been found guilty when he had actually been found not guilty.

The researchers point out that it is possible that jurors were expressing their own view of what they thought the verdict should have been. However, the research stated that it seems some jurors were confused, unclear or uncertain about the verdict. If jurors do not know what the verdict was immediately after that verdict has been given, then it creates doubts about how much of the case the jurors had understood.

12.7.6 Fraud trials

Fraud trials with complex accounts being given in evidence can create special problems for jurors. Even jurors who can easily cope with other evidence may have difficulty understanding a fraud case. These cases are also often very long, so that the jurors have to be able to be away from their own work for months. A long fraud trial can place a great strain on jurors. Such cases also become very expensive, both for the prosecution and for the defendants.

The Roskill Committee in 1986 suggested that juries should not be used for complex fraud cases. There have recently been two provisions made in Acts of Parliament for this to happen.

In the Criminal Justice Act 2003 there is provision for the prosecution to apply for trial by a judge alone in:

- complex fraud cases or
- where there has already been an effort to tamper with a jury in the case.

However, this is not yet in force and the provision is subject to an affirmative resolution. This means that it cannot be brought into effect without both Houses voting for it.

In the Domestic Violence, Crime and Victims Act 2004 there is a special provision for cases where there are a large number of counts on the indictment. This would allow a trial of sample

Key facts

Advantages	Disadvantages
Public confidence Considered to be a fundamental part of a democratic society New qualifications for jury service mean that almost everyone can serve on a jury	High acquittal rates undermine confidence in the criminal justice system Doing jury service is unpopular
Jury equity *Ponting's Case*	Perverse verdicts *Randle and Pottle* *Kronlid*
Open system of justice Involves members of the public	Media influence Reporting may influence the decision *Taylor and Taylor*
Secrecy of the jury room protects jurors from pressure	Secrecy means that: ● the reasons for the decision are not known ● the jury's understanding of the case cannot be checked (*Mirza*) Exception: *Young* (*Stephen*)
Impartiality Having 12 members with no direct interest in the case should cancel out any bias	Bias In some cases there has been racial bias *Sander v UK*

Figure 12.3 Key facts chart of advantages and disadvantages of jury trial

counts with a jury and then, if the defendant was convicted on those, the remainder could be tried by a judge alone. This provision has not yet been used.

12.7.7 High acquittal rates

Juries are often criticised on the grounds that they acquit too many defendants. The figures usually quoted in support of this are that about 60 per cent of those who plead not guilty at the Crown Court are acquitted. However, this figure does not give a true picture of the workings of juries as it includes cases discharged by the judge and those in which the judge directed an acquittal. When these decisions are excluded from the statistics it is found that juries actually acquit in less than 40 per cent of cases.

12.7.8 Other disadvantages

The compulsory nature of jury service is unpopular, so that some jurors may be against the whole system, while others may rush their verdict in order to leave as quickly as possible. Jury service can be a strain, especially where jurors have to listen to horrific evidence. Jurors in the Rosemary West case were offered counselling after the trial to help them cope with the evidence they had had to see and hear.

Jury 'nobbling' does occur and in some cases jurors have had to be provided with police protection. In order to try to combat this, the Criminal Procedure and Investigations Act 1996 allows for a retrial to be ordered if someone is subsequently proved to have interfered with the jury.

The use of juries makes trials slow and expensive. This is because each point has to be explained carefully to the jury and the whole procedure of the case takes longer.

12.8 Special problems of using juries in civil cases

12.8.1 Amount of damages

Juries in civil cases decide both the liability of the parties in the case and also the amount of damages that will be awarded. The awards vary greatly as each jury has its own ideas and does not follow past cases. The amount is, therefore, totally unpredictable which makes it difficult for lawyers to advise on settlements. Judges look back to past awards when deciding awards of damages in personal injury cases, and then apply an inflation factor so that there is consistency between similar cases. Juries in defamation cases cause particular problems with very large awards; one judge called it 'Mickey Mouse' money.

Until 1990 the Court of Appeal had no power to correct awards which were thought to be far too high. But under s 8 of the Courts and Legal Services Act 1990 the Court of Appeal has special powers in such cases. The Court of Appeal can order a new trial or substitute such sum as appears proper to the court, if they feel the damages were excessive or inadequate. This power was first used in a case brought by the MP Teresa Gorman where the Court of Appeal reduced the damages awarded to her by the jury from £150,000 to £50,000. It was also used in *Rantzen v Mirror Group Newspapers* (1993) when the award to Esther Rantzen, the founder of 'Childline' (a charity set up to help abused children) over allegations that she had deliberately kept quiet about the activities of a suspected child abuser, was reduced from £250,000 to £110,000.

12.8.2 Unreasoned decision

The jury does not have to give a reason either for its decision or for the amount it awards. A judge always gives a judgment, this makes it easier to see if there are good grounds for an appeal.

12.8.3 Bias

The problems of bias in civil cases is different to that encountered in criminal cases. In some defamation cases the claimants and/or the defendants may be public figures so that jurors will know and possibly hold views about them. Alternatively there is the fact that the defendant in a defamation case is often a newspaper and jurors may be biased against the press or may feel that 'they can afford to pay'.

12.8.4 Cost

Civil cases are expensive and the use of a jury adds to this as the case is likely to last longer. At the end of the case the losing party will have to pay all the costs of the case which may amount to hundreds of thousands of pounds.

12.9 Alternatives to jury trial

Despite all the problems of using juries in criminal cases, there is still a strong feeling that they are the best method available. However, if juries are not thought suitable to try serious criminal cases, what alternative form of trial could be used?

12.9.1 Trial by a single judge

This is the method of trial in the majority of civil cases which is generally regarded as producing a fairer and more predictable result.

However, there appears to be less public confidence in the use of judges to decide all serious criminal cases. The arguments against this form of trial are that judges become case-hardened and prosecution-minded. They are also from a very elite group and would have little understanding of the background and problems of defendants. Individual prejudices are more likely than in a jury where the different personalities should go some way to eliminating bias. But, on the other hand, judges are trained to evaluate cases and they are now being given training in racial awareness. This may make them better arbiters of fact than an untrained jury.

12.9.2 A panel of judges

In some continental countries, cases are heard by a panel of three or five judges sitting together. This allows for a balance of views, instead of the verdict of a single person. However, it still leaves the problems of judges becoming case-hardened and prosecution-minded and coming from an elite background. The other difficulty is that there are not sufficient judges and our system of legal training and appointment would need a radical overhaul to implement this proposal. It would also be expensive.

12.9.3 A judge plus lay assessors

Under this system the judge and two lay people would make the decision together. This method is used in the Scandinavian countries. It provides the legal expertise of the judge, together with lay participation in the legal system by ordinary members of the public. The lay people could either be drawn from the general public, using the same method as is used for selecting juries at

present or a special panel of assessors could be drawn up as in tribunal cases. This latter suggestion would be particularly suitable for fraud cases.

12.9.4 A mini-jury

Finally, if the jury is to remain, then it might be possible to have a smaller number of jurors. In many continental countries when a jury is used there are nine members. For example, in Spain, which reintroduced the use of juries in certain criminal cases in 1996, there is a jury of nine. Alternatively a jury of six could be used for less serious criminal cases that at the moment can have a full jury trial, as occurs in some American states.

Examination Questions

(a) Explain the role of juries in **both** criminal cases **and** civil cases.

(b) Discuss the arguments for abolishing juries.

OCR Specimen paper

Chapter 13

Funding and provision of services

When faced with a legal problem, the average person will usually need expert help from a lawyer. Most often the need is just for advice, but some people may need help in starting court proceedings and/or presenting their case in court. For the ordinary person seeking legal assistance there are three main difficulties:

1. Lack of knowledge
   Many people do not know where their nearest solicitor is located or, if they do know this, they do not know which solicitor specialises in the law involved in their particular case.

2. Fear of dealing with lawyers
   People feel intimidated when dealing with lawyers.

3. Cost
   Solicitors charge from about £100 an hour for routine advice from a small local firm to over £600 an hour for work done by a top city firm of solicitors in a specialist field.

Figure 13.1 Organisation of public funding under the Legal Services Commission

13.1 Access to justice

Where a person cannot get the help they need it is said they are being denied access to justice. Access to justice involves both an open system of justice and also being able to fund the costs of a case.

There have been various schemes aimed at making the law more accessible to everyone. One of the earliest was the Citizens' Advice Bureaux which started in 1938 and now operates in most towns.

However, the problem of cost still remains a major hurdle. The cost of civil cases in the High Court will run into thousands of pounds. Even in the cheaper County Court the cost will possibly be more than the amount of money recovered in damages. There is the additional risk in all civil cases that the loser has to pay the winner's costs.

In criminal cases a person's liberty may be at risk and it is essential that they should be able to defend themselves properly.

For these reasons the Government has run schemes to help those in lower income brackets with funding cases. The first scheme was started in 1949 and altered many times over the years. In 2000 a new scheme was started and this is the one currently in use.

13.2 The Legal Services Commission

The present funding scheme is overseen by the Legal Services Commission. This body was set up by the Access to Justice Act 1999. The Commission is responsible for identifying the needs and priorities of funding and developing the delivery of legal services in accordance with those needs.

In civil cases it is responsible for managing the Community Legal Service Fund which pays for legal funding in suitable cases. The Commission also has a role in respect of criminal legal aid managing the Criminal Defence Service.

For both civil and criminal cases the Legal Services Commission can make contracts with providers of legal services so that the providers can do legal work and be paid from Government funds. Providers include solicitors and not-for-profit organisations such as the Citizens Advice Bureau offering advice on legal matters.

Figure 13.1 shows the organisation of the public funding under the Legal Services Commission.

As civil and criminal cases have separate funding and systems, we will consider the funding of civil matters in the next section 13.3 and then the funding of criminal cases in section 13.4.

13.3 Government funding in civil cases

The Community Legal Service is responsible for the funding of civil cases. It uses money from the Community Legal Service Fund for these cases.

13.3.1 The Community Legal Service

The Community Legal Service provides services for civil matters in the following ways:

- Legal Help – this covers advice but does not include issuing or conducting court proceedings
- Help at Court – this allows help (ie advice) and advocacy at a court or tribunal, although without formally acting as legal representative in the proceedings
- Legal representation – this covers all aspects of a case including starting or defending court proceedings and any advocacy needed in the case
- Support Funding – this allows partial funding of cases which are otherwise being paid for privately, eg a very high-cost case under a conditional fee agreement.

In order to qualify for any of these services the applicant has to show that their income and their capital assets are below set levels (see 13.3.3).

13.3.2 The Community Legal Service Fund

Each year, when the Government budget is drawn up, a set amount is given for helping people fund legal cases. The total amount of the legal aid budget is over £2.2 billion. Most of this will be spent on criminal cases, but some of the money goes to the Community Legal Service Fund to deal with civil matters.

There are two problems with this. First, there is a limit or cap on the amount given by the budget. When this runs out there is no more money. Second, criminal cases take priority on funding and so there may not be enough left for civil

cases. This can lead to civil cases which have merit being refused funding just because the money has run out.

13.3.3 Financial limits on funding

A person applying to use one of the services provided by the Community Legal Service must show that they do not have enough money to pay for their own lawyer. In order to decide if the applicant is poor enough to qualify for Government funded help, their income and capital are considered.

People receiving Income Support or Income-Based Job Seekers' Allowance automatically qualify, assuming their disposable capital is below the set level. For all other applicants their gross income is considered first. If a person's gross income is above £2,435 per month (limits for 2007–08) then they do not qualify for any of the schemes provided by the Community Legal Service.

Disposable income

If the person's gross income is below £2,435 then their disposable income has to be calculated by starting with their gross income and taking away:

- tax and National Insurance
- housing costs
- childcare costs or maintenance paid for children
- an allowance for themselves and for each dependant.

If the amount left after making all deductions is below a minimum level (this was £290 a month in 2007–08), the applicant does not have to pay any contribution towards their funding. If the amount left is above a maximum level (this was £672 per month in 2007–08) the person will not qualify for any of the schemes provided by the Community Legal Service.

Where the disposable income is between the minimum level and the maximum level, the person applying for legal help has to pay a monthly contribution. The more in excess of the

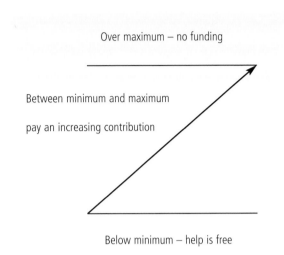

Over maximum – no funding

Between minimum and maximum

pay an increasing contribution

Below minimum – help is free

Figure 13.2 Minimum and maximum limits for legal aid

minimum the greater the amount of the contribution. This idea of minimum and maximum levels is shown in Figure 13.2

Note that the figures for the limits on income are increased slightly each year. You will be able to find the current figures on the Community Legal Service's website www.legalservices.gov.uk.

Disposable capital

Disposable capital is the assets of the person, such as money in a bank or savings account, stocks and shares or expensive jewellery. In order to qualify for funding to take a court case there is a maximum limit for disposable capital of £8,000. If the assets are over £8,000 they must use their own money to fund any legal case, although once they have spent the money in excess of £8,000 they can become eligible for funding. Even where the disposable capital is below £8,000 they can be asked to pay a contribution towards their case.

Where a person owns a home the value of that home is taken into account in deciding the disposable capital. This is so even though the person may have a large mortgage. Only the first £100,000 of any mortgage is deducted from the value of the home. This rule means that people are regarded as having too much disposable

capital because of the value of their house, but in reality they have no spare money.

13.3.4 Advice in civil cases

When people have a legal problem the first thing they want is advice. The Community Legal Service provides various services to try to make sure that advice is easily available. One of these is a telephone service, CLS Direct. This receives nearly a million calls a year. Many of the calls are from those in disadvantaged sections of society.

The Community Legal Service also has a website offering advice. This is at www.clsdirect.org.uk. This allows access to people in remote areas of the country and also to those who have difficulty travelling. As every public library has an online computer available for people to use, it also means that the poorest of society can also have access to advice on the website.

Community Legal Advice Centres

In 2006 Community Legal Advice Centres (CLACs) were started. These are a one-stop service providing advice on debt, welfare benefits, community care, housing and employment. The first two such centres were set up in Leicester and Gateshead. The Legal Services Commission intends that there will eventually be about 75 CLACs.

Service providers

People can also get advice from a solicitor or a not-for-profit organisation that has a contract with the Community Legal Service to give advice under the Legal Help scheme. To receive advice in this way the person has to come within the financial limits explained in 13.3.3 above.

13.3.5 Legal representation

This is where the Community Legal Service pays for the whole of a court case including paying for a lawyer to represent you in court. Legal representation is available to both claimants and defendants.

In deciding whether a person should receive help with funding, two matters are taken into consideration. These are:

- the finances of the person (means test) and
- the merits of the case (merits test).

In addition there are general criteria that are considered such as the importance of the case.

Means test

The person wanting representation paid from Government funds must show that they qualify financially. The level of income and capital are explained above in section 13.3.3.

Merits test

In order to receive help with funding a court case, there must be a realistic chance of the case succeeding. Also, the cost of bringing the case must not be greater than the likely damages (amount of money the court will award).

General criteria

As well as the means and merits tests, there are other factors which will be considered. These include:

- the availability of money in the Community Legal Service Fund
- the importance of the matters for the individual
- whether the case can be funded in another way, such as through a conditional fee agreement (see section 13.7)
- the conduct of the individual
- the public interest.

So, even if a person is poor enough to qualify for help and has a very good chance of winning the case, they may still not get funding if there is not enough money in the Community Legal Service Fund or if they could use another way of resolving the dispute.

13.3.6 Excluded matters

Not every civil matter can qualify for public funding. Certain types of civil case are excluded from public funding. These are:

- cases of negligence, even where the negligence caused death or serious injury. The only ones which can get public funding are cases of negligence by doctors or other health service workers
- conveyancing
- boundary disputes
- making of wills
- matters involving trust law
- most cases of defamation or malicious falsehood
- company law, partnership law or anything arising from carrying on a business.

Funding is normally available for any other type of case in the courts. This covers the County Court, the High Court and the appeal courts. The only exception is for claims of less than £5,000. These are dealt with as small claims and cannot receive public funding for such a case.

It is also not possible to get funding for most cases before tribunals. There are a few exceptions, such as the Mental Health Tribunals, where funding is available. The Mental Health Tribunal makes decisions on whether people detained under the Mental Health Acts should be released into the community. As such cases involve the liberty of the individual, public funding is allowed.

13.3.7 Problems with funding of civil cases

'Advice deserts'

There is evidence that not enough legal service providers have contracts. This is partly due to the smaller numbers of contracts made with providers by the Legal Services Commission and partly due to the fact that many solicitors are finding that the rates of pay are so low, it is not economically viable for solicitors to continue in the scheme. This is creating what have been called 'advice deserts'.

The problem of 'advice deserts' was considered by the Constitutional Affairs Select Committee in 2004. In the evidence to the Committee, even the Legal Services Commission acknowledged that:

 It is clear that there are parts of England and Wales in which the need for publicly funded legal services is not currently being met.

In their report the Select Committee gave the position in Northumberland as an example. There were no housing law advisers and no one with a contract for immigration law in Northumberland. Furthermore, there were only two contracts for employment law in the area. People have to travel a long way to see a lawyer. This can be expensive and is difficult for people on low incomes, those caring for small children or those who have a disability which makes it difficult to travel.

Since 2004 the position has been getting worse as more solicitors have stopped doing Government-funded legal work. With so few legal service providers in certain areas, people who want help may have to travel long distances to find it.

Eligibility levels

Even where there are enough legal services providers in an area, only people with very low levels of income and capital can qualify for help. In 2004 the Select Committee on Constitutional Affairs which investigated the adequacy of the provision of civil legal aid pointed out that:

At present, the legal aid system is increasingly being restricted to those with no means at all. There is a substantial risk that many people of modest means but who are home owners will fall out of the ambit of legal aid. In many cases this may amount to a serious denial of access to justice.

Key facts

Managing body	Community Legal Service
Different levels of help and representation available	● Legal Help – advice only ● Help at Court – advice and limited representation at court ● Legal Representation – covers all aspects of case ● Support Funding – partial funding of a very high-cost case
Means test	Strict means test on gross income, disposable income and disposable capital for all services
Merits test for Legal Representation	Whether the case has a reasonable chance of success and the damages will be worth more than the costs. Other criteria including: ● can the matter be funded in another way? ● are there funds available?
Problems	● number of solicitors is decreasing ● financial level of eligibility excludes people of modest means ● capping of fund together with increasing criminal expenditure means that less is available for civil cases ● not available for PI cases or employment tribunal cases

Figure 13.3 Key facts chart on public funding in civil cases

Lack of funds

The fact that there is a limit on the amount given by the budget means that some cases will not be funded as there is no money left for them. Also, the fact that criminal cases take priority on funding means there may not be enough left for civil cases. This can lead to civil cases which have merit being refused funding just because the money has run out.

Non-availability

As set out in section 13.3.5, funding is not available for all civil claims. Claims for damages for personal injury are excluded from the scheme. Any such case has to be paid for privately or through a conditional fee agreement (see section 13.7). This works well where people have suffered minor injuries, but it can be argued that it creates difficulties for people who have been left with serious disabilities. They need all the help they can get to make sure they receive adequate compensation.

It can also be argued that people bringing employment claims against large companies are disadvantaged by being unable to receive public funding to bring their case. The company will be able to afford a lawyer and will be at an advantage in the case.

 Internet Research

Look for the Funding Code Criteria.

This can be found on the website for the Legal Services Commission at **www.legalservices.gov.uk**.

Try searching for Funding Code **or** from the main page click on 'About legal aid', then 'Who can get it' and 'Testing eligibility' – there should then be links to the Funding Code.

13.4 Government funding in criminal cases

13.4.1 The Criminal Defence Service

Under the Access to Justice Act 1999, the Legal Services Commission was required to establish a Criminal Defence Service. This service is aimed at:

 securing that individuals involved in criminal investigation or proceedings have access to such advice, assistance and representation as the interests of justice require.

The Criminal Defence Service offers the following schemes:

- duty solicitor schemes
- advice and assistance
- representation.

Only the last one allows for full representation throughout the case.

13.4.2 Advice in criminal cases

The two advice schemes run by the Criminal Defence Service are:

- duty solicitors
- advice and assistance.

Duty solicitors

The Access to Justice Act 1999 states that the Legal Services Commission shall fund such advice and assistance as it considers appropriate for individuals who are arrested and held in custody at a police station or other premises. This provides those held at a police station with free legal advice.

This is an important right to protect the liberty of the individual. Originally this meant that anyone held was eligible to receive free advice from a duty solicitor.

However, since May 2004, the work that can be done by duty solicitors has been reduced. They can no longer normally attend at a police station where the client is detained:

- for a non-imprisonable offence
- on a warrant
- in breach of bail conditions
- for drink-driving offences.

A duty solicitor can still attend for the above in situations where the client is vulnerable, eg a youth, mentally ill, cannot speak English. They can also attend where the client complains of serious maltreatment by the police.

Telephone advice

One of the problems in the 1990s with duty solicitor schemes was that, in many cases, the solicitor did not attend at the police station but merely gave advice over the telephone. Although this was viewed as a defect in the scheme, telephone advice has now become the Government's preferred method of action for duty solicitors. Since 2004 solicitors should advise by telephone and only attend at the police station if they can show that attendance was expected to 'materially progress the case'.

Advice and assistance

Advice and assistance can be given by solicitors who have a contract with the Legal Services Commission to do criminal legal aid. It is limited to one hour's work. Normally it is just for advice, but it can include advocacy if the solicitor has applied for a representation order which has been refused.

Normally there is a means test for advice and assistance and only those on low incomes will qualify. In 2007–08 only defendants with income below £95 per week and capital of less than £1,000 were allowed to receive advice under this scheme.

The exception to the means test is that a duty solicitor at a Magistrates' Court can still see all defendants in custody under the advice and assistance scheme. This is free for everyone in custody, as it is important to protect defendants' human rights.

13.4.3 Representation

In order to get representation, the defendant has to qualify under the 'interests of justice' test. Also, for cases in the Magistrates' Courts, the defendant is means tested as well.

Interests of justice

A defendant will only get help with legal funding for representation in court if he can show that he comes within at least one of the five 'interests of justice' factors. These factors are:

- the individual would be likely to lose his liberty or livelihood or suffer serious damage to his reputation
- the case will involve consideration of a point of law
- the individual is unable to understand the proceedings in court or to state his own case
- the case may involve the tracing, interviewing or expert cross-examination of witnesses
- it is in the interests of another person that the individual is represented (eg in a rape case).

Means testing

As well as having to qualify under the 'interests of justice' test, defendants who are being tried in the Magistrates' Courts are also means tested.

Those who are on income support, defendants under the age of 16 and those under 18 in full-time education automatically pass the means test. For everyone else, the test starts with a first-stage simple means test which is calculated on gross annual income. If their income is too high on this test then the defendant does not qualify for legal aid. If a defendant's income is below a certain level, they qualify. For those in the middle bracket, they are further means tested to calculate their disposable income.

The levels allowed are very low. This means that about three-quarters of adults do not qualify for legal aid in criminal cases. This is particularly worrying, as the Government intends to introduce means testing for cases in the Crown Court. These are more serious and more expensive, so it is important that defendants should have access to legal help.

13.4.4 The Carter reforms

In July 2006 a report by Lord Carter, *Legal Aid – A Market-based Approach to Reform*, was published. The aim of this report is to reduce spending on criminal legal aid by more than 20 per cent over the next four years. This may seem a lot but comparative research by Carter on spending in other countries showed that the UK spends more than 10 times more than its nearest rival. There appeared to be no obvious reason for this difference.

The Government intends bringing in Lord Carter's main proposals. These are:

- 'best-value' tendering for legal aid contracts based on quality, capacity and price from 2009
- fixed fees for solicitors carrying out legal aid work in police stations (including cutting costs related to travelling and waiting times)
- revised graduated fees for Crown Court advocates – this will give junior barristers more for the 1- to 10-day cases, but cut fees for longer cases
- a new graduated fee scheme for Crown Court litigators to reward earlier preparation and resolution of cases.

The legal profession claim that these reforms will make Government-funded legal work uneconomic to do. There is a real risk the numbers of solicitors who do such work will be dramatically reduced. This will make it difficult for defendants to find a lawyer to represent them.

13.4.5 Public Defender Service

The Public Defender Service started in 2001. It has State-employed lawyers who represent defendants in criminal cases in four areas. There used to be eight offices, but four of them were closed in 2007 as they were not cost-effective.

When the service started, critics pointed out that the system meant that the State, which was

prosecuting the defendant (through the Crown Prosecution Service), was also defending the defendant (through the Public Defender Service). It has been suggested that this could mean that Public Defender Service lawyers might not be as independent as lawyers in private practice.

Evaluation

An evaluation of the PDS was published at the beginning of 2007. This found that there were positive aspects to the use of the PDS. In particular, lawyers from the service were more likely to attend at a police station to advise clients being held there. Where this happened, clients were less likely to be charged with an offence than those who used lawyers from private practice.

However, defendants who were charged and represented by the PDS were more likely to plead guilty in the Magistrates' Courts. This did not appear to have any advantage for the defendant in the way of pleading to a lower level offence or receiving a lesser sentence than those represented by private lawyers.

The evaluation found that the cost-effectiveness of the PDS was not as good as for private firms. During the first three years of its operation the average case costs for the PDS ranged from between 40 per cent to just over 90 per cent higher than the cost of private firms.

13.4.6 Problems with funding of criminal cases

'Interests of justice' test

This test is applied very strictly. Even where a defendant is charged with an offence for which a prison sentence can be given, for example theft, it does not necessarily mean that he will pass the 'interests of justice' test. The rule is that there must be a real risk of imprisonment.

This has the effect that defendants, who have several previous convictions for theft, will qualify for legal help as they are likely to be imprisoned. However, someone with no previous convictions

Key facts

Managing body	Criminal Defence Service
Different levels of help and representation available	● duty solicitor at the police station ● advice and assistance ● legal representation
Merits test for representation	Whether it is in the interests of justice ● defendant at risk of losing liberty, livelihood or reputation ● substantial point of law involved ● defendant unable to understand proceedings ● involves tracing, interview or expert cross-examination of witnesses ● is in the interests of another person
Means test	Duty solicitor free of charge and not means tested Means testing for representation in Magistrates' Courts cases
Problems	● strict application of 'interests of justice' test ● strict means test so that three-quarters of adults cannot qualify ● lack of solicitors doing publicly funded criminal law work ● does the Public Defender Service give good service?

Figure 13.4 Key facts chart on public funding in criminal cases

is not likely to be sent to prison. So, if they are pleading not guilty, they will have to represent themselves or pay for private legal help.

Means test

This is also a strict test. The levels of income allowed are very low. About three-quarters of adults do not qualify for legal aid in criminal cases. If means testing is extended to the Crown Court where it is more expensive to defend a case, then there is a real risk of injustice due to lack of availability of legal help.

Lack of lawyers

The Government has cut the fees paid to lawyers for criminal cases. Fixed fees are being brought in which do not take account of the true amount of work that may need to be done. As a result, fewer solicitors are taking on Government-funded legal work. This makes it more difficult for defendants to find a local solicitor to take their case.

Activity

Advise the people in the following scenarios whether publicly funded help/representation is available and what problems they may encounter in trying to get funding.

1. Ali has been charged with theft of a laptop computer from a shop. He works as an IT specialist and has no previous convictions.
2. Bernice has been left paralysed from the waist down after being hit by a car when she was standing at a bus stop.
3. Connor believes he has been unfairly dismissed from his job. He wants to make a claim in an employment tribunal.
4. Davina has had building work done at her home. The company are in breach of contract and it has cost Davina £10,000 to have the work made good. She wishes to make a claim for this amount. She owns her house but has a mortgage of £140,000.

Budget

The budget given by the Government for legal funding has not risen in line with inflation. This means that the Legal Services Commission has less money to allocate for funding.

13.5 Advice agencies

A number of different advice schemes are available. The main ones are Citizens' Advice Bureaux and Law Centres. However, there are other agencies which offer advice on specific legal topics. These include trade unions which will help members with work-related legal problems. There are also charities such as Shelter which offers advice to people with housing problems.

These will offer advice free to anyone who has a problem of the type they deal in. About 450 not-for-profit organisations have contracts from the Community Legal Service for providing advice under the Government advice schemes.

13.5.1 Citizens' Advice Bureaux

These were first set up in 1938 and today there are about one thousand throughout the country with a bureau existing in most towns. They give general advice free to anyone on a variety of issues mostly connected to social welfare problems and debt, but they also advise on some legal matters. They can also provide information on which local solicitors do legal aid work or give cheap or free initial interviews. Many have arrangements under which solicitors may attend at the bureau once a week or fortnight to give more qualified advice on legal matters.

As well as being available for anyone to get advice, the Legal Services Commission has awarded contracts for some CABx to provide Government-funded advice.

13.5.2 Law Centres

These offer a free, non means-tested legal service to people in their area. The first Law Centre opened in North Kensington in 1970. This stated its aims as providing 'a first class solicitor's service to the people . . . a service which is easily accessible, not intimidating, to which they can turn for guidance as they would to their family doctor, or as someone who can afford it would turn to his family solicitor'.

Their aim is to provide free legal advice (and sometimes representation) in areas where there are few solicitors.

Funding is a major problem for Law Centres. However, the Community Legal Service has given funding for some centres.

Key facts

Government-funded schemes	Advice agencies	Lawyers
Community Legal Service website offering advice	Citizens' Advice Bureaux	Some solicitors offer a free half-hour first interview
CLS Direct telephone service	Law Centres	Free Representation Unit run by barristers
Community Legal Advice Centres	Legal insurance	Pay privately for advice
Legal Help scheme – means tested and only available to those on low incomes		

Figure 13.5 Key facts chart on where to get advice in civil cases

13.5.3 Other advice agencies
Schemes run by lawyers

Some solicitors offer a free half-hour first interview. Local CABx will have a list of solicitors who offer the service.

Another service offered by solicitors is the Accident Legal Advice Service (ALAS) which is aimed at helping accident victims claim compensation. In addition, the Law Society runs Accident Line – a free telephone service to put accident victims in contact with solicitors who do personal injury work.

The Bar runs the Free Representation Unit (FRU) which helps people who are ineligible for legal aid present their case in court. Under this scheme barristers give their time free and represent clients in court at no cost. More than 2,000 cases are dealt with each year by the FRU.

Insurance

Another way of funding a court case is by legal insurance. Most motor insurance policies offer cover (for a small amount extra) for help with legal fees in cases arising from road accidents and there are also policies purely for insurance against legal costs.

Key facts

Service	Community Legal Service	Criminal Defence Service	Privately paid lawyer
Types of case	Civil only	Criminal only	All types
Finance	Only available for those on low incomes	Means tested in Magistrates' Courts and only available for those on low incomes	Available to anyone who can afford to pay Conditional fee agreements can be used for civil cases
Availability	Not available for personal injury, defamation or small claims Not available for most tribunals	Free advice for anyone detained at a police station Representation only if it is in the interests of justice	
Merits	Must have a good chance of success **and** the cost must not be more than the likely damages	● risk of losing liberty, livelihood, reputation ● substantial point of law involved ● defendant unable to understand proceedings ● involves tracing, interviewing or expert cross-examination of witnesses ● is in the interests of another person	Will usually only take a case on a conditional fee if there is a very high chance of success
Comment	Set budget Only available if there are sufficient funds Decreasing number of solicitors	Lack of solicitors doing publicly-funded criminal law work	Expensive – up to £600 an hour for City lawyers Liable to pay other side's costs if lose case

Figure 13.6 Key facts chart comparing sources of legal service

13.6 Private funding

Anyone who can afford it can pay for a solicitor and/or a barrister to deal with a legal matter. There are firms of solicitors in most towns. However, some solicitors specialise in certain types of work. If your legal problem is on an unusual area of law, then it may be necessary to travel to another town to find a solicitor who can deal with it.

The bigger firms of solicitors work in the major cities, in particular London. They often specialise in commercial law and the majority of their clients are businesses.

Consulting a solicitor can be expensive. The average cost of solicitor outside London is about £150 an hour. For a big London firm of solicitors, the charges are usually at least £600 an hour and can be as much as £1,000 an hour.

On issues of civil law it is also possible to consult a barrister directly, without going to a solicitor first. This can be cheaper than using a solicitor because barristers do not have such high business expenses as solicitors.

13.7 Conditional fees

One of the main problems of taking a case to court is that it is difficult to estimate how long it will last or how much it will cost. If a person is funding their own case, this is a major problem for them. Also, if they lose the case they may have to pay the costs of the other party. The combined costs of the case can be many thousands of pounds. In order to overcome these problems, a conditional fee agreement (CFA) can be used in all civil cases except family cases.

CFAs cannot be used in criminal cases.

13.7.1 How conditional fees work

The solicitor and client agree on the fee that would normally be charged for such a case. The agreement will also set out what the solicitor's success fee will be if he wins the case.

Many conditional fee agreements will be made on the basis that if the case is lost, the client pays

nothing. Because of this sort of agreement, the scheme is often referred to as 'no win, no fee'. However, some solicitors may charge a lower level fee, for example half the normal fee, even if the case is lost.

If the case is won the client has to pay the normal fee plus the success fee.

13.7.2 Success fee

The success fee can be up to 100 per cent of the normal fee. However, most agreements will include a 'cap' on the success fee, which prevents it from being more than 25 per cent of the damages (amount of money) that the client wins as compensation. This protects the client from having to pay more than he or she won as compensation. Even so, it can mean that the client is left with very little of their damages. This is easier to understand by looking at the examples given in Figure 13.7.

When conditional fee agreements were first allowed by the Courts and Legal Services Act 1990, the client had to pay the success fee themselves and could not claim it back for the other side as part of their cost of the case. This meant that clients often ended up with very little even though they had won the case, so the Access to Justice Act 1999 changed the rules to allow reasonable levels of success fees to be claimed as costs from the losing party.

What level of success fee that could be claimed back as costs has been the subject of many disputes. Eventually rules set down what level could be claimed. These depend on when the case is settled. If the case is settled at an early stage then the defendant (or in most cases, his insurers) will only have to pay 12.5 per cent of any success fee. This can mean that the successful claimant has to pay the rest of the success fee to his own solicitor. It will depend on what was agreed in the conditional fee agreement.

However, if the other side refuse to settle and then lose the case in court, the rules allow the claimant to get back 100 per cent of the success fee as costs from the other side.

Agreement

Normal fee	£4,000
Fee if case is lost	NIL
Success fee	£2,000
Cap on success fee	25% of damages

Possible results of case	Client pays	
Case is lost	Nothing	
Case is won: client gets £50,000 damages	£6,000	(£4,000 + £2,000)
Case is won: client gets £6,000 damages	£5,500	(£4,000 + £1,500*)

*This £1,500 is because the success fee cannot be more than 25% of the damages

Figure 13.7 Illustration of conditional fees

Case example

An example of a case in which a success fee of 100 per cent was ordered to be paid by the losing party is *Campbell v Mirror Group Newspapers Ltd (No 2)* (2005).

In this case the model Naomi Campbell successfully sued the *Daily Mirror* for libel and breach of privacy when the paper published an article and photos of her. She was awarded £3,500 in damages. The case had been originally tried at the High Court and then appealed to the Court of Appeal. For both these court actions Campbell had paid her lawyers' legal costs in the ordinary way.

When the case went to the House of Lords, Campbell entered into conditional fee agreements with both her solicitors and the barrister who represented her in the House of Lords. The agreements allowed for success fees of 95 per cent and 100 per cent respectively. Campbell won the case in the House of Lords and then claimed the success fees as part of her costs from Mirror Group Newspapers (MGN). The success fees came to almost £280,000 and this, added to the normal fees, made the total bill for her costs over £1 million. MGN challenged the amount of the

success fees on two points:

1. the amount was disproportionate and
2. the risk of having to pay large sums in costs was an infringement of the human right to freedom of expression: it effectively acted as a 'gag' on the media as it could prevent them from publishing items.

In the House of Lords, the Law Lords ruled that the cost of the success fees was proportionate because it reflected the reality of conditional fee agreements. Successful cases had to be paid more to allow for losses in other cases. If this was not so, then solicitors would not take on cases unless winning was virtually certain. People with cases in which the end result was difficult to predict would not be able to find a solicitor to take the case under a CFA.

The Lords also held that success fees did not infringe the media's freedom of expression. Using CFAs with a success fee was the only way most people could bring defamation cases against newspapers. If success fees were not allowed then the media would be free to make defamatory statements, as those affected could not afford to bring cases against them.

13.7.3 Insurance premiums

Although the client will often not have to pay anything to his own lawyer if the case is lost, they will usually have to pay the costs of the other side. This can leave the client with a very large bill to pay. To help protect against this, it is possible to insure against the risk. This type of insurance is known as 'after-the-event' insurance. So, if the case is lost, your insurers will pay the other side's costs.

In order to get insurance it is necessary to pay a premium (a sum of money) to the insurance company. Premiums for 'after-the-event' insurance are usually quite expensive. This premium usually has to be paid in advance of the decision in the case. This can cause problems to people who cannot afford the cost of the premium. Also, until the Access to Justice Act 1999, the insurance premium could not be claimed as costs from the losing party.

Matters have now improved as the law allows the premium to be claimed from the losing party. Also some solicitors have made arrangements with insurance companies that the premium need not be paid in advance.

13.7.4 Advantages of conditional fee agreements

CFAs provide access to justice. They allow people who could not afford to pay their own legal fees to bring cases. This is particularly important for personal injury cases, as Government legal aid is not available for such cases. It is also important in defamation cases as these will also not normally be given Government funding.

This access to justice is shown by the fact that thousands of claims have been brought using CFAs.

Allowing a successful claimant using a CFA to reclaim the success fee and the insurance premium makes CFAs fairer. Previously, people found that a large proportion of the damages they won as compensation for injuries was taken up by having to pay the success fee and the insurance premium.

As the solicitor only gets a fee if the case is won, the client will feel confident in the solicitor's commitment to the case. The solicitor benefits with higher fees from winning the case.

Solicitors will not want to take on cases which have no chance of success. This should prevent hopeless cases being started and wasting court time.

13.7.5 Disadvantages of conditional fee agreements

Surveys and research into CFAs suggests that there are still problems with such agreements. Research in 1998 by Sheffield University found that:

- The poorest clients could not afford to pay insurance premiums or other expenses such as a payment for a medical report. These normally have to be paid for at the beginning of a case and although they can be claimed back if the case is won, that may be two or three years later.
- Those with cases which were not certain to win found it difficult to find a solicitor prepared to take on the case.
- The amount of work needed to be done on some types of personal injury case, especially accidents at work, made it difficult to estimate the cost. In such cases solicitors found that the case had cost them more than the combined fee plus success fee.

In 2004 a report, *No Win, No Fee, No Chance* by James Sandbach, published by the Citizens' Advice Bureau, identified several problems with CFAs. These included:

- Consumers are subjected to high-pressure sales tactics, including salesmen approaching accident victims in hospital.
- Few consumers seem to understand the risks and liabilities of CFAs. These are not properly explained to them and they may be misled into thinking the system is genuinely 'no win, no fee' but can then find that there are hidden and unpredictable costs.

Key facts

How conditional fee agreements work	● the client and solicitor agree on the normal fee and on a success fee if the case is won ● the success fee can be up to 100% of the normal fee ● if the case is lost, most clients will pay nothing to their own solicitor ● after-the-event insurance is usually taken out to protect against the risk of paying the other's costs if the case is lost
Advantages of CFAs	● provide access to justice for those who cannot get Government funding and cannot afford to pay in the normal way ● client will feel confident in solicitor's commitment to case ● hopeless cases will not be taken on, saving court time
Disadvantages of CFAs	● clients cannot afford to pay insurance premiums or other expenses ● consumers may be subjected to high-pressure sales tactics ● consumers do not understand the risks and liabilities of CFAs and may be misled by sales persons ● some claims end in 'zero gain' ● solicitors do not want to take on high-risk claims or low-value claims: this can deny access to justice.

Figure 13.8 Key facts chart on conditional fee agreements

● Where insurance premiums are paid for with loan finance, this in addition to other legal costs, can be more than compensation awarded. In some cases consumers even owe money at the end of the process. The whole claims process is turned into a 'zero gain' for consumers and denies effective access to compensation.

● Solicitors do not want to take on high-risk claims or low-value claims. This can deny people access to justice, especially as Government funding is no longer available for personal injury cases.

@ Internet Research

Find websites of solicitors' firms in which they explain how conditional fee agreements work. You should be able to find such sites by entering the phrase 'conditional fee agreement' in Google or another search engine.

When you have found the sites, look at two different ones and compare what they say about CFAs.

Examination Questions

(a) Describe the various types of publicly funded advice and representation available in criminal cases.

(b) Discuss the problems of publicly funded criminal advice and representation.

OCR Specimen Paper

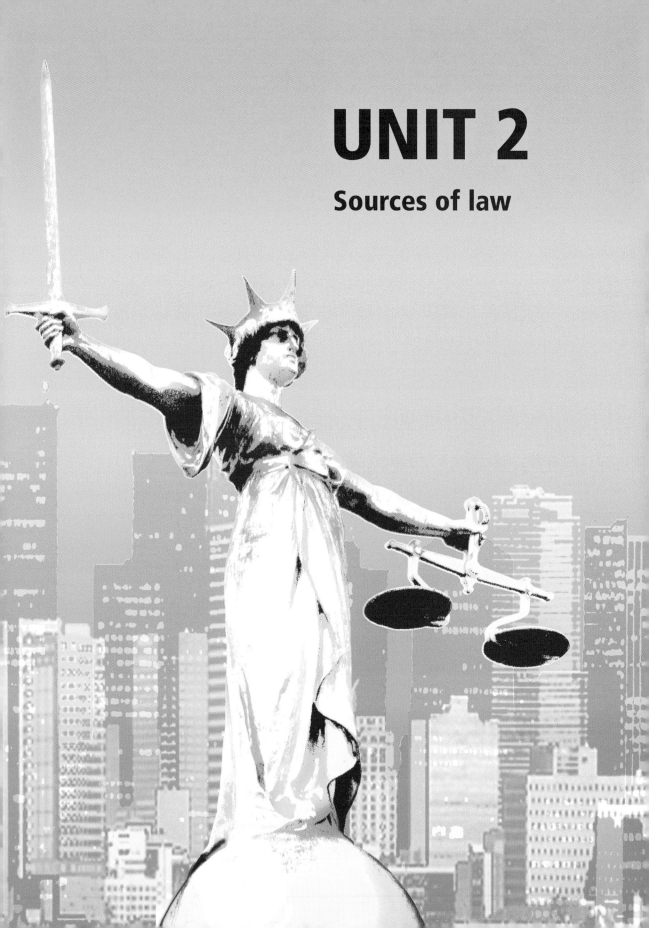

UNIT 2

Sources of law

Chapter 14

Judicial precedent

J udicial precedent refers to the source of law where past decisions of the judges create law for future judges to follow. This source of law is also known as case-law. It is a major source of law, both historically and today.

14.1 The doctrine of precedent

The English system of precedent is based on the Latin maxim *stare decisis et non quieta movere* (usually shortened to *stare decisis*). This means stand by what has been decided and do not unsettle the established. This supports the idea of fairness and provides certainty in the law.

14.1.1 Judgments

Precedent can only operate if the legal reasons for past decisions are known, so at the end of a case there will be a judgment. This is a speech made by the judge (or judges) hearing the case giving the decision and explaining the reasons for the decision. In a judgment the judge usually gives a summary of the facts of the case, reviews the arguments put to him by the advocates in the case, and then explains the principles of law he is using to come to the decision.

These principles are the important part of the judgment and are known as the *ratio decidendi* which means 'the reason for deciding' (and is

pronounced 'ray-she-o dess-id-end-i'). This is what creates a precedent for judges to follow in future cases. The rest of the judgment is known as *obiter dicta* ('other things said').

It is also worth realising that there can be more than one speech at the end of a case depending on the number of judges hearing the case. In courts of first instance there will be only one judge and therefore one judgment. However, in the appeal courts (the Divisional Courts, the Court of Appeal and the House of Lords) cases are heard by at least two judges up to a maximum of seven judges in the House of Lords, therefore there can be more than one judgment.

The fact that there are two or more judges does not mean that there will always be several judgments as it is quite common for one judge to give the judgment and the other judge/judges simply to say 'I agree'! However, in cases where there is a particularly important or complicated point of law, more than one judge may want to explain his legal reasoning on the point. This can cause problems in later cases as each judge may have had a different reason for his decision, so there will be more than one *ratio decidendi*.

14.1.2 *Ratio decidendi*

As already stated, this is the only part of the judgment which forms a precedent. A major problem when looking at a past judgment is to divide the *ratio decidendi* from the *obiter dicta*, as older judgments are usually in a continuous form, without any headings specifying what is meant to be part of the *ratio* and what is not. This means that the person reading the judgment (especially a judge in a later case) will have to decide what the *ratio* is. Sir Rupert Cross defined the *ratio decidendi* as 'any rule expressly or impliedly treated by the judge as a necessary step in reaching his conclusion'. Michael Zander says that it is 'a proposition of law which decides the case, in the light or in the context of the material facts'.

It depends on the level of the court making the decision as to whether the *ratio* has to be followed by a later court (a binding precedent) or whether it merely has to be considered by that court.

14.1.3 *Obiter dicta*

The remainder of the judgment is called *obiter dicta* ('other things said') and judges in future cases do not have to follow it. Sometimes a judge will speculate on what his decision would have been if the facts of the case had been different. This hypothetical situation is part of the *obiter dicta* and the legal reasoning put forward in it may be considered in future cases, although, as with all *obiter* statements, it is not binding precedent.

As well as learning the Latin phrases *ratio decidendi*, *obiter dicta* and *stare decisis* there are some English phrases which are important for understanding the concept of judicial precedent. These are 'original precedent', 'binding precedent' and 'persuasive precedent'.

14.1.4 Original precedent

If the point of law in a case has never been decided before, then whatever the judge decides will form a new precedent for future cases to follow. It is an original precedent. As there are no past cases for the judge to base his decision on, he is likely to look at cases which are the closest in principle and he may decide to use similar rules. This way of arriving at a judgment is called reasoning by analogy.

14.1.5 Binding precedent

This is a precedent from an earlier case which must be followed even if the judge in the later case does not agree with the legal principle. A binding precedent is only created when the facts of the second case are sufficiently similar to the original case and the decision was made by a court which is senior to (or in some cases the same level as) the court hearing the later case.

14.1.6 Persuasive precedent

This is a precedent that is not binding on the court, but the judge may consider it and decide that it is a correct principle so he is persuaded that he should follow it. Persuasive precedent comes from a number of sources, as explained below:

Courts lower in the hierarchy

Such an example can be seen in *R v R* (1991), where the House of Lords agreed with and followed the same reasoning as the Court of Appeal in deciding that a man could be guilty of raping his wife.

Decisions of the Judicial Committee of the Privy Council

This court is not part of the court hierarchy in England and Wales and so its decisions are not binding, but, since many of its judges are also members of the House of Lords, their judgments are treated with respect and may often be followed. An example of this can be seen in the law on remoteness of damage in the law of tort and the decision made by the Privy Council in the case of *The Wagon Mound (No 1)* (1961). In later cases courts in England and Wales followed the decision in this case.

This also happened in *A-G for Jersey v Holley* (2005) when the majority of the Privy Council (six out of nine judges) ruled that in the defence of provocation, a defendant is to be judged by the standard of a person having ordinary powers of self-control. This was contrary to an earlier judgment of the House of Lords. As a result, there were conflicting decisions from the House of Lords and the Privy Council. Although a decision by the Privy Council is not binding on English courts, in *R v Mohammed* (2005) the Court of Appeal followed *Holley* rather than the decision in *Smith*. Then in *R v James; R v Karimi* (2006), a five-member Court of Appeal confirmed that the decision in *Holley* should be followed by courts in England and Wales.

Statements made *obiter dicta*

An example of this is the law on duress as a defence to a criminal charge, where the House of Lords in *R v Howe* (1987) ruled that duress could not be a defence to a charge of murder. In the judgment the Lords also commented, as an *obiter* statement, that duress would not be available as a defence to someone charged with attempted murder. When, later, in *R v Gotts* (1992) a defendant charged with attempted murder tried to argue that he could use the defence of duress, the *obiter* statement from *Howe* was followed as persuasive precedent by the Court of Appeal.

A dissenting judgment

Where a case has been decided by a majority of judges (for example, 2–1 in the Court of Appeal), the judge who disagreed will have explained his reasons. If that case goes on appeal to the House of Lords, or if there is a later case on the same point which goes to the House of Lords, it is possible that the House of Lords may prefer the dissenting judgment and decide the case in the same way. The dissenting judgment has persuaded them to follow it.

Decisions of courts in other countries

Where another country uses the same ideas of common law as in our system, their decisions may be considered. This includes countries such as Canada, Australia and New Zealand.

14.2 The hierarchy of the courts

In England and Wales our courts operate a very rigid doctrine of judicial precedent which has the effect that:

- every court is bound to follow any decision made by a court above it in the hierarchy
- in general, appellate courts (courts which hear appeals) are bound by their own past decisions.

So the hierarchy of the courts is the next important point to get clear. Which courts come

 Internet Research

Judgments of cases are available on several Internet sites. One free site is **www.bailii.org**.

Try to find the case of *R v James: R v Karimi* (2006) using this site.

Tips

❯ look at the database for England and Wales,

then within that choose 'Court of Appeal (Criminal Division)'

❯ browse the year 2006

❯ the case will be indexed as *James, R v* and it was heard in January 2006.

Figure 14.1 Cascade model of judicial precedent operating in the hierarchy of the courts

where in the hierarchy? Figure 14.1 shows this in the form of a cascade model and Figure 14.2 gives each court and its position in respect of the other courts. The position of each court is also considered in this section and in sections 14.3 and 14.4.

14.2.1 Appellate courts

Appellate courts are those hearing appeals.

The European Court of Justice

Since 1973, the highest court affecting our legal system is the European Court of Justice. For points of European law, a decision made by this court is binding on all other courts in England and Wales. However, there are still laws which are unaffected by European Union law and for these the House of Lords is the supreme court. An

important feature of the European Court of Justice is that it is prepared to overrule its own past decisions if it feels it is necessary. This flexible approach to past precedents is seen in other legal systems in Europe, and is a contrast to the more rigid approach of our national courts.

House of Lords

The most senior national court is the House of Lords and its decisions bind all other courts in the English legal system. The House of Lords is not bound by its own past decisions, although it will generally follow them. This point is discussed in detail in section 14.3.

Court of Appeal

At the next level down in the hierarchy is the Court of Appeal which has two divisions: Civil

Court	Courts bound by it	Courts it must follow
European Court	All courts	None
House of Lords	All other courts in the English legal system	European Court
Court of Appeal	Itself (with some exceptions) Divisional Courts All other lower courts	European Court House of Lords
Divisional Courts	Itself (with some exceptions) High Court All other lower courts	European Court House of Lords Court of Appeal
High Court	County Court Magistrates' Court	European Court House of Lords Court of Appeal Divisional Courts
Crown Court	Possibly Magistrates' Court	All higher courts

County Court and Magistrates' Court do not create precedent and are bound by all higher courts

Figure 14.2 The courts and precedent

and Criminal. Both divisions of the Court of Appeal are bound to follow decisions of the European Court of Justice and the House of Lords. In addition, they must usually follow past decisions of their own; although there are some limited exceptions to this rule. Also the Court of Appeal (Criminal Division) is more flexible where the point involves the liberty of the subject. The position of the two divisions is discussed in detail in section 14.4.

Divisional Courts

The three Divisional Courts (Queen's Bench, Chancery and Family) are bound by decisions of the European Court of Justice, the House of Lords and the Court of Appeal. In addition, the Divisional Courts are bound by their own past decisions, although they operate similar exceptions to those operated by the Court of Appeal.

14.2.2 Courts of first instance

The term 'court of first instance' means any court where the original trial of a case is held. The appellate courts considered in section 14.2.1 do not hear any original trials. They only deal with appeals from decisions of other courts. Quite often an appeal will be about a point of law. This allows the appellate courts to decide the law and this is why the appellate courts are much more important than courts of first instance when it comes to creating precedent.

Courts of first instance rarely create precedent. They must follow the decisions of the courts above them.

The High Court

This is bound by decisions of all the courts above and in turn it binds the lower courts. High Court judges do not have to follow each others' decisions but will usually do so. In *Colchester Estates (Cardiff) v Carlton Industries plc* (1984) it was held that where there were two earlier decisions which conflicted, then, provided the first decision had been fully considered in the later case, that later decision should be followed.

Inferior courts

These are the Crown Court, the County Court and the Magistrates' Court. They are bound to follow decisions by all higher courts and it is unlikely that a decision by an inferior court can create precedent. The one exception is that a ruling on a point of law by a judge in the Crown Court technically creates precedent for the Magistrates' Court. However, since such rulings are rarely recorded in the law reports, this is of little practical effect.

14.3 The House of Lords

The main debate about the House of Lords is the extent to which it should follow its own past decisions and the ideas on this have changed over the years.

Originally the view was that the House of Lords had the right to overrule past decisions, but gradually during the nineteenth century this more flexible approach disappeared. By the end of that century, in *London Street Tramways v London County Council* (1898), the House of Lords held that certainty in the law was more important than the possibility of individual hardship being caused through having to follow a past decision.

So from 1898 to 1966 the House of Lords regarded itself as being completely bound by its own past decisions unless the decision had been made *per incuriam*, that is 'in error'. However, this idea of error referred only to situations where a decision had been made without considering the effect of a relevant statute.

This was not felt to be satisfactory. The law could not alter to meet changing social conditions and opinions, nor could any possible 'wrong' decisions be changed by the courts. If there was

an unsatisfactory decision by the House of Lords, then the only way it could be changed was by Parliament passing a new Act of Parliament.

This happened in the law about intention as an element of a criminal offence. The House of Lords in *DPP v Smith* (1961) had ruled that an accused could be guilty of murder if a reasonable person would have foreseen that death or very serious injury might result from the accused's actions. This decision was criticised as it meant that the defendant could be guilty even if he had not intended to cause death or serious injury, nor even realised that his actions might have that effect. Eventually Parliament changed the law by passing the Criminal Justice Act 1967.

14.3.1 The Practice Statement

It was realised that the House of Lords should have more flexibility. For today's system of judicial precedent the critical date is 1966, when the Lord Chancellor issued a Practice Statement announcing a change to the rule in *London Street Tramways* v *London County Council*. The Practice Statement said:

> Their Lordships regard the use of precedent as an indispensable foundation upon which to decide what is the law and its application to individual cases. It provides at least some degree of certainty upon which individuals can rely in the conduct of their affairs, as well as a basis for orderly development of legal rules.
>
> Their Lordships nevertheless recognise that the rigid adherence to precedent may lead to injustice in a particular case and also unduly restrict the proper development of the law. They propose, therefore, to modify their present practice and while treating former decisions of this House as normally binding, to depart from a previous decision when it appears right to do so.

In this connection they will bear in mind the danger of disturbing retrospectively the basis on which contracts, settlement of property and fiscal arrangements have been entered into and also the especial need for certainty as to the criminal law. This announcement is not intended to affect the use of precedent elsewhere than in this House.

14.3.2 Use of the Practice Statement

Since 1966, this Practice Statement has allowed the House of Lords to change the law if it believes that an earlier case was wrongly decided. It has the flexibility to refuse to follow an earlier case when 'it appears right to do so'. This phrase is, of course, very vague and gives little guidance as to when the House of Lords might overrule a previous decision. In fact the House of Lords has been reluctant to use this power, especially in the first few years after 1966. The first case in which the Practice Statement was used was *Conway v Rimmer* (1968), but this only involved a technical point on discovery of documents.

The first major use did not occur until 1972 in *Herrington v British Railways Board* (1972), which involved the law on the duty of care owed to a child trespasser. The earlier case of *Addie v Dumbreck* (1929) had decided that an occupier of land would only owe a duty of care for injuries to a child trespasser, if those injuries had been caused deliberately or recklessly. In *Herrington* the Lords held that social and physical conditions had changed since 1929, and the law should also change.

There was still great reluctance in the House of Lords to use the Practice Statement, as can be seen by the case of *Jones v Secretary of State for Social Services* (1972). This case involved the interpretation of the National Insurance (Industrial Injuries) Act 1946 and four out of the seven judges hearing the case regarded the earlier decision in *Re Dowling* (1967) as being wrong. Despite this the Lords refused to overrule that

earlier case, preferring to keep to the idea that certainty was the most important feature of precedent. The same attitude was shown in *Knuller v DPP* (1973) when Lord Reid said:

> Our change of practice in no longer regarding previous decisions of this House as absolutely binding does not mean that whenever we think a previous precedent was wrong we should reverse it. In the general interest of certainty in the law we must be sure that there is some very good reason before we so act.

From the mid-1970s onwards the House of Lords showed a little more willingness to make use of the Practice Statement. For example, in *Miliangos v George Frank (Textiles) Ltd* (1976) the House of Lords used the Practice Statement to overrule a previous judgment that damages could only be awarded in sterling. Another major case was *Pepper v Hart* (1993) where the previous ban on the use of *Hansard* in statutory interpretation was overruled.

In *Horton v Sadler and another* (2006) the House of Lords used the Practice Statement to depart from a previous decision of its own. The case involved a personal injury claim, but the point of law being decided was about the power to allow service out of time under s 33 of the Limitation Act 1980. The House of Lords departed from their decision in *Walkley v Precision Forgings Ltd* (1979).

The Law Lords departed from *Walkley* for three reasons:

- it unfairly deprived claimants of a right that Parliament had intended them to have
- it had driven the Court of Appeal to draw distinctions which were correct but were so fine as to reflect no credit on the area of law and
- it went against the clear intention of Parliament.

Lord Bingham in his speech considered the issue of departing from a previous decision. He pointed out that the case was not one in which contracts,

Key facts

1898	House of Lords decides in the case of *London Street Tramways* that it is bound to follow its own previous decisions
1966	Issue of the Practice Statement House of Lords will depart from previous decisions when 'it is right to do so'
1968	First use of Practice Statement in *Conway v Rimmer* Only involves technical law on discovery of documents
1972	First major use of Practice Statement in *Herrington v British Railways Board* on the duty of care owed to child trespassers
1980s and 1990s	House of Lords shows an increasing willingness to use Practice Statement to overrule previous decisions, eg *R v Shivpuri* (criminal attempts); *Pepper v Hart* (use of *Hansard* in statutory interpretation)
2003	Practice Statement used to overrule the decision in *Caldwell* on recklessness in the criminal law

Figure 14.3 Key facts chart for the operation of judicial precedent in the House of Lords

settlements of property or fiscal arrangements had been entered into, nor did it involve the criminal law where certainty was particularly important. Also, there would not be any detriment to public administration caused by departing from the previous decision.

14.3.3 The Practice Statement in criminal law

The Practice Statement stressed that criminal law needs to be certain, so it was not surprising that the House of Lords did not rush to overrule any judgments in criminal cases. The first use in a criminal case was in *R v Shivpuri* (1986) which overruled the decision in *Anderton v Ryan* (1985) on attempts to do the impossible. The interesting point was that the decision in *Anderton* had been made less than a year before, but it had been severely criticised by academic lawyers. In *Shivpuri* Lord Bridge said:

> I am undeterred by the consideration that the decision in *Anderton v Ryan* was so recent. The Practice Statement is an effective abandonment of our pretension to infallibility. If a serious error embodied in a decision of this House has distorted the law, the sooner it is corrected the better.

In other words, the House of Lords recognised that they might sometimes make errors and the most important thing then was to put the law right. Where the Practice Statement is used to overrule a previous decision, that past case is then effectively ignored. The law is now that which is set out in the new case.

Another important case on the use of the Practice Statement in criminal law is *R v G and R* (2003). In this case the House of Lords used the Practice Statement to overrule the earlier decision of *Caldwell* (1982) on the law of criminal damage. In *Caldwell* the House of Lords had ruled that recklessness included the situation where the defendant had not realised the risk of his actions causing damage, but an ordinary careful person would have realised there was a risk. In *R v G and R* it was held that this was the wrong test to use. The Law Lords overruled *Caldwell* and held that a defendant is only reckless if he realises that there is a risk of damage and goes ahead and takes that risk.

Activity

Read the following passage which comes from an extra explanatory note which was given to the press when the Practice Statement was issued and answer the questions below.

'The statement is one of great importance, although it should not be supposed that there will frequently be cases in which the House thinks it right not to follow their own precedent. An example of a case in which the House might think it right to depart from a precedent is where they consider that the earlier decision was influenced by the existence of conditions which no longer prevail, and that in modern conditions the law ought to be different.

One consequence of this change is of major importance. The relaxation of the rule of judicial precedent will enable the House of Lords to pay greater attention to judicial decisions reached in the superior courts of the Commonwealth, where they differ from earlier decisions of the House of Lords. That could be of great help in the development of our own law. The superior courts of many other countries are not rigidly bound by their own decisions and the change in the practice of the House of Lords will bring us more into line with them.'

Questions

1. Why is the Practice Statement of great importance?

2. Does the note suggest that the Practice Statement is likely to be used often?

3. Do you agree that 'in modern conditions the law ought to be different'? Give reasons and examples to support your answer.

4. Why should the House of Lords want to consider decisions from Commonwealth countries? What authority do such decisions have in the English legal system?

This case shows that the House of Lords is becoming more prepared to use the Practice Statement where they think it is 'right to do so'.

14.4 The Court of Appeal

As already stated there are two divisions of this court (the Civil Division and the Criminal Division) and the rules for precedent are not quite the same in these two divisions.

14.4.1 Decisions of courts above it

Both divisions of the Court of Appeal are bound by decisions of the European Court of Justice and the House of Lords. This is true even though there have been attempts in the past, mainly by Lord Denning, to argue that the Court of Appeal should not be bound by the House of Lords. In *Broome v Cassell & Co Ltd* (1971) Lord Denning refused to follow the earlier decision of the House of Lords in *Rookes v Barnard* (1964) on the circumstances in which exemplary damages could be awarded.

Again, in the cases of *Schorsch Meier GmbH v Henning* (1975) and *Miliangos v George Frank (Textiles) Ltd* (1976) the Court of Appeal refused to follow a decision of the House of Lords in *Havana Railways* (1961) which said that damages could only be awarded in sterling (English money). Lord Denning's argument for refusing to follow the House of Lords' decision was that the

Comment

Should the Court of Appeal have to follow House of Lords' decisions?

The main argument in favour of the Court of Appeal being able to ignore House of Lords' decisions is that very few cases reach the House of Lords, so that if there is an error in the law it may take years before a suitable case is appealed all the way to the House of Lords. The cases of *Schorsch Meier* and *Miliangos* illustrate the potential for injustice if there is no appeal to the House of Lords. What would have happened if the Court of Appeal in *Schorsch Meier* had decided that it had to follow the House of Lords' decision in *Havana Railways*? It is quite possible that the later case of *Miliangos* would not have even been appealed to the Court of Appeal. After all, why waste money on an appeal when there have been previous cases in both the Court of Appeal and the House of Lords ruling on that point of law? The law would have been regarded as fixed and it might never have been changed.

On the other hand, if the Court of Appeal could overrule the House of Lords, the system of precedent would break down and the law would become uncertain. There would be two conflicting precedents for lower courts to choose from. This would make it difficult for the judge in the lower court. It would also make the law so uncertain that it would be difficult for lawyers to advise clients on the law. However, since the case of *Miliangos*, there has been no further challenge by the Court of Appeal to this basic idea (in our system of judicial precedent) that lower courts must follow decisions of courts above them in the hierarchy.

currency. The case of *Schorsch Meier GmbH v Henning* was not appealed to the House of Lords, but *Miliangos v George Frank (Textiles) Ltd* did go on appeal to the Lords, where it was pointed out that the Court of Appeal had no right to ignore or overrule decisions of the House of Lords. The more unusual feature of *Miliangos* was that the House of Lords then used the Practice Statement to overrule its own decision in *Havana Railways*.

14.4.2 Human rights cases

Section 2(1)(a) of the Human Rights Act 1998 states that courts must take into account any judgment or decision of the European Court of Human Rights. In the case of *Re Medicaments (No 2), Director General of Fair Trading v Proprietary Association of Great Britain* (2001) the Court of Appeal refused to follow the decision of the House of Lords in *R v Gough* (1993) because it was slightly different to decisions of the European Court of Human Rights.

The *Director General* case was about whether a decision should be set aside because of the risk of bias on the part of one of the panel. In *Gough* the test for bias included the appeal court deciding whether there was a real danger that the tribunal was biased. The Court of Appeal said that in the European Court of Human Rights cases the emphasis was on the impression which the facts would give on an objective basis. This they claimed was a 'modest adjustment' of the test in *Gough*. However, this appears to be one situation in which the Court of Appeal need not follow a House of Lords decision.

14.4.3 The Court of Appeal and its own decisions

The first rule is that decisions by one division of the Court of Appeal will not bind the other division. However, within each division, decisions are normally binding, especially for the Civil Division. This rule comes from the case of *Young v Bristol Aeroplane Co Ltd* (1944) and the only

economic climate of the world had changed, and sterling was no longer a stable currency; there were some situations in which justice could only be done by awarding damages in another exceptions allowed by that case are:

- Where there are conflicting decisions in past Court of Appeal cases, the court can choose which one it will follow and which it will reject.
- Where there is a decision of the House of Lords which effectively overrules a Court of Appeal decision, the Court of Appeal must follow the decision of the House of Lords.
- Where the decision was made *per incuriam*, that is carelessly or by mistake because a relevant Act of Parliament or other regulation has not been considered by the court.

The rule in *Young's case* was confirmed in *Davis v Johnson* (1979). The Court of Appeal refused to follow a decision made only days earlier regarding the interpretation of the Domestic Violence and Matriminial Proceedings Act 1976. The case went to the House of Lords on appeal where the Law Lords, despite agreeing with the actual interpretation of the law, ruled that the Court of Appeal had to follow its own previous decisions and said that they 'expressly, unequivocally and unanimously reaffirmed the rule in *Young v Bristol Aeroplane*'.

Since this case the Court of Appeal has not challenged the rule in *Young's* case, though it has made some use of the *per incuriam* exception allowed by *Young's* case. For example in *Williams v Fawcett* (1986) the Court refused to follow previous decisions because these had been based on a misunderstanding of the County Court rules dealing with the procedure for committing to prison those who break court undertakings. In *Rickards v Rickards* (1989) the court refused to follow a case it had decided in 1981. This was because of the fact that, in the previous case, it had misunderstood the effect of a House of Lords' decision. Even though the court did not follow its

Activity

Read the following comments by Lord Scarman in his judgment in *Tiverton Estates Ltd v Wearwell Ltd* (1975) and answer the questions below.

'The Court of Appeal occupies a central, but intermediate position in our legal system. To a large extent, the consistency and certainty of the law depend upon it . . . If, therefore, one division of the court should refuse to follow another because it believed the other's decision to be wrong, there would be a risk of confusion and doubt arising where there should be consistency and certainty.

The appropriate forum for the correction of the Court of Appeal's errors is the House of Lords, where the decision will at least have the merit of being final and binding, subject only to the House's power to review its own decisions. The House of Lords as the court of last resort needs this power of review; it does not follow that an intermediate court needs it.'

Questions

1. Why did Lord Scarman describe the Court of Appeal as occupying 'a central but intermediate position'?

2. Do you agree with his view that there would be a 'risk of confusion and doubt' if the Court of Appeal was not obliged to follow its own past decisions?

3. Describe the situations in which the Court of Appeal may refuse to follow its own past decisions.

4. Why does the House of Lords need the power of review?

Key facts

General rules for Court of Appeal	Comment
Bound by European Court of Justice	Since 1972 all courts in England and Wales are bound by the European Court of Justice.
Bound by House of Lords	This is because the House of Lords is above the Court of Appeal in the court hierarchy. Also necessary for certainty in the law. Court of Appeal tried to challenge this rule in *Broome v Cassell* (1971) and also in *Miliangos* (1976). The House of Lords rejected this challenge. The Court of Appeal must follow decisions of the House of Lords.
Bound by its own past decisions	Decided by the Court of Appeal in *Young's* case (1944), though there are minor exceptions (see below). In *Davis v Johnson* (1979) the Court of Appeal tried to challenge this rule but the House of Lords confirmed that the Court of Appeal had to follow its own previous decisions.
Exceptions	**Comment**
Exceptions in *Young*'s case	Court of Appeal need not follow its own previous decisions where: ● there are conflicting past decisions ● there is a House of Lords' decision which effectively overrules the Court of Appeal decision ● the decision was made *per incuriam* (in error).
Limitation of *per incuriam*	Only used in 'rare and exceptional cases' (*Rickards v Rickards* (1989)).
Special exception for the Criminal Division	If the law has been 'misapplied or misunderstood' (*R v Gould* (1968)).

Figure 14.4 Key facts chart for the Court of Appeal and the doctrine of precedent

own previous decision Lord Donaldson said that it would only be in 'rare and exceptional cases' that the Court of Appeal would be justified in refusing to follow a previous decision. *Rickards v Rickards* was considered a 'rare and exceptional' case because the mistake was over the critical point of whether the court had power to hear that particular type of case. Also it was very unlikely that the case would be appealed to the House of Lords.

14.4.4 The Court of Appeal (Criminal Division)

The Criminal Division, as well as using the exceptions from *Young's* case, can also refuse to follow a past decision of its own if the law has been 'misapplied or misunderstood'. This extra exception arises because in criminal cases people's liberty is involved. This idea was recognised in *R v Taylor* (1950). The same point was made in *R v Gould* (1968). Also in *R v Spencer* (1985) the judges said that there should not in general be any difference in the way that precedent was followed in the Criminal Division and in the Civil Division, 'save that we must remember that we may be dealing with the liberty of the subject and if a departure from authority is necessary in the interests of justice to an appellant, then this court should not shrink from so acting'.

14.5 The Judicial Committee of the Privy Council

The Judicial Committee of the Privy Council hears appeals from some Commonwealth countries and from places such as the Channel Islands.

14.5.1 Judges

The judges include the Law Lords and also judges who have held high judicial office in countries which still use it as their final court of appeal. Normally a panel of five judges sits to hear an appeal. There can, however, be more judges on the panel where the case is particularly important.

14.5.2 The Privy Council and precedent

The Judicial Committee of the Privy Council is not part of the English legal system and its decisions are not binding on English courts. However, its decisions are persuasive precedent which courts in England and Wales may decide to follow.

Normally the Judicial Committee of the Privy Council will follow decisions of the House of Lords. The exception to this is where the point of law has developed differently in the country from which the appeal has come. In such a situation the court is not bound by House of Lords' decisions and can decide to follow the law of the particular country.

An unusual case was *A-G for Jersey v Holley* (2005), which was an appeal from Jersey on the law of provocation (a special partial defence to murder). An extra large panel of nine judges, all of whom were also Law Lords, was used to decide the case. They refused, by a majority of six judges to three, to follow a previous decision by the House of Lords in *R v Smith (Morgan James)* (2000), even though the law in Jersey was the same as in England. The judges in the majority actually said that the decision in *Smith* was wrong.

This created problems when the same point of law came before the Court of Appeal (Criminal Division) in a later case. Should the Court of Appeal follow the House of Lords' decision in *Smith* or should it follow the Privy Council decision in *Holley*? Normally the Court of Appeal would be bound by any decision of the House of Lords. However, the Court of Appeal took the unusual decision to follow the ruling by the Privy Council rather than that of the House of Lords. This was mainly because the decision in *Holley* was made by six judges from the House of Lords, even though the case was actually dealt with by the Privy Council.

14.6 Distinguishing, overruling and reversing

14.6.1 Distinguishing

This is a method which can be used by a judge to avoid following a past decision which he would otherwise have to follow. It means that the judge finds that the material facts of the case he is deciding are sufficiently different for him to draw a distinction between the present case and the previous precedent. He is not then bound by the previous case.

Two cases demonstrating this process are *Balfour v Balfour* (1919) and *Merritt v Merritt* (1971). Both cases involved a wife making a claim against her husband for breach of contract. In *Balfour* it was decided that the claim could not succeed because there was no intention to create legal relations; there was merely a domestic arrangement between a husband and wife and so there was no legally binding contract. The second case was successful because the court held that the facts of the two cases were sufficiently different in that, although the parties were husband and wife, the agreement was made after they had separated. Furthermore the agreement was made in writing. This distinguished the case from *Balfour*; the agreement in *Merritt* was not just a domestic arrangement but meant as a legally enforceable contract.

14.6.2 Overruling

This is where a court in a later case states that the legal rule decided in an earlier case is wrong. Overruling may occur when a higher court overrules a decision made in an earlier case by a lower court, for example the House of Lords overruling a decision of the Court of Appeal. It can also occur where the European Court of Justice overrules a past decision it has made; or when the House of Lords uses its power under the Practice Statement to overrule a past decision of its own.

An example of this was seen in *Pepper v Hart* (1993) when the House of Lords ruled that *Hansard* (the record of what is said in Parliament) could be consulted when trying to decide what certain words in an Act of Parliament meant. This decision overruled the earlier decision in *Davis v Johnson* (1979) when the House of Lords had held that it could not consult *Hansard*.

14.6.3 Reversing

This is where a court higher up in the hierarchy overturns the decision of a lower court on appeal in the same case. For example, the Court of Appeal may disagree with the legal ruling of the High Court and come to a different view of the law; in this situation they reverse the decision made by the High Court.

14.7 Judicial law-making

Although there used to be a school of thought that judges did not actually 'make' new law but merely declared what the law had always been, today it is well recognised that judges do use precedent to create new law and to extend old principles. There are many areas of law which owe their existence to decisions by the judges.

Law of contract

Nearly all the main rules which govern the formation of contracts come from decided cases.

Many of the decisions were made in the nineteenth century, but they still affect the law today.

Tort of negligence

The law of negligence in the law of tort is another major area which has been developed and refined by judicial decisions. An important starting point in this area of law was the case of *Donoghue v Stevenson* (1932) in which the House of Lords, when recognising that a manufacturer owed a duty of care to the 'ultimate consumer', created what is known as the 'neighbour test'. Lord Atkin in his judgment in the case said: 'You must take reasonable care to avoid acts or omissions which you can reasonably foresee would be likely to injure your neighbour.' This concept has been applied by judges in several different situations, so that the tort of negligence has developed into a major tort.

There have also been major developments in case-law on liability for nervous shock where there has been negligence. The House of Lords laid down the guidelines for this area of law in the case of *Alcock v Chief Constable of South Yorkshire* (1991) which involved claims made by people who had lost relatives in the Hillsborough tragedy.

Criminal law

In criminal law the judges have played a major role in developing the law on intention. For example, it is only because of judicial decisions that the intention for murder covers not only the intention to kill but also the intention to cause grievous bodily harm. Judicial decisions have also effectively created new crimes, as in *Shaw v DPP* (1962) which created the offence of conspiracy to corrupt public morals and *R v R* (1991) when it was decided that rape within marriage could be a crime.

However, there have been cases in which the House of Lords has refused to change the law, saying that such a change should only be made

Comment

Should judges make law?

It is argued that it is wrong for judges to make law. Their job is to apply the law. It is for Parliament to make the law. Parliament is elected to do this but judges are not. This means that law-making by judges is undemocratic.

But, in reality judges have to make law in some situations. The first is where a case involves a legal point which has never been decided before. As there is no law on it, the judge in the case has to make a decision. After all, the parties in the case would not want the judge to refuse to deal with the case; they want the matter decided.

The second area is more controversial. This is where judges overrule old cases and in doing so create new law. It is important for the law to be updated in this way. Law for the twenty first century needs to be based on today's society and values. Law decided a hundred years or more ago may no longer be suitable. Ideally, Parliament should reform the law, but Parliament is sometimes slow to do this. If judges never overruled old cases, then the law might be 'out of date'.

An example of this is the case of *R v R* (1991). In this case a man was charged with raping his wife. The point the court had to decide was whether, by being married, a woman automatically consented to sex with her husband and could never say 'no'. The old law dated back to 1736 when it was said that 'by their mutual matrimonial consent the wife hath given up her herself in this kind to her husband, which she cannot retract'. In other words, once married, a woman was always assumed to consent and could not go back on this. This was still held to be the law in *R v Miller* (1954), even though the wife had already started divorce proceedings. Parliament had not done anything to reform this law.

So, when the case of *R v R* came before the courts, the judges had to decide whether to follow the old law, or whether they should change the law to match the ideas of the late twentieth century. In the House of Lords, the judges pointed out that 'the status of women and the status of a married woman in our law have changed quite dramatically. A husband and wife are now for all practical purposes equal partners in marriage'. As a result it was decided that if a wife did not consent to sex then her husband could be guilty of rape. The House of Lords stated that the common law (judge-made law) 'is capable of evolving in the light of changing social, economic and cultural developments'. This clearly recognises that judges in the House of Lords can, and will, change the law if they think it necessary.

by Parliament. This happened in *C v DPP* (1995) when it refused to abolish the presumption that children between 10 and 14 were incapable of having the necessary intention to commit a crime. (This presumption meant that there always had to be evidence that the child knew he or she was doing something which was seriously wrong.) In fact the Government did change the law later in the Crime and Disorder Act 1998.

Key facts

Concept	Definition	Comment
stare decisis	Stand by what has been decided	Follow the law decided in previous cases for certainty and fairness
ratio decidendi	Reason for deciding	The part of the judgment which creates the law
obiter dicta	Others things said	The other parts of the judgment – these do not create law
binding precedent	A previous decision which has to be followed	Decisions of higher courts bind lower courts
persuasive precedent	A previous decision which does not have to be followed	The court may be 'persuaded' that the same legal decision should be made
original precedent	A decision in a case where there is no previous legal decision or law for the judge to use	This leads to judges 'making' law
distinguishing	A method of avoiding a previous decision because facts in the present case are different	eg *Balfour v Balfour* not followed in *Merritt v Merritt*
overruling	A decision which states that a legal rule in an earlier case is wrong	eg in *Pepper v Hart* the House of Lords overruled *Davis v Johnson* on the use of *Hansard*
reversing	Where a higher court in the same case overturns the decision of the lower court	This can only happen if there is an appeal in the case

Figure 14.5 Key facts chart for Precedent and Acts of Parliament

14.8 Precedent and Acts of Parliament

Although judges can and do make law, precedent is subordinate to statute law, delegated legislation and European regulations. This means that if (for example) an Act of Parliament is passed and that Act contains a provision which contradicts a previously decided case, that case decision will cease to have effect; the Act of Parliament is now the law on that point. This happened when Parliament passed the Law Reform (Year and a Day Rule) Act in 1996. Up to then judicial decisions meant that a person could only be charged with murder or manslaughter if the victim died within a year and a day of receiving his injuries. The Act enacted that there was no time limit, and a person could be guilty even if the victim died several years later, so cases after 1996 follow the Act and not the old judicial decisions.

14.9 Advantages and disadvantages of precedent

As can be seen from the previous sections there are both advantages and disadvantages to the way in which judicial precedent operates in England and Wales. In fact it could be said that every advantage has a corresponding disadvantage.

14.9.1 Advantages

The main advantages are:

1. Certainty
   Because the courts follow past decisions, people know what the law is and how it is likely to be applied in their case; it allows lawyers to advise clients on the likely outcome of cases; it also allows people to operate their businesses knowing that financial and other arrangements they make are recognised by law. The House of Lords' Practice Statement points out how important certainty is.

2. Consistency and fairness in the law
   It is seen as just and fair that similar cases should be decided in a similar way, just as in any sport it is seen as fair that the rules of the game apply equally to each side. The law must be consistent if it is to be credible.

3. Precision
   As the principles of law are set out in actual cases the law becomes very precise; it is well illustrated and gradually builds up through the different variations of facts in the cases that come before the courts.

4. Flexibility
   There is room for the law to change as the House of Lords can use the Practice Statement to overrule cases. The ability to distinguish cases also gives all courts some freedom to avoid past decisions and develop the law. However, the system could be made more flexible if the English courts adopt the same attitude to precedent as in some other countries. For example, in the United States of America a previous precedent is likely to be ignored if it fails to meet with academic approval. In other words, if there is considerable criticism of the decision by leading academic lawyers, judges in later cases are likely to take note of that criticism and rule differently. This has happened in England in the case of *R v Shivpuri* (1986), but this was a rare happening, while in America it occurs more frequently.

5. Time-saving
   Precedent can be considered a useful time-saving device. Where a principle has been established, cases with similar facts are unlikely to go through the lengthy process of litigation.

The main advantages have been summed up very neatly as follows:

> The main advantages of the precedent system are said to be certainty, precision and flexibility. Legal certainty is achieved in theory at least, in that if the legal problem raised has been solved before, the judge is bound to adopt that solution. Precision is achieved by the sheer volume of reported cases containing solutions to innumerable factual situations. No code or statute could ever contain as much.
>
> Flexibility is achieved by the possibility of decisions being overruled and by the possibility of distinguishing and confining the operation of decisions which appear unsound.

14.9.2 Disadvantages

However, there are disadvantages as follows:

1. Rigidity
   The fact that lower courts have to follow decisions of higher courts, together with the fact that the Court of Appeal has to follow its own past decisions, can make the law too inflexible so that bad decisions made in the past may be perpetuated. There is the added problem that so few cases go to the House of Lords. Change in the law will only take place if parties have the courage, the persistence and the money to appeal their case.

2. Complexity
   Since there are nearly half a million reported cases it is not easy to find all the relevant case law even with computerised databases.

Another problem is in the judgments themselves, which are often very long with no clear distinction between comments and the reasons for the decision. This makes it difficult in some cases to extract the *ratio decidendi*; indeed in *Dodd's Case* (1973) the judges in the Court of Appeal said they were unable to find the *ratio* in a decision of the House of Lords.

3. Illogical distinctions
   The use of distinguishing to avoid past decisions can lead to 'hair-splitting' so that some areas of the law have become very complex. The differences between some cases may be very small and appear illogical.

4. Slowness of growth
   Judges are well aware that some areas of the law are unclear or in need of reform; however, they cannot make a decision unless there is a case before the courts to be decided. This is one of the criticisms of the need for the Court of Appeal to follow its own previous decisions, as only about 50 cases go to the House of Lords each year. There may be a long wait for a suitable case to be appealed as far as the House of Lords.

14.10 Law reporting

In order to follow past decisions there must be an accurate record of what those decisions were. Written reports have existed in England and Wales since the thirteenth century, but many of the early reports were very brief and, it is thought, not always accurate. The earliest reports from about 1275 to 1535 were called Year Books, and contained short reports of cases, usually written in French. From 1535 to 1865 cases were reported by individuals who made a business out of selling the reports to lawyers. The detail and accuracy of these reports varied enormously. However, some are still occasionally used today.

In 1865 the Incorporated Council of Law

Reporting was set up – this was controlled by the courts. Reports became accurate, with the judgment usually noted down word for word. This accuracy of reports was one of the factors in the development of the strict doctrine of precedent. These reports still exist and are published according to the court that the case took place in. For example, case references abbreviated to 'Ch' stand for 'Chancery' and the case will have been decided in the Chancery Division; while 'QB' stands for 'Queen's Bench Division'.

There are also other well-established reports today, notably the All England series (abbreviated to 'All ER') and the Weekly Law Reports ('WLR'). Newspapers and journals also publish law reports, but these are often abbreviated versions in which the law reporter has tried to pick out the essential parts of the judgment.

14.10.1 Internet law reports

All High Court, Court of Appeal and House of Lords cases are now reported on the Internet. Some websites give the full report free; others give summaries or an index of cases. There are also subscription sites which give a very comprehensive service of law reports.

@ **Internet Research**

Search at least one website address and find a recent law report. Some suggestions for websites are given below.

www.lawreports.co.uk gives summaries of important cases in its Daily Law Notes section

www.parliament.uk gives reports of House of Lords cases

www.bailii.org has cases from the Court of Appeal and below.

Examination Questions

Read the source material below and answer the questions which follow.

Lord Denning carried on a one-man campaign to secure a change of practice in the Court of Appeal. The attack was on two fronts. First, he asserted that the Court of Appeal was no longer bound by decisions of the House of Lords. Second, he claimed that the Court of Appeal was no longer bound to follow its own decisions as a general rule, and not just in the exceptional circumstances laid down in *Young v Bristol Aeroplane* (1944). These exceptions are:

1. Where its own previous decisions conflict, the Court of Appeal must decide which to follow and which to reject.

2. The Court of Appeal must follow a later decision of the House of Lords if its own previous decision conflicts with it.

3. The Court of Appeal need not follow its own previous decision if it were made *per incuriam* (in error).

Lord Denning's views were based on the Practice Statement itself, which, he alleged, had transformed the *stare decisis* (doctrine of precedent) principle in the Court of Appeal as well as the House of Lords. But this approach ignored the closing words of the Practice Statement that it was not intended to affect the use of precedent anywhere other than in the House of Lords.

Adapted from *The English Legal Process*,
Terence Ingham

Answer all parts

(a) Using the source and other cases, describe the powers of the Court of Appeal.

(b) Consider each of the following situations and explain whether or not the Court of Appeal can depart from the previous decision.

(i) A case concerning a death resulting from medical negligence was heard by the Court of Appeal (Civil Division). A year later, a similar issue is being heard by the Court of Appeal (Criminal Division).

(ii) A case concerning breach of contract was decided by the Court of Appeal (Civil Division). Days later a similar issue is heard by the same court but the judges now feel that the decision should be different.

(iii) A case concerning murder was decided by the House of Lords. The Court of Appeal (Criminal Division) believes the decision of the House of Lords is out of date.

(c) (i) The source refers to *stare decisis*.

Describe the concept of *stare decisis* using the source and cases to illustrate your answer.

(ii) Discuss whether or not the powers of the Court of Appeal within the doctrine of precedent should be extended.

OCR G142 June 2007

Chapter 15

Acts of Parliament

I n today's world there is often a need for new law to meet new situations. Clearly, the method of judicial law-making through precedents is not suitable for major changes to the law, nor is it a sufficiently quick, efficient law-making method for a modern society. The other point to be made is that judges are not elected by the people, and in a democracy, the view is that laws should only be made by the elected representatives of society. So, today, the main legislative body in the United Kingdom is Parliament.

Laws passed by Parliament are known as Acts of Parliament or statutes, and this source of law is usually referred to as 'statute law'. About 60–70 Acts are passed each year. In addition to Parliament as a whole enacting law, power is delegated to Government Ministers and their departments to make detailed rules and regulations, which supplement Acts of Parliament. These regulations are delegated legislation (see Chapter 16) and are called statutory instruments.

15.1 Parliament

Parliament consists of the House of Commons and the House of Lords. Under the normal procedure both Houses must vote in favour of a Bill before it can become a new Act of Parliament.

15.1.1 The House of Commons

The people who sit in the House of Commons are referred to as Members of Parliament (MPs). These members of the House of Commons are elected by the public, with the country being divided into constituencies and each of these returning one Member of Parliament (MP). There

The Houses of Parliament

must be a general election at least once every five years, though such an election can be called sooner by the Prime Minister. In addition, there may be individual by-elections in constituencies where the MP has died or retired during the current session of Parliament. The Government of the day is formed by the political party which has a majority in the House of Commons.

15.1.2 The House of Lords

At the end of 2007 the House of Lords consisted of:

- 92 hereditary peers
- life peers
- the judges who are the Law Lords
- the most senior bishops in the Church of England.

Originally most of the members of the House of Lords were hereditary peers. During the twentieth century the awarding of a title for life (a life peerage) became more common. The Prime Minister nominated people who should receive a

title for their lifetime, but this title would not pass on to their children. The title was then awarded by the Monarch. In this way people who had served the country and were thought to be suitable members of the House of Lords were able to bring their expertise to the House. Most life peerages were given to former politicians who had retired from the House of Commons. For example, Margaret Thatcher, who had been Prime Minister in the 1980s, was made a life peer.

15.1.3 Reform of the House of Lords

By 1999, there were over 1,100 members of the House of Lords, of whom 750 were hereditary peers. The Labour Government decided that in a modern society an inherited title should not automatically allow someone to participate in making law. They felt that some of the members should be elected and some should be nominated. To help decide exactly what reforms should be made, a Royal Commission (known as the Wakeham Commission) was set up to consider how members of the House of Lords should be selected. In the meantime the right of most of the hereditary peers to sit in the House of Lords was abolished in November 1999. Only 92 hereditary peers were allowed to continue to be members of the House of Lords.

The Wakeham Commission reported in 2000 and recommended that one-third of the House should be elected. Also, that there should be a limit on the system of political patronage whereby the Prime Minister nominates people to the House of Lords. The Commission recommended that an independent Appointments Commission could reject poorly qualified nominees and also be able to appoint 'people's peers'.

In 2001 some so-called people's peers were appointed to the House of Lords by the Prime Minister. These were supposed to be ordinary people who had been recommended by other ordinary people. However, the list was mainly of already famous people, rather than 'Mr Joe Public'.

This was meant to be a temporary solution while the Government consulted on the final make-up of the House of Lords. However, there have been major disagreements about how many of the House of Lords should be elected by the general public and how many should be nominated (and by whom). As a result the reform of the House of Lords has not been completed.

Judges in the House of Lords

The most senior court in England and Wales is also usually referred to as the House of Lords. In fact its full title is the Judicial Committee of the House of Lords. Only the 12 Law Lords are allowed to sit on this judicial committee. Take care not to confuse the House of Lords in its legislative (law-making) function with the House of Lords as an appeal court.

It is agreed that judges should not sit as part of Parliament. So a new Supreme Court will replace the Judicial Committee of the House of Lords. When this court starts work, probably in 2009, the judges will cease to be members of the House of Lords and will no longer sit in Parliament.

15.2 Influences on parliamentary law-making

15.2.1 The Government programme

When a Government is formed, it will have a programme of reforms it wishes to carry out. These will have been set out in its party manifesto on which it asked people to vote for it in the General Election. Also, at the start of each parliamentary session, the Government announces (in the Queen's Speech) what particular laws it intends introducing during that session. So most new legislation is likely to arise from Government policy.

15.2.2 European Union law

However, there are other influences on what law is enacted: European Union law can lead to new Acts of Parliament which are passed in order to bring our law in line with the European law. This may be to implement a specific European Regulation or Directive, as in the case of the Consumer Protection Act 1987, or because a decision of the European Court of Justice has shown that our law does not conform with the Treaty of Rome, as with the Sex Discrimination Act 1986. The effect of European law is considered in more detail in Chapter 18.

15.2.3 Other influences

Other outside influences include proposals for law reform put forward by law reform agencies, commissions or inquiries into the effectiveness of existing law. These law reform agencies are dealt with in detail in Chapter 19. In addition specific events may also play a role in formulating the law. A particularly tragic example was the massacre in March 1996 of 16 young children and their teacher in Dunblane by a lone gunman. After this there was an inquiry into the laws on gun-ownership. By March 1997 Parliament passed the Firearms (Amendment) Act 1997 banning private ownership of most handguns.

Another major example of an event leading to new law was the terrorist attack on the Twin Towers in New York in September 2001. (This is often referred to as '9/11'.) Following this our Parliament passed the Anti-Terrorism, Crime and Security Act 2001.

Pressure groups may also cause the Government to reconsider the law on certain areas. This was seen in 1994 when the Government agreed to reduce the age of consent for homosexual acts in private from 21 to 18. Then in 2000 the age of consent was further reduced to 16. Another clear example of the Government bowing to public opinion and the efforts of pressure groups was the introduction of the Disability Discrimination Act 1995. This Act gave disabled people certain rights in relation to employment. It also stated that they should have access to shops and hotels and other services.

The Civil Partnership Act 2004 gave the right to same-sex couples to register their partnership and have a civil ceremony. This was the result of changing attitudes to same-sex partnerships.

15.3 The pre-legislative process

On major matters a Green Paper may be issued by the Minister with responsibility for that matter. A Green Paper is a consultative document on a

Activity

Read the following article and answer the questions below.

Judge reprieves Dempsey, the harmless pit bull

A High Court judge, who reprieved a pit bull terrier from death row yesterday, savaged the Dangerous Dogs Act (1991) which he said would have sent a 'perfectly inoffensive animal to the gas chamber'.

Dempsey, dubbed Britain's most expensive dog after a long legal battle to save her, will be returned to her overjoyed owner after Lord Justice Staughton and Mr Justice Rougier quashed a destruction order by Ealing Magistrates' Court in 1992.

Dempsey's only crime was being the wrong kind of dog, Judge Rougier said. Magistrates sentenced her to be destroyed after the nephew of her owner, Dianne Fanneran, took her muzzle off in public when she became ill, and she was spotted by a policeman.

Mr Justice Rougier said: 'It seems to me that, while acknowledging the need to protect the public . . . the Dangerous Dogs Act bears all the hallmarks of an ill-thought-out piece of legislation, no doubt drafted in response to another pressure group . . . '

The Act was rushed through in 1991 by the then Home Secretary, Kenneth Baker, after pit bull terriers attacked a man in Lincoln and a 6-year-old girl in Bradford. It requires them to be put down unless they are neutered, tattooed, microchipped, registered, muzzled and kept on a lead in public.

Taken from an article by Clare Dyer
in *The Guardian*, 23 November 1995

Questions

1. Why was the Dangerous Dogs Act 1991 passed?

2. Why was Dempsey in breach of the Act?

3. What did Mr Justice Rougier say about the Act?

4. How might this problem with the Act have been avoided by the Government when formulating the legislation?

topic in which the Government's view is put forward with proposals for law reform. Interested parties are then invited to send comments to the relevant Government Department, so that a full consideration of all sides can be made and necessary changes made to the Government's proposals. Following this the Government will publish a White Paper with its firm proposals for new law.

Consultation before any new law is framed is valuable as it allows time for mature consideration. Governments have been criticised for sometimes responding in a 'knee-jerk' fashion to incidents and, as a result, rushing law through that has subsequently proved to be unworkable. This occurred with the Dangerous Dogs Act 1991.

15.4 Introducing an Act of Parliament

The great majority of Acts of Parliament are introduced by the Government – these are initially drafted by lawyers in the civil service who are known as Parliamentary Counsel to the Treasury. Instructions as to what is to be included and the effect the proposed law is intended to have are given by the Government Department responsible for it.

15.4.1 Bills

When the proposed Act has been drafted it is published, and at this stage is called a Bill. It will only become an Act of Parliament if it successfully completes all the necessary stages in Parliament. Even at this early stage there are difficulties, as the draftsmen face problems in trying to frame the Bill. It has to be drawn up so that it represents the Government's wishes, while at the same time using correct legal wording so that there will not be any difficulties in the courts applying it. It must be unambiguous, precise and comprehensive. Achieving all of these is not easy, and there may be unforeseen problems with the language used, as discussed in the chapter on

statutory interpretation. On top of this there is usually pressure on time, as the Government will have a timetable of when they wish to introduce the draft Bill into Parliament.

15.4.2 Private Members' Bills

Ballot

Bills can also be sponsored by individual MPs. The parliamentary process allows for a ballot each parliamentary session in which 20 private members are selected who can then take their turn in presenting a Bill to Parliament. The time for debate of Private Members' Bills is limited, usually only being debated on Fridays, so that only the first six or seven members in the ballot have a realistic chance of introducing a Bill on their chosen topic.

Relatively few Private Members' Bills become law, but there have been some important laws passed as the result of such Bills. A major example was the Abortion Act 1967 which legalised abortion in this country. More recent examples are the Marriage Act 1994, which was introduced by Giles Brandreth, the MP for Chester. This allowed people to marry in any registered place, not only in Register Offices or religious buildings. Another example is the Household Waste Recycling Act 2003 which places local authorities under a duty to recycle waste.

10-minute rule

Backbenchers can also try to introduce a Bill through the '10-minute' rule, under which any MP can make a speech of up to 10 minutes supporting the introduction of new legislation. This method is rarely successful unless there is no opposition to the Bill, but some Acts of Parliament have been introduced in this way, for example the Bail (Amendment) Act 1993 which gave the prosecution the right to appeal against the granting of bail to a defendant. Members of the House of Lords can also introduce Private Members' Bills.

Public Bills

A public Bill involves matters of public policy which will affect either the whole country or a large section of it. Most of the Government Bills are in this category, for example the Constitutional Reform Act 2005 or the Legal Services Act 2007 which will probably be an Act by the time this book is published.

Private Bills

A small number of Bills are designed to pass a law which will affect only individual people or corporations. These do not affect the whole community. They are known as Private Bills. A recent example of such a Bill as this was the Whitehaven Harbour Bill which was passed by Parliament and is now the Whitehaven Harbour Act 2007. This transferred all rights and obligations in respect of the harbour from three separate companies to the Whitehaven Harbour Commissioners.

15.5 The process in Parliament

In order to become an Act of Parliament, the Bill will usually have to be passed by both Houses of Parliament, and in each House there is a long and complex process (see Figure 15.1). A Bill may start in either the House of Commons or the House of Lords, with the exception of finance Bills which must start in the House of Commons. All Bills must go through the stages explained below:

First Reading

This is a formal procedure where the name and main aims of the Bill are read out. Usually no discussion takes place, but there will be a vote on whether the House wishes to consider the Bill further. The vote may be verbal: this is when the Speaker of the House asks the members as a whole how they vote and the members shout out 'Aye' or 'No'. If it is clear that nearly all members are in agreement, either for or against, there is no need for a more formal vote. If it is not possible to

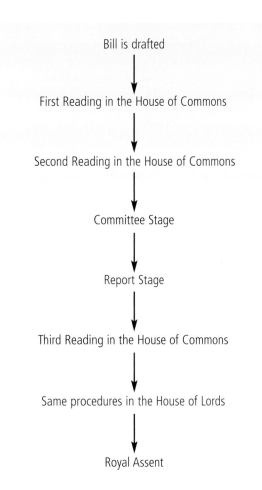

Figure 15.1 Flow chart of the passing of an Act of Parliament starting in the House of Commons

judge whether more people are shouting 'Aye' or 'No' there will be a formal vote in which the members of the House vote by leaving the Chamber and then walking back in through one of two special doors on one side or the other of the Chamber. There will be two 'tellers' positioned at each of these two voting doors to make a list of the Members voting on each side. These tellers count up the number of MPs who voted for and against and declare these numbers to the Speaker in front of the members of the House.

Second Reading

This is the main debate on the whole Bill in which MPs debate the principles behind the Bill.

The debate usually focuses on the main principles rather than the smaller details. Those MPs who wish to speak in the debate must catch the Speaker's eye, since the Speaker controls all debates and no-one may speak without being called on by the Speaker. At the end of this a vote is taken in the same way as for the First Reading; obviously there must be a majority in favour for the Bill to progress any further.

Committee Stage

At this stage a detailed examination of each clause of the Bill is undertaken by a committee of between 16 and 50 MPs. This is usually done by what is called a Standing Committee, which, contrary to its name, is a committee chosen specifically for that Bill. The membership of such a committee is decided 'having regard to the qualifications of those members nominated and to the composition of the House'. So, although the Government will have a majority, the opposition and minority parties are represented proportionately to the number of seats they have in the House of Commons. The members of Parliament nominated for each Standing Committee will usually be those with a special interest in, or knowledge of, the subject of the Bill which is being considered. For finance Bills the whole House will sit in committee.

Report Stage

At the Committee stage amendments to various clauses in the Bill may have been voted on and passed, so this report stage is where the committee report back to the House on those amendments. (If there were no amendments at the Committee stage, there will not be a 'Report' stage – instead the Bill will go straight on to the Third Reading.) The amendments will be debated in the House and accepted or rejected. Further amendments may also be added. The Report stage has been described as 'a useful safeguard against a small Committee amending a Bill against the wishes of the House, and a necessary opportunity for second thoughts'.

Third Reading

This is the final vote on the Bill. It is almost a formality since a Bill which has passed through all the stages above is unlikely to fail at this late stage. In fact in the House of Commons there will only be an actual further debate on the Bill as a whole if at least six MPs request it. However, in the House of Lords there may sometimes be amendments made at this stage.

The House of Lords

If the Bill started life in the House of Commons it is now passed to the House of Lords where it goes through the same five stages outlined above and, if the House of Lords makes amendments to the Bill, then it will go back to the House of Commons for it to consider those amendments. If the Bill started in the House of Lords then it passes to the House of Commons.

Royal Assent

The final stage is where the Monarch formally gives approval to the Bill and it then becomes an Act of Parliament. This is now a formality and, under the Royal Assent Act 1961, the Monarch will not even have the text of the Bills to which she is assenting; she will only have the short title. The last time that a Monarch refused assent was in 1707, when Queen Anne refused to assent to the Scottish Militia Bill.

@　**Internet Research**

Look to see what Bills are going through Parliament at the moment. You can find this at **www.parliament.uk**.

Try to find one Bill that is currently going through the House of Commons and a different Bill that is currently going through the House of Lords.

Key facts

Green Paper	Consultation document on possible new law
White Paper	Government's firm proposals for new law
First Reading	Formal introduction of Bill into the House of Commons
Second Reading	Main debate on Bill's principles
Committee Stage	Clause by clause consideration of the Bill by a select committee
Report Stage	Committee reports suggested amendments back to the House of Commons
Third Reading	Final debate on the Bill
Repeat of process in the House of Lords	All stages are repeated BUT if the House of Lords votes against the Bill, it can go back to the House of Commons and, under the Parliament Acts 1911 and 1949, become law if the House of Commons passes it for the second time (rare occurrence)
Royal Assent	A formality – normally Acts of Parliament come into force at midnight after receiving the Royal Assent

Figure 15.2 Key facts chart for the legislative process

15.5.1 The Parliament Acts 1911 and 1949

The power of the House of Lords to reject a Bill is limited by the Parliament Acts 1911 and 1949. These allow a Bill to become law even if the House of Lords rejects it, provided that the Bill is re-introduced into the House of Commons in the next session of Parliament and passes all the stages again there.

The principle behind the Parliament Acts is that the House of Lords is not an elected body, and its function is to refine and add to the law rather than oppose the will of the democratically elected House of Commons. In fact there have only been four occasions when this procedure has been used to by-pass the House of Lords after they had voted against a Bill. Since 1949 the Parliament Acts have only been used on four occasions. These were for the:

- War Crimes Act 1991
- European Parliamentary Elections Act 1999
- Sexual Offences (Amendment) Act 2000
- Hunting Act 2004.

15.5.2 Commencement of an Act

Following the Royal Assent the Act of Parliament will come into force on midnight of that day, unless another date has been set. However, there has been a growing trend for Acts of Parliament not to be implemented immediately. Instead, the Act itself states the date when it will commence or passes responsibility on to the appropriate Minister to fix the commencement date. In the latter case the Minister will bring the Act into force by issuing a commencement order. This can cause problems of uncertainty, as it is difficult to discover which sections of an Act have been brought into force.

It may be that some sections or even a whole Act will never become law. An example of this is the Easter Act 1928, which was intended to fix the date of Easter Day. Although this Act passed all the necessary parliamentary stages, and was given the Royal Assent, it has never come into force.

It can be seen that with all these stages it usually takes several months for a Bill to be passed. However, there have been occasions

ELIZABETH II   c. **19**

Law Reform (Year and a Day Rule) Act 1996

1996 CHAPTER 19

An Act to abolish the "year and a day rule" and, in consequence of its abolition, to impose a restriction on the institution in certain circumstances of proceedings for a fatal offence. [17th June 1996]

B E IT ENACTED by the Queen's most Excellent Majesty, by and with the advice and consent of the Lords Spiritual and Temporal, and Commons, in this present Parliament assembled, and by the authority of the same, as follows:—

1. The rule known as the "year and a day rule" (that is, the rule that, for the purposes of offences involving death and of suicide, an act or omission is conclusively presumed not to have caused a person's death if more than a year and a day elapsed before he died) is abolished for all purposes.

Abolition of "year and a day rule".

2.—(1) Proceedings to which this section applies may only be instituted by or with the consent of the Attorney General.

Restriction on institution of proceedings for a fatal offence.

(2) This section applies to proceedings against a person for a fatal offence if—

    (a) the injury alleged to have caused the death was sustained more than three years before the death occurred, or

    (b) the person has previously been convicted of an offence committed in circumstances alleged to be connected with the death.

(3) In subsection (2) "fatal offence" means—

    (a) murder, manslaughter, infanticide or any other offence of which one of the elements is causing a person's death, or

    (b) the offence of aiding, abetting, counselling or procuring a person's suicide.

2   c. **19**   *Law Reform (Year and a Day Rule) Act 1996*

(4) No provision that proceedings may be instituted only by or with the consent of the Director of Public Prosecutions shall apply to proceedings to which this section applies.

(5) In the application of this section to Northern Ireland—

(a) the reference in subsection (1) to the Attorney General is to the Attorney General for Northern Ireland, and

(b) the reference in subsection (4) to the Director of Public Prosecutions is to the Director of Public Prosecutions for Northern Ireland.

Short title, commencement and extent.

3.—(1) This Act may be cited as the Law Reform (Year and a Day Rule) Act 1996.

(2) Section 1 does not affect the continued application of the rule referred to in that section to a case where the act or omission (or the last of the acts or omissions) which caused the death occurred before the day on which this Act is passed.

(3) Section 2 does not come into force until the end of the period of two months beginning with the day on which this Act is passed; but that section applies to the institution of proceedings after the end of that period in any case where the death occurred during that period (as well as in any case where the death occurred after the end of that period).

(4) This Act extends to England and Wales and Northern Ireland.

© Crown copyright 1996

PRINTED IN THE UNITED KINGDOM BY MIKE LYNN
Controller and Chief Executive of Her Majesty's Stationery Office
and Queen's Printer of Acts of Parliament

Figure 15.3 The Law Reform (Year and a Day Rule) Act 1996

where all parties have thought a new law is needed urgently and an Act has been passed in less than 24 hours. This happened with the Northern Ireland Bill in 1972.

15.5.3 Example of an Act

Figure 15.3 is a reproduction of the Law Reform (Year and a Day Rule) Act 1996. This shows what an Act of Parliament looks like. The name of the Act is given immediately under the Royal coat of arms and underneath the name '1996 CHAPTER 19' means that it was the nineteenth Act to be passed in 1996. Next follows a short statement or preamble about the purpose of the Act. Then there is a formal statement showing that the Act has been passed by both Houses of Parliament

and received the Royal Assent; this is included in all Acts. After this comes the body of the Act, which is set out in sections; this is an unusually short Act as it has only three sections.

Section 1 abolishes the 'year and a day rule'. Note that the Act actually refers to it in those terms; this is because the rule was a part of the common law and was never written down in any statute. Section 2 sets out when the consent of the Attorney-General is needed before a prosecution can be started. The last section gives the name by which the Act may be cited and it also sets out that the Act does not apply to cases in which the incident which led to death occurred before the Act was passed. Section 3 is concerned with the commencement of the Act; this sets the commencement date for s 2 at two months after the Act is passed. As s 1 is not specifically mentioned, the normal rule that an Act comes into effect on midnight of the date on which it receives the Royal Assent applies to that section.

15.6 Criticisms of the legislative process

There are many criticisms which can be made about the legislative process. The Renton Committee in 1975 said there were four main categories of complaint:

1. The language used in many Acts was obscure and complex.

2. Acts were 'over-elaborate' because draftsmen tried to provide for every contingency.

3. The internal structure of many Acts was illogical with sections appearing to be out of sequence, making it difficult for people to find relevant sections.

4. There was a lack of clear connection between Acts, so that it was not easy to trace all the Acts on a given topic. In addition, the frequent practice of amending small parts of one Act by passing another increased the difficulty of finding out what the law was.

The Committee made 81 recommendations, but only about half of these have been fully implemented.

15.6.1 Lack of accessibility

Ideally, the laws of the land should be easily accessible to citizens but there are some major problems which create difficulties. As already mentioned, it is difficult to discover which Acts and/or which sections have been brought into force.

An example of problems with knowing what sections are in force is the Criminal Justice Act 2003 which has 339 sections and several Schedules. Only 11 sections came into force when the Royal Assent was given. Some more came into force four weeks after the Royal Assent.

 Internet Research

Find the commencement section or schedule in an Act of Parliament.

This can be done on the Internet at **www.opsi.gov.uk**. There is usually a list of contents at the start of an Act.

Many of the other 300-plus sections have been brought into effect a few at a time over a period of time. Five years after the Act was passed, some of the sections had still not been brought into effect.

Where sections are brought into effect at different times, it is difficult to know what the law is. This prevents law from being easily accessible.

15.6.2 Other problems

Many statutes are amended by later statutes so that it is necessary to read two or sometimes more Acts together to make sense of provisions. The law may also be added to by delegated legislation in the form of statutory instruments. All this increases the difficulty of discovering the law that is actually in force.

The language used in Acts is not always easily understood and apart from the obvious difficulties this causes it also results in many cases going to court. In fact about 75 per cent of cases heard by the House of Lords in its judicial capacity each year involve disputes over the interpretation of Acts.

15.7 Parliamentary sovereignty

Parliamentary law is sovereign over other forms of law in England and Wales. This means that an Act of Parliament can completely overrule any custom, judicial precedent, delegated legislation or previous Act of Parliament. This is also referred to as parliamentary supremacy.

The concept of the sovereignty of parliamentary law is based on the idea of democratic law-making. A member of Parliament is elected by the voters in the constituency, so that in theory that MP is participating in the legislative process on the behalf of those voters. However, this is a very simplistic view since:

- MPs usually vote on party lines rather than how their particular constituents wish
- Many MPs are elected by only a very small majority and if there were several candidates in the election, it may well be that the MP was only actually voted for by about 30 per cent or even fewer of the voters
- Parliamentary elections only have to take place once every five years, so that an MP who votes against the wishes of his constituents is not immediately replaced.

In addition, the ideal concept of democracy is lost because much of the drafting of parliamentary law is done by civil servants who are not elected. Finally, there is the point that the House of Lords is not an elected body.

15.7.1 Definition of parliamentary sovereignty

The most widely recognised definition of parliamentary sovereignty or supremacy was given by Dicey in the nineteenth century. He made three main points:

1. Parliament can legislate on any subject-matter
2. No Parliament can be bound by any previous Parliament, nor can a Parliament pass any Act that will bind a later Parliament
3. No other body has the right to override or set aside an Act of Parliament.

Legislating on any subject-matter

There are no limits on what Parliament can make laws about. It can make any law it wants. For example, in the past, Parliament changed the rule on who should succeed to the throne. This was in 1700, when Parliament passed the Act of Settlement which stated that the children of King James II (who were the direct line of the monarchy) could not succeed to the throne.

Parliament can also change its own powers. It did this with the Parliament Acts 1911 and 1949, which placed limits on the right of the House of Lords to block a Bill by voting against it (see section 15.5.1).

Cannot bind successor

Each new Parliament should be free to make or change what laws it wishes. Parliament cannot be bound by a law made by a previous Parliament, and can repeal any previous Act of Parliament.

There are, however, some laws that have become such an important part of the British constitution that they cannot realistically be repealed. For example, the Act of Settlement in 1700 changed the line of succession to the throne. It affected who was entitled to become king or queen. Realistically, after 300 years, this cannot now be repealed.

There are other modern limitations which have been self-imposed by Parliament. These are dealt with in section 15.7.2 below.

Cannot be overruled by others

This rule is kept to even if the Act of Parliament may have been passed because of incorrect information. This was shown by *British Railways Board v Pickin* (1974). A private Act of Parliament, the British Railways Act 1968, was enacted by Parliament. Pickin challenged the Act on the basis that that the British Railways Board had fraudulently concealed certain matters from Parliament. This alleged fraud had led to Parliament passing the Act which had the effect of depriving Pickin of his land or proprietary rights. The action was struck out because no court is entitled to go behind an Act once it has been passed. A challenge cannot be made to an Act of Parliament even if there was fraud.

15.7.2 Limitations on parliamentary sovereignty

There are now some limitations on Parliament's sovereignty, but all these limits have been self-imposed by previous Parliaments. The main limitations are through:

● membership of the European Union
● the effect of the Human Rights Act 1998.

Membership of the European Union

The United Kingdom joined the European Union in 1973. In order to become a member, Parliament passed the European Communities Act 1972. Although, as Parliament passed that Act, it is theoretically possible for a later Parliament to pass an Act withdrawing from the European Union, political reality means that this is very unlikely. Membership of the EU affects so much of our law and political system.

Membership of the EU means that EU laws take priority over English law even where the English law was passed after the relevant EU law. This was shown by the Merchant Shipping Act 1988, which set down rules for who could own or manage fishing boats registered in Britain. The Act stated that 75 per cent of directors and shareholders had to be British. The European Court of Justice ruled that this was contrary to European Union law, under which citizens of all Member States can work in other Member States. The Merchant Shipping Act 1988 could not be effective so far as other EU citizens were concerned.

Human Rights Act 1998

This states that all Acts of Parliament have to be compatible with the European Convention on Human Rights. It is possible to challenge an Act on the ground that it does not comply with the Convention. Under s 4 of the Human Rights Act, the courts have the power to declare an Act incompatible with the Convention.

This happened in *H v Mental Health Review Tribunal* (2001). When a patient was making an application to be released, the Mental Health Act 1983 placed the burden of proof on the patient to show that he should be released. Human rights meant that it should be up to the State to justify the continuing detention of such a patient. The court made a declaration that the law was not compatible with human rights. Following this declaration of incompatibility, the Government changed the law.

However, a declaration of incompatibility does not mean that the Government has to change the law. Also, if Parliament wishes it can pass a new Act which contravenes the European Convention on Human Rights.

Examination Questions

See end of Chapter 16.

Delegated legislation

Delegated legislation is law made by some person or body other than Parliament, but with the authority of Parliament. That authority is usually laid down in a 'parent' Act of Parliament known as an enabling Act which creates the framework of the law and then delegates power to others to make more detailed law in the area. An example of enabling Acts is the Access to Justice Act 1999 which gave the Lord Chancellor wide powers to alter various aspects of the legal funding schemes. Another example is the Criminal Justice Act 2003 which gives the Secretary of State the power to make delegated legislation in several areas. One of these powers enables a code of practice to be created for the use of conditional cautions. A conditional caution is used instead of taking an offender to court.

16.1 Types of delegated legislation

There are three different types of delegated legislation. These are:

- Orders in Council
- statutory instruments
- bylaws.

16.1.1 Orders in Council

The Queen and the Privy Council have the authority to make Orders in Council. The Privy Council is made up of the Prime Minister and other leading members of the Government. So this type of delegated legislation effectively allows the Government to make legislation without going through Parliament. Its main use today is to give legal effect to European Directives (see

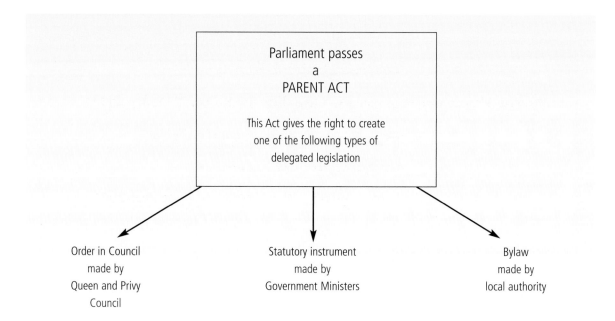

Figure 16.1 Different types of delegated legislation

Chapter 18). However, the Privy Council has power to make law in emergency situations under the Emergency Powers Act 1920 and the Civil Contingencies Act 2004. Occasionally, Orders in Council will be used to make other types of law. For example, in 2003 an Order in Council was used to alter the Misuse of Drugs Act 1971 so as to make cannabis a Class C drug (see Figure 16.2).

16.1.2 Statutory instruments

The term 'statutory instruments' refers to rules and regulations made by Government Ministers. Ministers and Government Departments are given authority to make regulations for areas under their particular responsibility. This means that, for example, the Lord Chancellor has power regarding the legal aid schemes, while the Minister for Transport is able to deal with necessary road traffic regulations. The use of statutory instruments is a major method of law-making as there are about 3,000 statutory instruments brought into force each year.

There are many Acts which give a Minister of State the power to make delegated legislation. Some examples are:

- Constitutional Reform Act 2005
  Section 65 gives the Lord Chancellor the power to issue guidance on the procedures for the Judicial Appointments Commission which recommends who should be appointed as a judge (see section 9.3.2).
- Serious Organised Crime and Police Act 2005
  Section 27 gives the Secretary of State the power to make regulations requiring equipment used by the Serious Crime Agency to satisfy certain levels of design and performance.

These examples show that very different powers can be given to Ministers.

The Legislative and Regulatory Reform Act 2006

In addition to specific Acts giving Ministers powers to make statutory instruments, the Legislative and Regulatory Reform Act 2006 gives Ministers power to make *any* provision by order if

2003 No. 3201

DANGEROUS DRUGS

The Misuse of Drugs Act 1971 (Modification) (No. 2) Order 2003

Made   *10th December 2003*

Coming into force   *29th January 2004*

At the Court at Buckingham Palace, the 10th day of December 2003

Present,

The Queen's Most Excellent Majesty in Council

Whereas a draft of this Order has been laid before Parliament on the recommendation of the Advisory Council on the Misuse of Drugs and has been approved by a resolution of each House of Parliament;

Now, therefore, Her Majesty, in pursuance of section 2(2) of the Misuse of Drugs Act 1971[1], is pleased, by and with the advice of Her Privy Council, to order, and it is hereby ordered, as follows: –

1. This Order may be cited as the Misuse of Drugs Act 1971 (Modification) (No. 2) Order 2003 and shall come into force on 29th January 2004.

2. – (1) Schedule 2 to the Misuse of Drugs Act 1971[2] (which specifies the drugs which are subject to control under that Act) shall be amended as follows.

(2) In paragraph 1(a) of Part I of that Schedule, "Cannabinol, except where contained in cannabis or cannabis resin" and "Cannabinol derivatives" shall be deleted.

(3) In paragraph 1(a) of Part II of that Schedule, "Cannabis and cannabis resin" shall be deleted.

(4) In paragraph 1(a) of Part III of that Schedule, there shall be inserted after "Camazepam", "Cannabinol", "Cannabinol derivatives" and "Cannabis and cannabis resin".

(5) In paragraph 1(d) of Part III of that Schedule, there shall be inserted after "above", "or of cannabinol or a cannabinol derivative".

A. K. Galloway
Clerk of the Privy Council

Figure 16.2 Example of an Order in Council

Definition of delegated legislation	Law made by bodies other than Parliament, but with the authority of Parliament through an enabling or parent Act		
	Types of delegated legislation	**Made by**	**Examples**
	Orders in Council	Made by Queen and Privy Council	The Misuse of Drugs Act 1971 (Modification) Order 2003
	Statutory instruments	Made by Government Ministers	Codes of Practice under PACE
	Bylaws	Made by local authorities	Local parking regulations

Figure 16.3 Types of delegated legislation

it will remove or reduce a 'burden' resulting from legislation. For this purpose a burden is defined as:

- a financial cost
- an administrative inconvenience
- an obstacle to efficiency, productivity or profitability
- a sanction which affects the carrying on of any lawful activity.

This means that Ministers can change Acts of Parliament, even though the original Act did not give them the power to do this. However, when the Legislative and Regulatory Reform Act was being discussed, the Government gave a clear undertaking that orders made under the Act would 'not be used to implement highly controversial reforms'.

16.1.3 Bylaws

These can be made by local authorities to cover matters within their own area; for example, a County Council can pass laws affecting the whole county, while a District or Town Council can only make bylaws for its district or town. Many local bylaws will involve traffic control, such as parking

restrictions.

Bylaws can also be made by public corporations and certain companies for matters within their jurisdiction which involve the public. This means that bodies such as the British Airports Authority and the railways can enforce rules about public behaviour on their premises. An example of such a bylaw is the smoking ban on the London Underground system.

16.2 The need for delegated legislation

1. Parliament does not have time to consider and debate every small detail of complex regulations.

2. In addition Parliament may not have the necessary technical expertise or knowledge required; for example, health and safety regulations in different industries need expert knowledge, while local parking regulations need local knowledge. Modern society has become very complicated and technical, so that it is impossible for members of Parliament to have all the knowledge needed to draw up

laws on controlling technology, ensuring environmental safety, dealing with a vast array of different industrial problems or operating complex taxation schemes. It is thought that it is better for Parliament to debate the main principles thoroughly, but leave the detail to be filled in by those who have expert knowledge of it.

3. Ministers can have the benefit of further consultation before regulations are drawn up. Consultation is particularly important for rules on technical matters, where it is necessary to make sure that the regulations are technically accurate and workable. In fact, some Acts giving the power to make delegated legislation set out that there must be consultation before the regulations are created. For example, before any new or revised police Code of Practice under the Police and Criminal Evidence Act 1984 is issued, there must be consultation with a wide range of people including:

   - persons representing the interests of police authorities
   - the General Council of the Bar
   - the Law Society.

4. As already seen, the process of passing an Act of Parliament can take a considerable time and in an emergency, Parliament may not be able pass law quickly enough. This is another reason why delegated legislation is sometimes preferred. It can also be amended or revoked easily when necessary, so that the law can be kept up to date, and Ministers can respond to new or unforeseen situations by amending or amplifying statutory instruments.

16.3 Control of delegated legislation

As delegated legislation in many instances is made by non-elected bodies and, since there are so many people with the power to make delegated legislation, it is important that there should be some control over this. Control is

exercised by Parliament and by the courts. In addition there may sometimes be a Public Inquiry before a law is passed on an especially sensitive matter, such as planning laws which may affect the environment.

16.3.1 Control by Parliament

This is fairly limited, though obviously Parliament has the initial control with the enabling Act which sets the boundaries within which the delegated legislation is to be made. In addition, a Delegated Powers Scrutiny Committee was established in 1993 in the House of Lords to consider whether the provisions of any Bills delegated legislative power inappropriately. It reports its findings to the House of Lords before the Committee stage of the Bill, but has no power to amend Bills. The main problem is that there is no general provision that the regulations made under the enabling Act have to be laid before Parliament for the MPs to consider them. However a few enabling Acts will say that this has to happen.

Affirmative resolutions

A small number of statutory instruments will be subject to an affirmative resolution. This means that the statutory instrument will not become law unless specifically approved by Parliament. The need for an affirmative resolution will be included in the enabling Act. For example, an affirmative resolution is required before new or revised police Codes of Practice under the Police and Criminal Evidence Act 1984 can come into force. One of the disadvantages of this procedure is that Parliament cannot amend the statutory instrument; it can only be approved, annulled or withdrawn.

Negative resolutions

Most other statutory instruments will be subject to a negative resolution, which means that the relevant statutory instrument will be law unless rejected by Parliament within 40 days. Individual Ministers may also be questioned by MPs in

Parliament on the work of their departments, and this can include questions about proposed regulations.

Scrutiny Committee

A more effective check is the existence of a Joint Select Committee on Statutory Instruments (formed in 1973), usually called the Scrutiny Committee. This committee reviews all statutory instruments and, where necessary, will draw the attention of both Houses of Parliament to points that need further consideration. However, the review is a technical one and not based on policy. The main grounds for referring a statutory instrument back to the Houses of Parliament are that:

- it imposes a tax or charge – this is because only an elected body has such a right
- it appears to have retrospective effect which was not provided for by the enabling Act
- it appears to have gone beyond the powers given under the enabling legislation or it makes some unusual or unexpected use of those powers
- it is unclear or defective in some way.

The Scrutiny Committee can only report back its findings; it has no power to alter any statutory instrument.

16.3.2 The Legislative and Regulatory Reform Act 2006

This Act sets out the procedure for the making of statutory instruments which are aimed at repealing an existing law in order to remove a 'burden' (see section 16.1.2). Under s 13 of the Act, the Minister making the statutory instrument must consult various people and organisations. These include:

- organisations which are representative of interests substantially affected by the proposals
- the Welsh Assembly in relation to matters upon which the Assembly exercises functions
- the Law Commission, where appropriate.

Orders made under this power of this Act must be laid before Parliament. There are three possible procedures:

1. Negative resolution procedure:
   where the Minister recommends that this procedure should be used, it will be used unless within 40 days one of the Houses of Parliament objects to this.

2. Affirmative resolution procedure:
   this requires both Houses of Parliament to approve the order: even though the Minister has recommended this procedure, Parliament can still require the super-affirmative resolution procedure to be used.

3. Super-affirmative resolution procedure:
   under this the Minister must have regard to:
   - any representations
   - any resolution of either House of Parliament
   - any recommendations by a committee of either House of Parliament who are asked to report on the draft order.

This super-affirmative resolution procedure gives Parliament more control over delegated legislation made under the Legislative and Regulatory Reform Act 2006. It is important that this is the position, as the Act gives Ministers very wide powers to amend Acts of Parliament.

16.3.3 Control by the courts

Delegated legislation can be challenged in the courts on the ground that it is *ultra vires*, ie it goes beyond the powers that Parliament granted in the enabling Act. This challenge to the validity of delegated legislation may be made through the judicial review procedure, or it may arise in a civil claim between two parties, or on appeal (especially case-stated appeals).

Any delegated legislation which is ruled to be *ultra vires* is void and not effective. This was illustrated by *R v Home Secretary, ex parte Fire Brigades Union* (1995) where changes made by the Home Secretary to the Criminal Injuries Compensation Scheme were held to have gone beyond the power given to him in the Criminal

Key facts

		Comment or Case
Reasons for delegated legislation	● Knowledge and expertise ● Saving of parliamentary time ● Can be changed more quickly than Acts of Parliament	
Disadvantages of delegated legislation	● Undemocratic ● Risk of sub-delegation ● Large volume ● Lack of publicity	
Control by Parliament	Negative resolution	Becomes law unless within 40 days there is an objection
	Affirmative resolution	Must be approved by both Houses of Parliament
	Scrutiny Committee	Reviews and can draw Parliament's attention to problems, but cannot amend
	Super-affirmative resolution	Only for SIs made under Legislative and Regulatory Reform Act 2006
Control by the courts	Judicial review to decide: ● if it is beyond the powers given in the enabling Act ● if it is unreasonable ● if it failed to follow correct procedure	*R v Home Secretary, ex parte Fire Brigades Union* (1995) *Aylesbury Mushroom case* (1972) *Strictland v Hayes* (1896)

Figure 16.4 Key facts chart for delegated legislation

Justice Act 1988.

The courts will presume that unless an enabling Act expressly allows it, there is no power to do any of the following:

● make unreasonable regulations – in *Strictland v Hayes Borough Council* (1896) a bylaw prohibiting the singing or reciting of any obscene song or ballad and the use of obscene language generally, was held to be unreasonable and so *ultra vires*, because it was too widely drawn in that it covered acts done in private as well as those in public
● levy taxes
● allow sub-delegation.

It is also possible for the courts to hold that delegated legislation is *ultra vires* because the correct procedure has not been followed. For example in the *Aylesbury Mushroom* case (1972) the Minister of Labour had to consult 'any organisation . . . appearing to him to be representative of substantial numbers of employers engaging in the activity concerned'. His failure to consult the Mushroom Growers' Association, which represented about 85 per cent of all mushroom growers, meant that his order establishing a training board was invalid as against mushroom growers, though it was valid in relation to others affected by the order, such as farmers, as the minister had consulted with the

National Farmers' Union.

In *R v Secretary of State for Education and Employment, ex parte National Union of Teachers* (2000) a High Court Judge ruled that a statutory instrument setting conditions for appraisal and access to higher rates of pay for teachers was beyond the powers given under the Education Act 1996. In addition, the procedure used was unfair as only four days had been allowed for consultation.

Statutory instruments can also be declared void if they conflict with European Union legislation.

16.4 Criticisms of the use of delegated legislation

1. The main criticism is that it takes law-making away from the democratically elected House of Commons and allows non-elected people to make law. This is acceptable provided there is sufficient control, but, as already seen, Parliament's control is fairly limited. This criticism cannot be made of bylaws made by local authorities since these are elected by local citizens.

2. Another problem is that of sub-delegation, which means that the law-making authority is handed down another level. This causes comments that much of our law is made by civil servants and merely 'rubber-stamped' by the Minister of that department.

3. The large volume of delegated legislation also gives rise to criticism since it makes it difficult to discover what the present law is. This problem is aggravated by a lack of publicity, as much delegated legislation is made in private in contrast to the public debates of Parliament.

4. Finally, delegated legislation shares with Acts of Parliament the same problem of obscure wording that can lead to difficulty in understanding the law. This difficulty of how to understand or interpret the law is dealt with in Chapter 17.

Examination Questions

Read the source material below and answer all the questions.

Exercise on legislation and delegated legislation

Source A

Parliament consists of three different elements: the House of Commons, the House of Lords and the Queen. Before a Bill can become an Act of Parliament, it must proceed through and be approved by both Houses of Parliament and must receive the Royal Assent.

Source B

In order to reduce pressure on parliamentary time, some Acts of Parliament often known as enabling (parent) Acts give Government Ministers or other authorities the power to regulate administrative details by means of 'delegated' or secondary legislation.

Delegated legislation mostly takes the form of Orders in Council, statutory instruments (SIs) and also bylaws made by local authorities for local issues.

These are as much the law as are Acts of Parliament. SIs are normally drafted by the legal department of the Ministry concerned and may be subject, when in draft, to consultations with interested parties. About 3,000 SIs are issued each year.

To minimise any risk that delegating powers to Government bodies (eg Ministers and local authorities) might undermine the authority of Parliament, such powers are normally only delegated to authorities directly accountable to Parliament.

The enabling Acts concerned sometimes provide for some measure of direct parliamentary control over proposed delegated legislation, by giving Parliament the opportunity to affirm or annul it.

Parliament always has the right to consider whether the SI is made in accordance with the powers that it delegated.

The courts can also control delegated legislation through the process of judicial review.

Adapted from **www.news.bbc.co.uk**

Answer all parts

(a) Source A refers to making an Act of Parliament. Describe how an Act of Parliament is created.

(b) Identify and explain the most suitable type of delegated legislation to implement law in the following situations:

(i) A national emergency such as the outbreak of war involving the UK.

(ii) Where an enabling Act authorises the issuing of regulations concerning

police powers.

(iii) The local imposition of penalties for dogs fouling footpaths.

(c) With reference to Source B:

(i) describe the controls on delegated legislation;

(ii) discuss the effectiveness of the controls of delegated legislation.

OCR G142 June 2007

For delegated legislation, see also part of question at the end of Chapter 18.

Chapter 17

Statutory interpretation

As seen in Chapter 15, many statutes are passed by Parliament each year. The meaning of the law in these statutes should be clear and explicit but this is not always achieved. In order to help with the understanding of a statute Parliament sometimes includes sections defining certain words used in that statute: such sections are called interpretation sections. In the Theft Act 1968, for example, the definition of 'theft' is given in section one, and then sections two to six define the key words in that definition. To help the judges with general words, Parliament has also passed the Interpretation Act 1978 which makes it clear that, unless the contrary appears, 'he' includes 'she', and singular includes plural.

17.1 The need for statutory interpretation

Despite the aids mentioned above, many cases come before the courts because there is a dispute over the meaning of an Act of Parliament. In such cases the court's task is to decide the exact meaning of a particular word or phrase. There are many reasons why the meaning may be unclear:

- A broad term
  There may be words designed to cover several possibilities; this can lead to problems as to how wide this should go. In the Dangerous Dogs Act 1991 there is a phrase: 'any dog of the type known as the pit bull terrier' which seems simple but has led to problems. What is meant by 'type'? Does it mean the same as 'breed'? In *Brock v DPP* (1993) this was the key point in dispute and the Queen's Bench Divisional Court decided that 'type' had a wider meaning than 'breed'. It could cover dogs which were not pedigree pit bull terriers, but had a substantial number of the characteristics of such a dog

Activity

Read the following law report and answer the questions below.

Lurking policemen not 'passengers'
Cheeseman v Director of Public Prosecutions

Before Lord Justice Bingham and Mr Justice Waterhouse
[Judgment October 19]

Police officers who witnessed a man masturbating in a public lavatory were not 'passengers' within the meaning of section 28 of the Town Police Clauses Act 1847 when they had been stationed in the lavatory following complaints.

The Queen's Bench Divisional Court so held in allowing an appeal by way of case stated by Ashley Frederick Cheeseman against his conviction by Leicester City Justices of an offence of wilfully and indecently exposing his person in a street to the annoyance of passengers.

Section 81 of the Public Health Amendment Act 1907 extended the meaning of the word 'street' in section 28 to include, *inter alia*, any place of public resort under the control of the local authority.

Mr Stuart Rafferty for the appellant: Mr David Bartlett for the prosecution.

LORD JUSTICE BINGHAM, concurring with Mr Justice Waterhouse, said that *The Oxford English Dictionary* showed that in 1847 when the Act was passed 'passenger' had a meaning, now unusual except in the expression 'foot-passenger' of 'a passer by or through: a traveller (usually on foot); a wayfarer'.

Before the meaning of 'street' was enlarged in 1907 that dictionary definition of passenger was not hard to apply: it clearly covered anyone using the street for ordinary purposes of passage or travel.

The dictionary definition could not be so aptly applied to a place of public resort such as a public lavatory, but on a commonsense reading when applied in context 'passenger' had to mean anyone resorting in the ordinary way to a place for one of the purposes for which people would normally resort to it.

If that was the correct approach, the two police officers were not 'passengers'. They were stationed in the public lavatory in order to apprehend persons committing acts which had given rise to earlier complaints. They were not resorting to that place of public resort in the ordinary way but for a special purpose and thus were not passengers.

Solicitors: Bray & Bray, Leicester: CPS Leicester.

The Times Law Report, 2 November 1990

Questions

1. In this case the meaning of the word 'street' was important. How did the court discover the meaning of the word in this case?

2. The meaning of the word 'passenger' was also important. How did the court discover what this word meant in 1847?

3. The court decided that 'passenger' meant 'a passer by or through; a traveller (usually on foot); a wayfarer'. Why did that definition not apply to the police officers who arrested the defendant?

4. The defendant was found not guilty because of the way the court interpreted 'passenger'. Do you think this was a correct decision? Give reasons for your answer.

- Ambiguity
  This is where a word has two or more meanings; it may not be clear which meaning should be used
- A drafting error
  The Parliamentary Counsel who drafted the original Bill may have made an error which has not been noticed by Parliament; this is particularly likely to occur where the Bill is amended several times while going through Parliament
- New developments
  New technology may mean that an old Act of Parliament does not apparently cover present-day situations. This is seen in the case of *Royal College of Nursing v DHSS* (1981) where medical science and methods had changed since the passing of the Abortion Act in 1967. This case is discussed more fully in section 17.5.1
- Changes in the use of language
  The meaning of words can change over the years. This was one of the problems in the case of *Cheeseman v DPP* (1990). *The Times* law report of this case is set out in the activity section on the previous page.

17.2 Literal approach versus purposive approach

The case of *Cheeseman* illustrates several of the problems of statutory interpretation. It is an example of the courts taking the words literally. However, it can be argued that the defendant was 'wilfully and indecently exposing his person in a street' and that he was caught doing that. Is it important whether the police officers were 'passengers'? After all, they were there because of previous complaints about this type of behaviour and presumably the defendant thought they were ordinary members of the public. Some people would argue that the whole purpose of the Act was to prevent this type of behaviour; this is the purposive approach to statutory interpretation – instead of looking at the precise meaning of each

word, a broader approach is taken.

This conflict between the literal approach and the purposive approach is one of the major issues in statutory interpretation. Should judges examine each word and take the words literally or should it be accepted that an Act of Parliament cannot cover every situation and that the meanings of words cannot always be exact? In European law the purposive approach is taken. The Treaty of Rome sets out general principles but without explicit details. As Lord Denning said of the Treaty in *Bulmer Ltd v Bollinger SA* (1974):

 It lays down general principles. It expresses its aims and purposes. All in sentences of moderate length and commendable style. But it lacks precision. It uses words and phrases without defining what they mean. An English lawyer would look for an interpretation clause, but he would look in vain. There is none. All the way through the Treaty there are gaps and lacunas. These have to be filled in by the judges.

In fact, since European treaties, regulations and directives are issued in several languages it would be difficult, if not impossible, to take the meanings of words literally. It is not always possible to have an exact translation from one language to another.

In English law the judges have not been able to agree on which approach should be used, but instead, over the years they have developed three different rules of interpretation. These are:

- the literal rule
- the golden rule
- the mischief rule.

These rules take different approaches to interpretation and some judges prefer to use one rule, while other judges prefer another rule. This means that in English law the interpretation of a statute may differ according to which judge is hearing the case. However, once an interpretation has been laid down, it may then form a precedent for future cases under the normal rules of judicial precedent. Since the three rules can result in very different decisions, it is important to understand them.

17.3 The literal rule

Under this rule courts will give words their plain, ordinary or literal meaning, even if the result is not very sensible. This idea was expressed by Lord Esher in *R v Judge of the City of London Court* (1892) when he said:

 If the words of an act are clear then you must follow them even though they lead to a manifest absurdity. The court has nothing to do with the question whether the legislature has committed an absurdity.

The rule developed in the early nineteenth century and was the main rule used for the first part of the twentieth century. It is still used as the starting point for interpreting any legislation.

17.3.1 Cases using the literal rule

The rule was used in *Whiteley v Chappell* (1868) where the defendant was charged under a section which made it an offence to impersonate 'any person entitled to vote'. The defendant had pretended to be a person whose name was on the voters' list, but who had died. The court held that the defendant was not guilty since a dead person is not, in the literal meaning of the words, 'entitled to vote'. Using the literal rule in this case made the law absurd.

The rule can also lead to what are considered harsh decisions. This occurred in *London & North Eastern Railway Co. v Berriman* (1946) where a railway worker was killed while doing maintenance work, oiling points along a railway line. His widow tried to claim compensation because there had not been a look-out man provided by the railway company in accordance

with a regulation under the Fatal Accidents Act which stated that a look-out should be provided for men working on or near the railway line 'for the purposes of relaying or repairing' it. The court took the words 'relaying' and 'repairing' in their literal meaning and said that oiling points was maintaining the line and not relaying or repairing so that Mrs Berriman's claim failed.

17.3.2 Advantages of the literal rule

The rule follows the words that Parliament has used. Parliament is our law-making body and it is right that judges should apply the law exactly as it is written. Using the literal rule to interpret Acts of Parliament means that unelected judges do not make law.

Using the literal rule should make the law more certain, as it should be interpreted exactly as it is written. This makes it easier for people to know what the law is and how judges will apply it.

17.3.3 Disadvantages of the literal rule

The literal rule assumes every Act will be perfectly drafted. In fact it is not always possible to word an Act so that it covers every situation that Parliament meant it to. This was seen in the case of *Whiteley v Chappell* (1868) where the defendant was not guilty of voting under another person's name (see 17.3.1 above).

Words may have more than one meaning, so that the Act is unclear. Often in dictionaries words are defined with several different meanings.

Following the words exactly can lead to unfair or unjust decisions. This was seen in *London & North Eastern Railway Co. v Berriman* (1946) (see 17.3.1 above).

With decisions such as *Whiteley v Chappell* and the *Berriman case*, it is not surprising that Professor Michael Zander has denounced the literal rule as being mechanical and divorced from the realities of the use of language.

17.4 The golden rule

This rule is a modification of the literal rule. The golden rule starts by looking at the literal meaning but the court is then allowed to avoid an interpretation which would lead to an absurd result. There are two views on how far the golden rule should be used. The first is very narrow and is shown by Lord Reid's comments in *Jones v DPP* (1962) when he said:

> It is a cardinal principle applicable to all kinds of statutes that you may not for any reason attach to a statutory provision a meaning which the words of that provision cannot reasonably bear. If they are capable of more than one meaning, then you can choose between those meanings, but beyond this you cannot go.

So under the narrow application of the golden rule the court may only choose between the possible meanings of a word or phrase. If there is only one meaning then that must be taken.

The second and wider application of the golden rule is where the words have only one clear meaning, but that meaning would lead to a repugnant situation (that is, a situation in which the court feels that using the clear meaning would produce a result which should not be allowed). In such a case the court will invoke the golden rule to modify the words of the statute in order to avoid this problem.

17.4.1 Cases using the golden rule

The narrow view of the golden rule can be seen in practice in *R v Allen* (1872). In this case s 57 of the Offences against the Person Act 1861 made it an offence to 'marry' whilst one's original spouse was still alive (and there had been no divorce). The word 'marry' can mean to become legally married to the other person or in a more general way it can mean that the person takes part or 'goes through' a ceremony of marriage.

The court decided that in the Offences Against the Person Act 1861 the word had this second meaning of 'go through a ceremony of marriage'. This was because a person who is still married to another person cannot legally marry anyone else so if the first meaning of being legally married was applied then there would be the absurd situation that no-one could ever be guilty of bigamy.

A very clear example of the use of the wider application of the golden rule was the case of *Re Sigsworth* (1935). In this case the son had murdered his mother. The mother had not made a will, so normally her estate would have been inherited by her next-of-kin according to the rules set out in the Administration of Justice Act 1925. This meant that the murderer son would have inherited as her 'issue'.

There was no ambiguity in the words of the Act, but the court was not prepared to let a murderer benefit from his crime, so it was held that the literal rule should not apply; the golden rule would be used to prevent the repugnant situation of the son inheriting. Effectively the court was writing into the Act that the 'issue' would not be entitled to inherit where they had killed the person they would be inheriting from.

17.4.2 Advantages of the golden rule

It respects the exact words of Parliament except in limited situations. Where there is a problem with using the literal rule, the golden rule provides an 'escape route'.

It allows the judge to choose the most sensible meaning where there is more than one meaning to the words in the Act. It can also provide sensible decisions in cases where the literal rule would lead to a repugnant situation. It would clearly have been unjust to allow the son in *Re Sigsworth* to benefit from his crime.

This shows how it can avoid the worst problems of the literal rule.

17.4.3 Disadvantages of the golden rule

It is very limited in its use, so it is only used on rare occasions. Another problem is that it is not always possible to predict when courts will use the golden rule.

Michael Zander has described it as a 'feeble parachute'. In other words, it is an escape route but it cannot do very much.

17.5 The mischief rule

This rule gives a judge more discretion than the other two rules. The definition of the rule comes from *Heydon's case* (1584), where it was said that there were four points the court should consider. These, in the original language of that old case, were:

1. 'What was the common law before the making of the Act?
2. What was the mischief and defect for which the common law did not provide?
3. What was the remedy the Parliament hath resolved and appointed to cure the disease of the commonwealth?
4. The true reason of the remedy.
   Then the office of all the judges is always to make such construction as shall suppress the mischief and advance the remedy.'

Under this rule therefore, the court should look to see what the law was before the Act was passed in order to discover what gap or 'mischief' the Act was intended to cover. The court should then interpret the Act in such a way that the gap is covered. This is clearly a quite different approach to the literal rule.

17.5.1 Cases using the mischief rule

The mischief rule was used in *Smith v Hughes* (1960) to interpret section 1(1) of the Street Offences Act 1959 which said 'it shall be an offence for a common prostitute to loiter or solicit in a street or public place for the purpose of prostitution'. The court considered appeals against conviction under this section by six different women. In each case the women had not been 'in a street'; one had been on a balcony

and the others had been at the windows of ground floor rooms, with the window either half open or closed. In each case the women were attracting the attention of men by calling to them or tapping on the window, but they argued that they were not guilty under this section since they were not literally 'in a street or public place'. The court decided that they were guilty, with Lord Parker saying:

> For my part I approach the matter by considering what is the mischief aimed at by this Act. Everybody knows that this was an Act to clean up the streets, to enable people to walk along the streets without being molested or solicited by common prostitutes. Viewed in this way it can matter little whether the prostitute is soliciting while in the street or is standing in the doorway or on a balcony, or at a window, or whether the window is shut or open or half open.

No, Romeo, I am not a prostitute!

Activity

Read the facts of the case set out below then apply the different rules of interpretation.

CASE: *Fisher v Bell* [1960] 1 QB 394

The Restriction of Offensive Weapons Act 1959 s 1(1)

'Any person who manufactures, sells or hires or offers for sale or hire or lends or gives to any other person – (a) any knife which has a blade which opens automatically by hand pressure applied to a button, spring or other device in or attached to the handle of the knife, sometimes known as a "flick knife" . . . shall be guilty of an offence.'

FACTS: The defendant was a shop keeper, who had displayed a flick knife marked with a price in his shop window; he had not actually sold any. He was charged under s1 (1) and the court had to decide whether he was guilty of offering the knife for sale. There is a technical legal meaning of 'offers for sale', under which putting an article in a shop window is not an offer to sell.

Questions

Consider the phrase 'offers for sale' and explain how you think the case would have been decided using:

(a) the literal rule

(b) the golden rule

(c) the mischief rule.

Note: The court's decision on the case is given in Appendix 1.

A similar point arose in *Eastbourne Borough Council v Stirling* (2000) where a taxi driver was charged with 'plying for hire in any street' without a licence to do so. His vehicle was parked on a taxi rank on the station forecourt. He was found guilty as, although he was on private land, he was likely to get customers from the street. The court referred to *Smith v Hughes* and said that it was the same point. A driver would be plying for hire in the street when his vehicle was positioned so that the offer of services was aimed at people in the street.

Another case in which the House of Lords used the mischief rule was *Royal College of Nursing v DHSS* (1981). In this case the wording of the Abortion Act 1967 which provided that a pregnancy should be 'terminated by a registered medical practitioner', was in issue. When the Act was passed in 1967 the procedure to carry out an abortion was such that only a doctor (a registered medical practitioner) could do it. From 1972 onwards improvements in medical techniques meant that the normal method of terminating a pregnancy was to induce premature labour with drugs. The first part of the procedure was carried out by a doctor, but the second part was performed by nurses without a doctor present. The court had to decide if this procedure was lawful under the Abortion Act. The case went to the House of Lords where the majority (three) of the judges held that it was lawful, whilst the other two said that it was not lawful.

The three judges in the majority based their decision on the mischief rule, pointing out that the mischief Parliament was trying to remedy was the unsatisfactory state of the law before 1967 and the number of illegal abortions. They also said that the policy of the Act was to broaden the grounds for abortion and ensure that they were carried out with proper skill in hospital. The other two judges took the literal view and said that the words of the Act were clear and that terminations could only be carried out by a registered medical practitioner. They said that the other judges were not interpreting the Act but 'redrafting it with a vengeance'.

It is clear that these three rules can lead to different decisions on the meanings of words and phrases. The activity on the previous page is based on a real case in which the different rules could result in different decisions.

17.5.2 Advantages of the mischief rule

The mischief rule promotes the purpose of the law as it allows judges to look back at the gap in the law which the Act was designed to cover. The emphasis is on making sure that the gap on the law is filled. This is more likely to produce a 'just' result.

The Law Commission prefers the mischief rule and, as long ago as 1969, recommended that it should be the only rule used in statutory interpretation.

17.5.3 Disadvantages of the mischief rule

There is the risk of judicial law-making. Judges are trying to fill the gaps in the law with their own views on how the law should remedy the gap. The case of *Royal College of Nursing v DHSS*

Key facts

Literal rule	Golden rule	Mischief rule
Words in their ordinary grammatical meaning	Can choose best interpretation of ambiguous words OR avoid an absurd/repugnant result	Looks at the gap in the law prior to the Act and interprets words to 'suppress the mischief'
Case: *LNER v Berriman* (1946) Not 'relaying or repairing' track, but was oiling points (maintenance) Literal approach – held maintenance was not within the literal meaning of the words 'relaying or repairing' Could not claim compensation	Case: *R v Allen* (1872) 'Marry' meant go through a ceremony of marriage Case: *Re Sigsworth* (1935) Son not allowed to inherit money from mother because he murdered her	Case: *Smith v Hughes* (1960) Prostitutes calling from a house to men in the street were 'soliciting in a street' This was the mischief that the Act was intended to prevent
Advantages of literal rule • leaves law-making to Parliament • makes law more certain	Advantages of golden rule • respects the words of Parliament as only used in limited situations • avoids the worst problems of the literal rule	Advantages of mischief rule • fills in the gaps in the law • promotes the purpose of the Act • produces 'just' results
Disadvantages of literal rule • assumes that every Act is perfectly drafted • words have more than one meaning • can lead to absurd results • can lead to unjust decisions	Disadvantages of golden rule • can only be used in limited situations • a 'feeble parachute' (Zander)	Disadvantages of mischief rule • risk of judicial law-making • not as wide as the purposive approach • limited to looking back to the law prior to the Act • can make law uncertain

Figure 17.1 Key facts chart on the three 'rules' of statutory interpretation

(see section 17.5.1) shows that judges do not always agree on the use of the mischief rule.

Use of the mischief rule may lead to uncertainty in the law. It is impossible to know when judges will use the rule and also what result it might lead to. This makes it difficult for lawyers to advise clients on the law.

The mischief rule is not as wide as the purposive approach (see section 17.6) as it is limited to looking back at the gap in the old. It cannot be used for a more general consideration of the purpose of the law.

17.6 The purposive approach

This goes beyond the mischief rule in that the court is not just looking to see what the gap was in the old law. The judges are deciding what they believe Parliament meant to achieve. The champion of this approach in English law was Lord Denning. His attitude towards statutory interpretation was shown when he said in the case of *Magor and St Mellons v Newport Corporation* (1950):

> We sit here to find out the intention of Parliament and carry it out, and we do this better by filling in the gaps and making sense of the enactment than by opening it up to destructive analysis.

However, his attitude was criticised by judges in the House of Lords when they heard the appeal in the case. Lord Simonds called Lord Denning's approach:

> a naked usurpation of the legislative function under the thin disguise of interpretation

and pointed out that:

> if a gap is disclosed the remedy lies in an amending Act.

Another judge, Lord Scarman, said:

> If Parliament says one thing but means another, it is not, under the historic principles of the common law, for the courts to correct it. The general principle must surely be acceptable in our society. We are to be governed not by Parliament's intentions but by Parliament's enactments.

This speech shows the problem with the purposive approach. Should the judges refuse to follow the clear words of Parliament? How do they know what Parliament's intentions were? Opponents of the purposive approach say that it is impossible to discover Parliament's intentions; only the words of the statute can show what Parliament wanted.

17.6.1 Cases using the purposive approach

The purposive approach was used in *R v Registrar-General, ex parte Smith* (1990), where the court had to consider s 51 of the Adoption Act 1976 which stated:

> (1) Subject to subsections (4) and (6), the Registrar-General shall on an application made in the prescribed manner by an adopted person a record of whose birth is kept by the Registrar-General and who has attained the age of 18 years supply to that person . . . such information as is necessary to enable that person to obtain a certified copy of the record of his birth . . .

Subsection (4) said that before supplying that information the Registrar-General had to inform the applicant about counselling services available. Subsection (6) stated that if the adoption was before 1975 the Registrar-General could not give the information unless the applicant had attended an interview with a counsellor.

The case involved the application by Charles Smith for information to enable him to obtain his

Literal approach	Purposive approach
Words taken in their ordinary grammatical meaning	Looks for the purpose of Parliament and interprets the law to ensure that purpose
Case: *LNER v Berriman* (1946) Not 'relaying or repairing' track, but was oiling points (maintenance) Literal approach – held maintenance was not within the literal meaning of the words 'relaying or repairing' Could not claim compensation	Case: *R (Quintavalle) v Sec of State for Health* (2003) Act stated embryo meant 'a live human embryo where fertilisation is complete' Embryos were created by cell nuclear replacement, so there was no fertilisation Purposive approach – Parliament could not have intended to distinguish between embryos The Act applied
Advantages of literal approach ● leaves law-making to Parliament ● makes law more certain	Advantages of purposive approach ● leads to justice in individual cases ● broad approach covering more situations ● fills in the gaps in the law ● allows for new technology
Disadvantages of literal approach ● assumes that every Act is perfectly drafted ● words have more than one meaning ● can lead to absurd results ● can lead to unjust decisions	Disadvantages of purposive approach ● leads to judicial law-making ● can make law uncertain ● difficult to discover the intention of Parliament

Figure 17.2 Comparing the literal approach and the purposive approach

birth certificate. Mr Smith had made his application in the correct manner and was prepared to see a counsellor. On a literal view of the Act the Registrar-General had to supply him with the information, since the Act uses the phrase 'shall . . . supply'.

The problem was that Mr Smith had been convicted of two murders and was detained in Broadmoor as he suffered from recurring bouts of psychotic illness. A psychiatrist thought that it was possible he might be hostile towards his natural mother.

This posed a difficulty for the court; should they apply the clear meaning of the words in this situation? The judges in the Court of Appeal decided that the case called for the purposive approach, saying that, despite the plain language of the Act, Parliament could not have

intended to promote serious crime. So, in view of the risk to the applicant's natural mother if he discovered her identity, they ruled that the Registrar-General did not have to supply any information.

In *R (Quintavalle) v Secretary of State* (2003) the House of Lords used the purposive approach in deciding that organisms created by cell nuclear replacement (CNR) came within the definition of 'embryo' in the Human Embryology and Fertilisation Act 1990.

Section 1(1)(a) of this Act states that 'embryo means a live human embryo where fertilisation is complete'. CNR was not possible in 1990 when the Act was passed and the problem is that fertilisation is not used in CNR. Lord Bingham said:

[T]he court's task, within permissible bounds of interpretation is to give effect to Parliament's purpose . . . Parliament could not have intended to distinguish between embryos produced by, or without, fertilisation since it was unaware of the latter possibility.

17.6.2 Advantages of the purposive approach

The purposive approach leads to justice in individual cases. It is a broad approach which allows the law to cover more situations than applying words literally. This means it can fill in the gaps in the law.

The purposive approach is particularly useful where there is new technology which was unknown when the law was enacted. This is demonstrated by *R (Quintavalle) v Secretary of State*, the embryo case explained in section 17.6.1. If the literal rule/approach had been used in that case, it would have been necessary for Parliament to make a new law to deal with the situation.

17.6.3 Disadvantages of the purposive approach

Using the purposive approach makes the law less certain. It also allows unelected judges to 'make' law as they are deciding what they think the law should be rather than using the words that Parliament enacted.

Another problem with the purposive approach is that it is difficult to discover the intention of Parliament. There are reports of debates in Parliament in *Hansard* (see section 17.7.2), but these give every detail of debates including those MPs who did not agree with the law that was under discussion. The final version of what Parliament agreed is the actual words used in the Act.

It also leads to uncertainty in the law. It is impossible to know when judges will use this approach or what result it might lead to. This makes it difficult for lawyers to advise clients on the law.

17.7 Finding Parliament's intention

There are certain ways in which the courts can try to discover the intention of Parliament and certain matters which they can look at in order to help with the interpretation of a statute.

17.7.1 Intrinsic aids

These are matters within the statute itself that may help to make its meaning clearer. The court can consider the long title, the short title and the preamble (if any). Older statutes usually have a preamble which sets out Parliament's purpose in enacting that statute. Modern statutes either do not have a preamble or contain a very brief one; for example the Theft Act 1968 states that it is an Act to modernise the law of theft. The long title may also explain briefly Parliament's intentions.

The other useful internal aids are any headings before a group of sections, and any schedules attached to the Act. There are often also marginal notes explaining different sections, but these are not generally regarded as giving Parliament's intention as they will have been inserted after the parliamentary debates and are only helpful comments put in by the printer.

17.7.2 Extrinsic aids

These are matters which are outside the Act – it has always been accepted that some external sources can help explain the meaning of an Act. These undisputed sources are:

- previous Acts of Parliament on the same topic
- the historical setting
- earlier case law
- dictionaries of the time.

As far as other extrinsic aids are concerned, attitudes have changed. Originally the courts had very strict rules that other extrinsic aids should not be considered; however, for the following three aids the courts' attitude has changed. These three main extrinsic aids are:

- *Hansard*: the official report of what was said in Parliament when the Act was debated
- reports of law reform bodies, such as the Law Commission, which led to the passing of the Act
- international conventions, regulations or directives which have been implemented by English legislation.

The use of *Hansard*

Until 1992 there was a firm rule that the courts could not look at what was said in the debates in Parliament. Some years earlier Lord Denning had tried to attack this ban on *Hansard* in *Davis v Johnson* (1979), which involved the interpretation of the Domestic Violence and Matrimonial Proceedings Act 1976. He admitted that he had indeed read *Hansard* before making his decision, saying:

> Some may say . . . that judges should not pay any attention to what is said in Parliament. They should grope about in the dark for the meaning of an Act without switching on the light. I do not accede to this view.

In the same case the House of Lords disapproved of this and Lord Scarman explained their reasons by saying:

> Such material is an unreliable guide to the meaning of what is enacted. It promotes confusion, not clarity. The cut and thrust of debate and the pressures of executive responsibility . . . are not always conducive to a clear and unbiased explanation of the meaning of statutory language.

However, in *Pepper v Hart* (1993) the House of Lords relaxed the rule and accepted that *Hansard* could be used in a limited way. This case was unusual in that seven judges heard the appeal, rather than the normal panel of five. These seven judges included the Lord Chancellor, who was the only judge to disagree with the use of *Hansard*. The majority ruled that *Hansard* could be consulted. Lord Browne-Wilkinson said in his judgment that:

> the exclusionary rule should be relaxed so as to permit reference to parliamentary materials where: (a) legislation is ambiguous or obscure, or leads to an absurdity; (b) the material relied on consists of one or more statements by a minister or other promoter of the Bill together if necessary with such other parliamentary material as is necessary to understand such statements and their effect; (c) the statements relied on are clear. Further than this I would not at present go.

So *Hansard* may be considered but only where the words of the Act are ambiguous or obscure or lead to an absurdity. Even then *Hansard* should only be used if there was a clear statement by the Minister introducing the legislation, which would resolve the ambiguity or absurdity. The Lord Chancellor opposed the use of *Hansard* on practical grounds, pointing out the time and cost it would take to research *Hansard* in every case.

The only time that a wider use of *Hansard* is permitted is where the court is considering an Act that introduced an international convention or European directive into English law. This was pointed out by the Queen's Bench Divisional Court in *Three Rivers District Council and others v Bank of England (No 2)* (1996). In such a situation it is important to interpret the statute purposively and consistently with any European materials and the court can look at ministerial statements, even if the statute does not appear to be ambiguous or obscure.

Since 1992 *Hansard* has been referred to in a number of cases, even sometimes when there did not appear to be any ambiguity or absurdity. The Lord Chancellor's predictions on cost have been

Key facts

	Brief definition	Case examples
Literal approach	● Approaching problems of statutory interpretation by taking the words at their face value	*Fisher v Bell* (1960)
Purposive approach	● Looking at the reasons why a law was passed and interpreting the words accordingly	*R v Registrar-General, ex parte Smith* (1990)
The 'three rules' Literal rule	● Words given ordinary, plain, grammatical meaning	*Whiteley v Chappell* (1868)
Golden rule	● Avoids absurd or repugnant situations	*R v Allen* (1872)
Mischief rule	● Looks at the gap in the previous law and interprets the words 'to advance the remedy'	*Smith v Hughes* (1960)
Rules of language *Ejusdem generis*	● General words which follow a list are limited to the same kind	*Powell v Kempton Park* (1899)
Expressio unius	● The express mention of one thing excludes others	*Tempest v Kilner* (1846)
Noscitur a sociis	● A word is known by the company it keeps	*IRC v Frere* (1965)
Presumptions	● No change to common law ● Crown not bound ● *Mens rea* required ● No retrospective effect	*Leach v R* (1912) *Sweet v Parsley* (1970)
Aids to finding Parliament's intention	● Intrinsic – within the Act, eg interpretation section ● Extrinsic – outside the Act, eg *Hansard* ● Law Commission Reports	*Pepper v Hart* (1993) *Black Clawson* case (1975)

Figure 17.3 Key facts chart for statutory interpretation

confirmed by some solicitors, with one estimating that it had added 25 per cent to the bill. On other occasions it is clear that *Hansard* has not been helpful or that the court would have reached the same conclusion in any event.

Law reform reports

As with *Hansard*, the courts used to hold that reports by law reform agencies should not be considered by the courts. However this rule was relaxed in the *Black Clawson* case in 1975, when it was accepted that such a report should be looked at to discover the mischief or gap in the law which the legislation based on the report was designed to deal with (see Chapter 19 for more detail on law reform agencies).

International conventions

In *Fothergill v Monarch Airlines Ltd* (1980) the House of Lords decided that the original convention should be considered as it was possible that in translating and adapting the convention to our legislative process, the true meaning of the original might have been lost. The

House of Lords in that same case also held that an English court could consider any preparatory materials or explanatory notes published with an international convention. The reasoning behind this was that other countries allowed the use of such material, known as *travaux préparatoires*, and it should therefore be allowed in this country in order to get uniformity in the interpretation of international rules.

17.8 The effect of EU law

The purposive approach is the one preferred by most European countries when interpreting their own legislation. It is also the approach which has been adopted by the European Court of Justice (see Chapter 18) in interpreting European law.

Since the United Kingdom became a member of the European Union in 1973 the influence of the European preference for the purposive approach has affected the English courts in two ways. Firstly, they have had to accept that, at least for law which has been passed as a result of having to conform to a European law, the purposive approach is the correct one to use. Secondly, the fact that judges are having to use the purposive approach for European law is making them more accustomed to it and, therefore, more likely to apply it to English law.

17.8.1 Interpreting EU Law

Where the law to be interpreted is based on European law, the English courts must interpret it in the light of the wording and purpose of the European law. This is because the Treaty of Rome, which sets out the duties of European member states, says that all member states are required to:

> " take all appropriate measures . . . to ensure fulfilment of the obligations "

The European Court of Justice in the *Marleasing* case (1992) ruled that this included interpreting national law in the light and the aim of the European law.

An example of the English courts interpreting law by looking at the purpose of the relevant European Union law is *Diocese of Hallam Trustee v Connaughton* (1996). This case is discussed in full in the chapter on European law at section 18.3.1.

17.9 The effect of the Human Rights Act 1998

Section 3 of the Human Rights Act says that, so far as it is possible to do so, legislation must be read and given effect in a way which is compatible with the rights in the European Convention on Human Rights. This applies to any case where one of the rights is concerned, but it does not apply where there is no involvement of human rights.

An example of the effect of the Human Rights Act on interpretation is *Mendoza v Ghaidan* (2002). In this case the Court of Appeal ignored a House of Lords' judgment about the Rent Act 1977 which had been made prior to the implementation of the Human Rights Act.

The Rent Act applied where a person who had the tenancy of a house or flat died. If the tenant had been living in the property with their spouse, then the spouse had the right to take over the tenancy. The Rent Act also allowed unmarried partners to succeed to the tenancy as it stated that 'a person who was living with the original tenant as his or her wife or husband shall be treated as the spouse of the original tenant'.

In *Mendoza v Ghaidan* the question was whether same sex partners had the right to take over the tenancy. A House of Lords' decision, made before the Human Rights Act came into effect, had ruled that same sex partners did not have the right under the Rent Act to take over the tenancy.

The Court of Appeal held that the Rent Act had to be interpreted to conform to the European Convention on Human Rights which forbids discrimination on the ground of gender. In order to make the Act compatible with human rights, the Court of Appeal read the words 'living with the original tenant as his or her wife or husband' to mean 'as *if they were* his or her wife or husband'. This allowed same sex partners to have the same rights as unmarried opposite sex couples.

The Court of Appeal pointed out the importance of conforming to the Convention rights when they said:

> In order to remedy this breach of the Convention the court must, if it can, read the Schedule so that its provisions are rendered compatible with the Convention rights of the survivors of same-sex partnerships.

In 2004 the House of Lords confirmed the Court of Appeal's decision in this case.

17.10 Rules of language

Even the literal rule does not take words in complete isolation. It is common sense that the other words in the Act must be looked at to see if they affect the word or phrase which is in dispute. In looking at the other words in the Act the courts have developed a number of minor rules which can help to make the meaning of words and phrases clear where a particular sentence construction has been used. These rules, which also have Latin names, are:

- the *ejusdem generis* rule
- the express mention of one thing excludes others
- a word is known by the company it keeps.

17.10.1 The *ejusdem generis* rule

This states that where there is a list of words followed by general words, then the general words are limited to the same kind of items as the specific words. This is easier to understand by looking at cases. In *Powell v Kempton Park Racecourse* (1899) the defendant was charged with keeping a 'house, office, room or other place for betting'. He had been operating betting at what is

known as Tattersall's Ring, which is outdoors. The court decided that the general words 'other place' had to refer to indoor places since all the words in the list were indoor places and so the defendant was not guilty.

There must be at least two specific words in a list before the general word or phrase for this rule to operate. In *Allen v Emmerson* (1944) the court had to interpret the phrase 'theatres and other places of amusement' and decide if it applied to a funfair. As there was only one specific word, 'theatres', it was decided that a funfair did come under the general term 'other places of amusement' even though it was not of the same kind as theatres.

17.10.2 *Expressio unius exclusio alterius* (the mention of one thing excludes others)

Where there is a list of words which is not followed by general words, then the Act applies only to the items in the list. In *Tempest v Kilner* (1846) the court had to consider whether the Statute of Frauds 1677 (which required a contract for the sale of 'goods, wares and merchandise' of more than £10 to be evidenced in writing) applied to a contract for the sale of stocks and shares. The list 'goods, wares and merchandise' was not followed by any general words, so the court held that only contracts for those three types of things were affected by the statute; because stocks and shares were not mentioned they were not caught by the statute.

17.10.3 *Noscitur a sociis* (a word is known by the company it keeps)

This means that the words must be looked at in context and interpreted accordingly; it involves looking at other words in the same section or at other sections in the Act. Words in the same section were important in *Inland Revenue Commissioners v Frere* (1965), where the section set out rules for 'interest, annuities or other annual interest'. The first use of the word 'interest' on its own could have meant any interest paid, whether daily, monthly or annually. Because of the words 'other annual interest' in the section, the court decided that 'interest' only meant annual interest.

Other sections of the Act were considered by the House of Lords in *Bromley London Borough Council v Greater London Council* (1982). The issue in this case was whether the GLC could operate a cheap fare scheme on their transport systems, where the amounts being charged meant that the transport system would run at a loss. The decision in the case revolved around the meaning of the word 'economic'. The House of Lords looked at the whole Act and, in particular, at another section which imposed a duty to make up any deficit as far as possible. As a result they decided that 'economic' meant being run on business lines and ruled that the cheap fares policy was not legal since it involved deliberately running the transport system at a loss and this was not running it on business lines.

17.11 Presumptions

The courts will also make certain presumptions or assumptions about the law, but these are only a starting point. If the statute clearly states the opposite, then the presumption will not apply and it is said that the presumption is rebutted. The most important presumptions are:

1. A presumption against a change in the common law
   In other words it is assumed that the common law will apply unless Parliament has made it plain in the Act that the common law has been altered. An example of this occurred in *Leach v R* (1912), where the question was whether a wife could be made to give evidence against her husband under the Criminal Evidence Act 1898. Since the Act did not expressly say that

this should happen, it was held that the common law rule that a wife could not be compelled to give evidence still applied. If there had been explicit words saying that a wife was compellable then the old common law would not apply. This is now the position under s 80 of the Police and Criminal Evidence Act 1984, which expressly states that in a crime of violence one spouse can be made to give evidence against the other spouse.

2. A presumption that *mens rea* is required in criminal cases
   The basic common law rule is that no-one can be convicted of a crime unless it is shown that they had the required intention to commit it. In *Sweet v Parsley* (1970) the defendant was charged with being concerned with the management of premises which were used for the purposes of smoking cannabis. The facts were that the defendant was the owner of premises which she had leased out and the tenants had smoked cannabis there without her knowledge. She was clearly 'concerned in the management' of the premises and cannabis had been smoked there, but because she had no knowledge of the events she had no *mens rea*. The key issue was whether *mens rea* was required; the Act did not say there was any need for knowledge of the events. The House of Lords held that she was not guilty as the presumption that *mens rea* was required had not been rebutted.

3. A presumption that the Crown is not bound by any statute unless the statute expressly says so.

4. A presumption that legislation does not apply retrospectively
   This means that no Act of Parliament will apply to past happenings; each Act will normally only apply from the date it comes into effect.

Examination Questions

Read the source material below and answer the questions which follow.

Source A

Royal College of Nursing v DHSS (1981)

The wording of the Abortion Act 1967 provided that a pregnancy should be 'terminated by a registered medical practitioner'. From 1967 it was the practice that only doctors (registered medical practitioners) carried out the operation. From 1972 onwards, improvements in medical techniques meant that a nurse, without a doctor present, could perform some of the procedure. The court had to decide if a nurse's involvement was legal under the Abortion Act. The case went to the House of Lords where the majority (three) of the judges held that it was lawful, whilst the other two said that it was not lawful.

The three judges in the majority based their decision on the mischief rule, pointing out that the mischief Parliament was trying to remedy was the unsatisfactory state of the law before 1967 and the number of dangerous illegal abortions. The other two judges applied the literal rule and said that the words of the Act were clear and that only a 'registered medical practitioner' could carry out terminations.

Adapted from
The English Legal System, 4th edition

Source B

The courts can, when they are trying to find Parliamentary intention, sometimes use intrinsic and extrinsic aids. Intrinsic aids are things inside the Act, for example, the preamble, the long and short title. Extrinsic aids are things outside the Act, for example, case law, Law Commission reports, previous Acts of Parliament, Hansard and dictionaries.

Answer all parts

(a) Source A refers to the literal rule.

   Explain the literal rule using Source A and cases to illustrate your answer.

(b) Using Source B, identify and explain the most suitable extrinsic aid that could be used in the following situations

   (i) The House of Lords is considering an ambiguous word. The meaning of this word was discussed by Parliament during the passage of the Bill.

   (ii) The House of Lords is trying to cover a gap in the law left by an Act. This Act was based on the Law Commission's recommendations.

   (iii) The House of Lords is trying to find the plain, ordinary, literal meaning of a word. The word is not defined in the Act.

(c) (i) Source A refers to the mischief rule. Using Source A and other cases, explain how this rule is applied.

   (ii) Discuss the strengths and weaknesses of the mischief rule.

OCR G142 January 2007

Chapter 18

European law

O n 1st January 1973 the United Kingdom joined what was then the European Economic Community, and another source of law came into being: European law. Since then it has had increasing significance as a source of law. The European Economic Community was originally set up by Germany, France, Italy, Belgium, the Netherlands and Luxembourg in 1957 by the Treaty of Rome. The name 'European Union' was introduced by the Treaty of European Union in 1993. Denmark and Ireland joined at the same time as the United Kingdom. In the 1980s and 1990s Greece, Spain, Portugal, Austria, Finland and Sweden joined. Then on 1st May 2004 another ten countries joined the EU. These were Cyprus, Czech Republic, Estonia, Hungary, Latvia, Lithuania, Malta, Poland, Slovak Republic and Slovenia. The most recent members are Bulgaria and Romania who joined on 1st January 2007. There are now 27 Member States (see Figure 18.1).

18.1 The institutions of the European Union

In order to implement the aims of the Treaty of Rome, the European Union has a vast and complex organisation with institutions established by the Treaty of Rome. The main institutions which exercise the functions of the Union are:

- the Council of the European Union
- the Commission
- the European Parliament
- the European Court of Justice.

In addition there are a number of ancillary bodies, the most important of which is the Economic and Social Committee.

18.1.1 The Council of Ministers

The Government of each nation in the Union sends a representative to the Council. The Foreign Minister is usually a country's main representative, but a government is free to send any of its Ministers to Council meetings. This means that usually the Minister responsible for the topic under consideration will attend the meetings of the Council, so that the precise membership will vary

DATE	COUNTRIES JOINING	COMMENT
1957	Belgium France Germany Italy Luxembourg The Netherlands	These are the founder members Treaty of Rome signed
1973	Denmark Ireland United Kingdom	UK passes the European Communities Act 1972 on joining
1981	Greece	
1986	Portugal Spain	
1995	Austria Finland Sweden	
2004	Cyprus, Czech Republic, Estonia, Hungary, Latvia, Lithuania, Malta, Poland, Slovak Republic and Slovenia	
2007	Bulgaria Romania	

Figure 18.1 Chart showing the Member States of the European Union

with the subject being discussed. For example, the Minister for Agriculture will attend when the issue to be discussed involves agriculture. Twice a year government heads meet in the European Council or 'Summit' to discuss broad matters of policy. The Member States take it in turn to provide the President of the Council, each for a six-month period. To assist with the day-to-day work of the Council there is a committee of permanent representatives known as Coreper.

The Council is the principal decision-making body of the Union. Voting in the Council is on a weighted basis with each country having a number of votes roughly in proportion to the size of its population.

18.1.2 The Commission

This consists of 27 Commissioners who are supposed to act independently of their national origin. Each Member State has one Commissioner.

The Commissioners are appointed for a five-year term and can only be removed during this term of office by a vote of censure by the European Parliament. Each Commissioner heads a department with special responsibility for one area of Union policy, such as economic affairs, agriculture or the environment.

The Commission as a whole has several functions as follows:

● It is the motive power behind Union policy as it proposes policies and presents drafts of legislation to the Council for the Council's consideration. In its own booklet on Union law, the European Union says the relationship between the Commission and the Council can be briefly summarised by saying 'the Commission proposes and the Council disposes'.

● The Commission is also the 'guardian' of the treaties. It ensures that treaty provisions and other measures adopted by the Union are properly implemented. If a Member State has failed to implement Union law within its own country, or has infringed a Provision in some way, the Commission has a duty to intervene and, if necessary, refer the matter to the European Court of Justice. The Commission has performed this duty very effectively, and as a result there have been judgments given by the Court against Britain and other Member States.

● It is responsible for the administration of the Union and has executive powers to implement the Union's budget.

 Internet Research

Use the Internet to find out more about the European Commission. Find out who is the Commissioner for the United Kingdom. Try http://europa.eu.

18.1.3 The Assembly

Parliament's main function is to discuss proposals put forward by the Commission, but it has no direct law-making authority. The members of the European Parliament are directly elected by the people of the Member States in elections which take place once every five years. Within the Parliament the Members do not operate in national groups, but form political groups with those of the same political allegiance. The Assembly meets on average about once a month for sessions that can last up to a week. It has standing committees which discuss proposals made by the Commission and then report to the full Parliament for debate. Decisions made by the Parliament are not binding, though they will influence the Council of Ministers.

The main criticism is that the Parliament has no real power. However, the assent of Parliament is required to any international agreements the Union wishes to enter into. This allows it an important role in deciding whether new members should be admitted to the Union. It also has some power over the Union budget, especially in non-compulsory expenditure, where it has the final decision on whether to approve the budget or not.

18.2 The European Court of Justice

Its function is set out in Art 220 of the Treaty of Rome. This states that the Court must 'ensure that in the interpretation and application of the Treaty the law is observed'. The court sits in Luxembourg

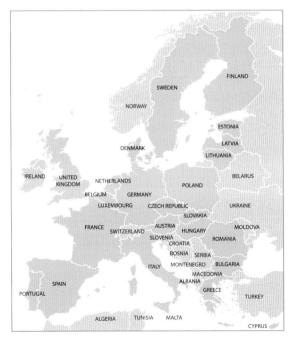

Figure 18.2 Map showing countries of the European Union

Figure 18.3 Role of the European Court of Justice

and has 27 judges, one from each Member State. For a full court, 11 judges will sit, but it also sits in chambers of five judges or three judges. Judges are appointed under Art 222 of the Treaty of Rome from those who are eligible for appointment to the highest judicial posts in their own country or who are leading academic lawyers. Each judge is appointed for a term of six years, and can be re-appointed for a further term of six years. The judges select one of themselves to be President of the Court.

The Court is assisted by nine Advocates General who also hold office for six years. Each case is assigned to an Advocate General whose task under Art 223 is to research all the legal points involved and 'to present publicly, with complete impartiality and independence, reasoned conclusions on cases submitted to the Court of Justice with a view to assisting the latter in the performance of its duties'.

18.2.1 Role of the court

The court's task is to ensure that the law is applied uniformly in all Member States (see Figure 18.3) and it does this by performing two key roles.

The first is that it hears cases to decide whether Member States have failed to fulfil obligations under the Treaties. Such actions are usually initiated by the European Commission, although they can also be started by another Member State. An early example of such a case was *Re Tachographs: The Commission v United Kingdom* (1979) in which the court held that the United Kingdom had to implement a Council Regulation on the use of mechanical recording equipment (tachographs) in road vehicles used for the carriage of goods (see section 18.2.2 for further information on the effect of Regulations).

18.2.2 Article 234 rulings

The second key function is that it hears references from national courts for preliminary rulings on points of European law. This function is a very important one since rulings made by the European Court of Justice are then binding on courts in all Member States. This ensures that the law is indeed uniform throughout the European Union.

Article 234

A request for a preliminary ruling is made under Article 234 of the Treaty of Rome. This says that:

 the Court of Justice shall have jurisdiction to give preliminary rulings concerning:

(a) the interpretation of treaties;

(b) the validity and interpretation of acts of the institutions of the Union;

(c) the interpretation of the statutes of bodies established by an act of the Council, where those statutes so provide.

Article 234 goes on to state that where there is no appeal from the national court within the national system, then such a court *must* refer points of European Law to the European Court of Justice. Other national courts are allowed to make an Art 234 reference, but as there is still an appeal available within their own system, such courts do not have to do so. They have a discretion (ie they can choose whether or not to refer the case).

Applied to the court structure in England and Wales, this means that the House of Lords must refer questions of European law, since it is the highest appeal court in our system. However, the Court of Appeal does not have to refer questions. It has a choice: it may refer if it wishes or it may decide the case without any referral. The same is true of all the lower courts in the English court hierarchy.

However, even courts at the bottom of the hierarchy can refer questions of law under Article 234, if they feel that a preliminary ruling is necessary to enable a judgment to be given. An example of this was in *Torfaen Borough Council v B & Q* (1990) when Cwmbran Magistrates' Court made a reference on whether the restrictions which then existed on Sunday were in breach of the Treaty of Rome.

Whenever a reference is made the European Court of Justice only makes a preliminary ruling on the point of law; it does not actually decide the case. The case then returns to the original court for it to apply the ruling to the facts in the case.

Key facts

Council of Ministers	● Consists of Ministers from each Member State ● Responsible for broad policy decisions ● Under Art 249 can issue regulations, directives and decisions
Commission	● 27 Commissioners whose duty it is to act in Union's interest ● Proposes legislation ● Tries to ensure the implementation of the Treaties and can bring court action against Member States who do not comply with EU law
Economic and Social Committee	● Non-elected consultative body to represent such groups as employers, employees, consumer associations, etc
Assembly or European Parliament	● Members voted for by electorate in each of the Member States ● Consultative body, has limited powers
European Court of Justice	● Judges from each Member State, assisted by Advocates General ● Rules on European law when cases are referred under Art 234

Figure 18.4 Key facts chart on the institutions of the European Union

18.2.3 Discretionary referrals

In *Bulmer v Bollinger* (1974) the Court of Appeal set out the approach to be used when deciding whether a discretionary referral should be made to the European Court of Justice. The guidelines are as follows:

- guidance on the point of law must be necessary to come to a decision in the case
- there is no need to refer a question which has already been decided by the European Court of Justice in a previous case
- there is no need to refer a point which is reasonably clear and free from doubt; this is known as the *'acte clair'* doctrine
- the court must consider all the circumstances of the case
- the English court retains the discretion on whether to refer or not.

The first case to be referred to the European Court of Justice by an English court was *Van Duyn v Home Office* (1974).

18.2.4 How the court operates

When compared with English courts there are several major differences in the way the European Court of Justice operates. First the emphasis is on presenting cases 'on paper'. Lawyers are required to present their arguments in a written form and there is far less reliance on oral presentation of a case. This requirement is, of course, partly because of the wide range of languages involved, though French is the traditional language of the Court. It also represents the traditional method of case presentation in other European countries. An interesting point to note is that the English system in some areas is now beginning to use this 'paper' submission.

A second major difference is the use of the Advocate General. This independent lawyer is not used in the English system. However in the European Court of Justice the Advocate General who was assigned to the case will present his findings on the law after the parties have made their submissions. The court, therefore, has the advantage of having all aspects of the law presented to them.

The deliberations of the judges are secret and where necessary the decision will be made by a majority vote. However, when the judgment is delivered, again in a written form, it is signed by all the judges who formed part of the panel, so that it is not known if any judges disagreed with the majority. This contrasts strongly with the English system, whereby a dissenting judge not only makes it known that he disagrees with the majority, but also usually delivers a judgment explaining his reasoning.

The other points to be noted are that the European Court of Justice is not bound by its own previous decisions and that it prefers the purposive approach to interpretation (see section 17.6 for an explanation of the purposive approach).

The court has wide rights to study extrinsic material when deciding the meaning of provisions and may study preparatory documents. The European Court of Justice is important, not only because its decisions are binding on English courts, but also because its attitude to interpretation is increasingly being followed by English courts. The European Court of Justice pointed this out in *von Colson v Land Nordrhein-Westfalen* (1984) when it said:

> national courts are required to interpret their national law in the light of the wording and the purpose of the directive.

18.3 European sources of law

These are classed as primary and secondary sources of law. Primary sources are mainly the Treaties, the most important of which is the Treaty of Rome itself. Secondary sources are legislation passed by the Institutions of the Union under Art 249 of the Treaty of Rome. The most important types of secondary legislation are regulations and directives, which are considered below.

Key facts

Type of law	Effect	Source
Treaties	Directly applicable Have direct effect (both vertically and horizontally) if give individual rights and are clear	Section 2(1) of the European Communities Act 1972 *Macarthys v Smith* (1979)
Regulations	Directly applicable Have direct effect (both vertically and horizontally) if give individual rights and are clear	Article 249 of the Treaty of Rome
Directives	NOT directly applicable Have vertical direct effect if give individual rights and are clear NO horizontal direct effect But individual can claim against State for loss caused by failure to implement	Article 249 of the Treaty of Rome *Marshall* case (1986) *Duke v GEC Reliance* (1988) *Francovich v Italian Republic* (1991)

Figure 18.5 Key facts chart showing effect of EU laws

18.3.1 Treaties

So far as our law is concerned all treaties signed by our head of government become part of English law automatically. This is as a result of the European Communities Act 1972, s 2(1) which states that:

> All such rights, powers, liabilities, obligations and restrictions from time to time created or arising by or under the Treaties and all such remedies and procedures from time to time provided for by or under the Treaties, as in accordance with the Treaties <u>are without further enactment to be given legal effect</u> or used in the United Kingdom, shall be recognised and available in law and be enforced, allowed and followed accordingly.

Direct effect

This not only makes Community law part of our law but also allows individuals to rely on it. In the case of *Van Duyn v Home Office* (1974) the European Court of Justice held that an individual was entitled to rely on Art 39 giving the right of freedom of movement. The Article had direct effect and conferred rights on individuals which could be enforced not only in the European Court of Justice, but also in national courts.

This means that citizens of the United Kingdom are entitled to rely on the rights in the Treaty of Rome and other treaties, even though those rights may not have been specifically enacted in English law. This is clearly illustrated by the case of *Macarthys Ltd v Smith* (1980). In this case Wendy Smith's employers paid her less than her male predecessor for exactly the same job. As the two people were not employed at the same time by the employer there was no breach of English domestic law. However, Wendy Smith was able to claim that the company which employed her was in breach of Art 141 of the Treaty of Rome over equal pay for men and women and this claim was confirmed by the European Court of Justice.

The growing influence of European law is shown in that British courts are now prepared to apply European Treaty law directly rather than wait for the European Court of Justice to make a ruling on the point. This is illustrated in *Diocese of Hallam Trustee v Connaughton* (1996). In this case the Employment Appeal Tribunal had to consider facts which had some similarity to the Wendy Smith case; Josephine Connaughton was employed as director of music by the Diocese of Hallam from 1990 to September 1994, at which time her salary was £11,138. When she left the position, the post was advertised at a salary of £13,434, but the successful applicant, a man, was actually appointed at a salary of £20,000. In other words, where in Wendy Smith's case she had discovered that her male predecessor was paid more than she was, in the *Connaughton* case it was the immediate successor who was receiving considerably higher pay.

The Employment Appeal Tribunal considered Art 141 of the Treaty of Rome and decided as a preliminary point that its provisions were wide enough to allow Miss Connaughton to make a claim, saying;

 We are sufficiently satisfied as to the scope of Article 141 so as to decide this appeal without further reference to the European Court of Justice.

Similarly the House of Lords in *R v Secretary of State ex parte EOC* (1994) decided, without referring the case to the European Court of Justice, that the longer period of qualification for redundancy for those working less than 16 hours a week discriminated against women and was contrary to Art 141.

18.3.2 Regulations

Under Art 249 of the Treaty of Rome the European Union has the power to issue regulations which are

 binding in every respect and directly applicable in each Member State.

Such regulations do not have to be adopted in any way by the individual states as Art 249 makes it clear that they automatically become law in each member country.

This 'direct applicability' point was tested in *Re Tachographs: Commission v United Kingdom* (1979), where a regulation requiring mechanical recording equipment to be installed in lorries was issued. The United Kingdom Government of the day decided not to implement the regulation, but to leave it to lorry owners to decide whether or not to put in such equipment. When the matter was referred to the European Court of Justice it was held that Member States had no discretion in the case of regulations. The wording of Art 249 was explicit and meant that regulations were automatically law in all Member States. States could not pick and choose which ones they would implement. In this way regulations make sure that laws are uniform across all the Member States.

Direct effect

Regulations have direct effect. This means that, provided a regulation is clear and gives rights to individuals, the regulation can be relied on by an individual in any case in the UK. Individuals can enforce the rights given by a regulation against both the State and any other person or business.

18.3.3 Directives

Directives are the main way in which harmonisation of laws within Member States is reached. There have been directives covering many topics including company laws, banking, insurance, health and safety of workers, equal rights, consumer law and social security.

As with regulations, it is Art 249 of the Treaty of Rome that gives the power to the Union to issue directives. There is, however, a difference from regulations in that Art 249 says such directives

 bind any Member State to which they are addressed as to the result to be achieved, while leaving to domestic agencies a competence as to form and means.

This means that Member States will pass their own laws to bring directives into effect (or implement them) and such laws have to be brought in within a time limit set by the European Commission.

The usual method of implementing directives in the United Kingdom is by Statutory Instrument. An example is the Unfair Terms in Consumer Contracts Regulations 1994, which implemented a directive aimed at giving consumers protection from unfair terms in contracts. Directives can, however, be implemented by other law-making methods. An example is the Consumer Protection Act 1987. A directive on liability for defective products was issued in July 1985. (By the way, this was some nine years after the proposal had first been put forward by the Commission!) The directive had to be implemented by 30th July 1988. This was done in this country by Parliament passing the Consumer Protection Act 1987, which came into force on 1st March 1988. Directives can also be implemented by an Order in Council made by the Privy Council.

Working Time Directive

Another example of a directive is the Working Time Directive which was issued in 1993. This directive gave detailed instructions of the maximum number of hours that should be worked, the rest periods and the amount of paid holiday to which workers were entitled. It should have been implemented by November 1996 but the United Kingdom Government did not implement it until October 1998, with the Working Time Regulations 1998.

Direct effect

Where Member States have not implemented a directive within the time laid down the European Court of Justice has developed the concept of 'direct effect'.

If the purpose of a directive is to grant rights to individuals and that directive is sufficiently clear, it may be directly enforceable by an individual against the Member State. This will be so even

though that State has not implemented the directive, or has implemented it in a defective way. The important point is that an individual who is adversely affected by the failure to implement only has rights against the State. This is because of the concepts of vertical effect and horizontal effect (see Figure 18.6).

Vertical direct effect

In *Marshall v Southampton and South West Hampshire Area Health Authority* (1986) the facts were that Miss Marshall was required to retire at the age of 62 whereas men doing the same work did not have to retire until age 65. Under the Sex Discrimination Act 1975 in English law this was not discriminatory. However, she was able to succeed in an action for unfair dismissal by relying on the Equal Treatment Directive 76/207. This directive had not been fully implemented in the United Kingdom but the European Court of Justice held that it was sufficiently clear and imposed obligations on the Member State. This ruling allowed Miss Marshall to succeed in her claim against her employers because her employers were 'an arm of the state'; ie they were considered as being part of the State. The directive had vertical effect allowing her to rely on it and take action against them.

The concept of the State for these purposes is quite wide, as it was ruled by the European Court of Justice in *Foster v British Gas plc* (1990) that it was:

> a body, whatever its legal form, which has been made responsible, pursuant to a measure adopted by the State, for providing a public service under the control of the State and has for that purpose special powers beyond those which result from the normal rules applicable in relations between individuals.

In view of this wide definition the House of Lords decided that British Gas, which at the time was a nationalised industry, was part of the State, and

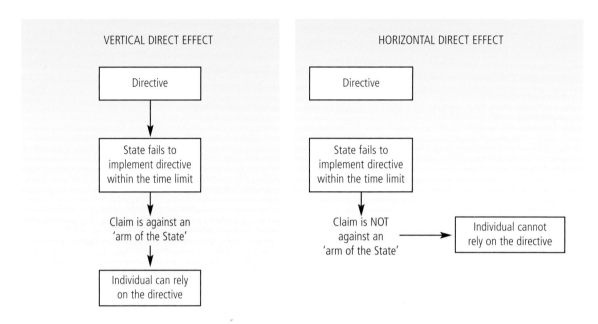

Figure 18.6 Diagram illustrating vertical and horizontal direct effect

Foster could rely on the Equal Treatment Directive.

The concept of vertical effect means that a Member State cannot take advantage of its own failure to comply with European law and implement a directive. Individuals can rely on the directive when bringing a claim against the State.

This concept of vertical effect was used in the case of *Gibson v East Riding of Yorkshire Council* (1999). In this case Mrs Gibson was employed as a part-time swimming instructor. She did not get paid holidays. The Employment Appeal Tribunal held that under the Working Time Directive she was entitled to four weeks' paid holiday from November 1996, the date that the directive should have been implemented. Her employers were an 'emanation of the State' and could not rely on the lack of domestic legislation to defeat her claim.

Horizontal direct effect

Directives which have not been implemented do not, however, give an individual any rights against other people. So, in *Duke v GEC Reliance Ltd* (1988), Mrs Duke was unable to rely on the Equal Treatment Directive as her employer was a private company. This illustrates that directives do not have horizontal effect and this has been confirmed by an Italian case, *Paola Faccini Dori v Recreb Srl* (1994), in which the Italian Government failed to implement Directive 85/447 in respect of consumer rights to cancel certain contracts. Dori could not rely on the directive in order to claim a right of cancellation against a private trader.

Duty to interpret national law in the light of directives

Even where a directive has not been implemented, national courts have a duty to interpret their national law in the light of the wording and purpose of any relevant directive.

This was pointed out by the European Court of Justice in the earlier case of *von Colson v Land Nordrhein-Westfalen* (1984) that

> national courts are required to interpret their national law in the light of the wording and the purpose of the directive.

Actions against the State for failure to implement a directive

Clearly it is unfair that these conflicting doctrines of vertical and horizontal effect should give rights to individuals in some cases and not in others. The European Court of Justice has developed another strategy under which it may be possible to take an action to claim damages against the Member State which has failed to implement the European directive. This was decided in *Francovich v Italian Republic* (1991) where the Italian Government failed to implement a directive aimed at protecting wages of employees whose employer became insolvent. As a result when the firm for which Francovich worked went into liquidation owing him wages, he sued the State for his financial loss. The European Court of Justice held that he was entitled to compensation. The court said that:

> Community law required the member states to make good damage caused by a failure to transpose a directive, provided three conditions were fulfilled;
>
> First, the purpose of the directive had to be to grant rights to individuals.
>
> Second, it had to be possible to identify the content of those rights on the basis of the provisions of the directive.
>
> Finally, there had to be a causal link between the breach of the state's obligations and the damage suffered.

In *R v HM Treasury, ex parte British Telecommunications plc* (1996) the European Court of Justice held that although a directive on telecommunications had been incorrectly implemented in English law, compensation was not payable as the breach of Community law was not sufficiently serious.

The principle of Member States being liable to pay compensation has been extended to other breaches by Member States of Community law. This was seen in the joined cases of *Brasserie du Pêcheur SA v Federation of Republic of Germany* and *R v Secretary of State for Transport, ex parte Factortame Ltd (No 4)* (1996) which are considered in section 18.4.

Comment

The importance of rulings of the European Court of Justice

The development of the concept of direct effect has been a very important one for the effectiveness of EU law. If the European Court of Justice had not developed this concept citizens of Member States would not have been able to enforce the rights given to them.

In particular where the Government has not implemented a directive, the rights of individuals in many important areas, especially employment law and discrimination, would have been lost. The rulings of the European Court of Justice have allowed individuals to rely on EU law in claims against the State or an arm of the State, and also forced the Government to implement EU law more fully.

The development of the *Francovich* principle has provided citizens with a remedy against the State, when otherwise they would not have had one. However, this brings its own problems as the European Court of Justice has no mechanism for enforcing its judgments.

Activity

Below in Source A are set out extracts from Arts 1 and 2 of the Equal Treatment Directive 76/207. Read these and then apply them, giving reasons for your decision, to the facts set out in Source B.

SOURCE A

Council Directive No. 76/207

Article 1

1. The purpose of this Directive is to put into effect in the Member States the principle of equal treatment as regards access to employment, including promotion, and to vocational training and as regards working conditions ... This principle is hereinafter referred to as the 'principle of equal treatment'.

Article 2

1. For the purposes of the following provisions, the principle of equal treatment shall mean that there shall be no discrimination whatsoever on the grounds of sex either directly or indirectly by reference in particular to marital or family status.
2. This Directive shall be without prejudice to the right of Member States to exclude from its field of application those occupational activities and, where appropriate, the training leading thereto, for which, by reason of their nature or the context in which they are carried out, the sex of the worker constitutes a determining factor.
3. This Directive shall be without prejudice to provisions concerning the protection of women, particularly as regards pregnancy and maternity.
4. This Directive shall be without prejudice to measures to promote equal opportunity for men and women, in particular by removing existing inequalities which affect women's opportunities in the areas referred to in Article 1(1).

SOURCE B

CASE FACTS: Amy Austin and Ben Bowen are employed by Green Gardens Ltd. There is a vacancy for a promotion to section manager, and both have applied for the post. Green Gardens have interviewed Amy and Ben and decided that both are equally qualified for the position. In this situation, if there are fewer women employed at the relevant level, Green Gardens have a policy of appointing the female applicant.

Ben complains that this is discriminatory and contrary to the Equal Treatment Directive.

18.4 Conflict between European law and national law

European law takes precedence over national law. This was first established in *Van Gend en Loos* (1963) which involved a conflict of Dutch law and European law on customs duty. The Dutch Government argued that the European Court of Justice had no jurisdiction to decide whether European law should prevail over Dutch law; that was a matter for the Dutch courts to decide. However, the European Court rejected this argument. In *Costa v ENEL* (1964) the European Court of Justice held that even if there was a later national law it did not take precedence over the European law. In this case the European Court of Justice said:

> the Member States have limited their sovereign rights, albeit within limited fields, and have thus created a body of law which binds both their nationals and themselves.

This conflict was seen clearly in the *Factortame* case (1990) when the European Court of Justice decided that Britain could not enforce the Merchant Shipping Act 1988. This Act had been passed to protect British fishermen by allowing vessels to register only if 75 per cent of directors and shareholders were British nationals. It was held that this contravened the Treaty of Rome.

This breach of Community law has had another effect as the European Court of Justice held in a later action in the joined cases of *Brasserie du Pêcheur SA v Federation of Republic of Germany* and *R v Secretary of State for Transport, ex parte Factortame Ltd (No 4) (1996)* that governments were liable for financial loss suffered as a result of their breach of European law. In *Brasserie du Pêcheur* a French company claimed that it was forced to discontinue exports of beer to Germany, because the German authorities considered that the beer did not comply with the purity requirements laid down in German law. In *Factortame* European fishermen claimed that they had been deprived of the right to fish as a result of the Merchant Shipping Act 1988. In both cases there was a claim for compensation from the State concerned.

The European Court of Justice held that Community law did give the right to compensation provided that three conditions were met. These were:

- the rule of Community law infringed must be intended to confer rights on individuals
- the breach must be sufficiently serious
- there must be a direct causal link between the breach of the obligation resting on the State and the damage sustained by the injured parties.

18.4.1 The effect of European law on the sovereignty of Parliament

From the cases given above it can be seen that Member States, including Britain, have definitely transferred sovereign rights to a Community created by them. None of the Member States can

Key facts

1963	*Van Gend en Loos*	European Court of Justice has right to decide whether Community law or national law prevails
1964	*Costa v ENEL*	European law takes precedence over national law
1974	*Van Duyn v Home Office*	Principle of direct applicability Citizens can rely directly on an article of the Treaty of Rome which confers rights on individuals
1986	*Marshall v Southampton etc Health Authority*	Vertical direct effect of directives In an action against the State individuals can rely on a directive which has not been implemented
1991	*Francovich v Italy*	Individual can claim compensation from State for its failure to implement directive
1996	*Brasserie du Pêcheur, ex parte Factortame No 4*	State liable to compensate for breaches of Community law

Figure 18.7 Key facts chart of some important decisions of the European Court of Justice

rely on its own law when it is in conflict with European Union law.

It is also a principle of the Treaty of Rome that no Member State may call into question the status of Community law as a system of uniformly and generally applicable law throughout the Community. It therefore follows from this, that Community law has priority over any conflicting law of Member States. This is true both of national laws which were enacted before the Community law and also of national laws which were enacted after the relevant Community law.

While Britain is a member of the European Union it is therefore true to say that the sovereignty of Parliament has been affected and that, in the areas it operates, European law has supremacy over national law.

Examination Questions

Read the source material below and answer the questions which follow.

Exercise on European Union law and delegated legislation

SOURCE A

In many ways the most important type of legislation is delegated legislation. This describes legislation made by a subordinate body (a body other than Parliament) authorised to make law by an Act of Parliament. The Health and Safety at Work Act 1974, for example, authorised a Government Minister to make new safety laws by issuing regulations (see **Source B**). Safety laws have to be complex and may need frequent updating. It would be impractical to put every complex change in the law through the full stages of Parliamentary procedure. Technically, regulations of this kind are known as statutory instruments.

> Adapted from *A Level Law*, AM Doudale, MP Furmston, SP Jones, CH Sherrin, Butterworths

SOURCE B

(This statutory instrument was introduced to implement an EU directive. In Marshall v Southampton and South West Hampshire Area Health Authority *(1986) it was stated that directives only have vertical direct effect, not horizontal direct effect. If Mrs Marshall had been employed by a private company she would have had no remedy.)*

The Health and Safety (Display Screen Equipment) Regulations 1992

Some Important Definitions

- **Display Screen Equipment used at workstations** *includes* computer monitors. Screens showing mainly TV or film pictures are *not* covered.
- **Users**: Uses the display screen equipment more or less daily and for continuous spells of an hour or more at a time.

The Regulations:

Regulation 1: requires every employer to perform a suitable and sufficient assessment of workstations to assess any health and safety risks and to take action to reduce those risks to the lowest extent possible.

Regulation 2: requires employers to plan the activities of those using workstations so that daily work is periodically interrupted by breaks or activity changes. These could be informal breaks away from the screen for a short period each hour.

Regulation 3: gives users the opportunity to have an appropriate eye and eyesight test as soon as practicable after requesting one and at regular intervals thereafter. The costs will be met by the employer.

> Adapted from the Regulations

(a) With reference to Source B, briefly explain with examples, the terms 'vertical direct effect' and 'horizontal direct effect'.

(b) Apply the content of the Health and Safety (Display Screen Equipment) Regulations 1992 in Source B to each of the situations described below:

   (i)   Mario is about to start a new job as a librarian in a small school. The job will require occasional use of a computer monitor. The Deputy Head is also the school Health and Safety Officer and is anxious to comply with all relevant legislation.

   (ii) Amir works as a telephone-sales representative. His regular daily work requires long periods of sustained concentration as he transfers information from customers onto a computer system. He is finding it increasingly difficult to sustain his concentration.

   (iii) Julie works as a receptionist in a busy office. Her daily work involves monitoring a TV screen (fed from security cameras) and constant use of a computer monitor to perform a variety of functions. She has started to suffer with blurred vision.

(c) (i) Source A refers to 'statutory instruments'. Describe with examples the nature of statutory instruments and the process of bringing them into force.

   (ii) Using Source A and other examples discuss the advantages and disadvantages of delegated legislation.

OCR Specimen Paper

Chapter 19

Law reform

19.1 Influences on law reform

It is important to keep the law under review and make sure that it is reformed when necessary. There are many influences on the way our law is formed and the impetus for reform can come from a number of sources. Some of these will have more effect than others. It is also possible that in some situations there may be conflicting interests about the way that the law should be reformed.

19.1.1 Parliament

Throughout any session of Parliament, the Government has the major say on what new laws will be put before the House of Commons and the House of Lords for discussion.

Queen's Speech

At the opening of each session of Parliament (usually once a year) the Government announces its plans for new laws in that session. This is done in the Queen's Speech. This speech is written for the Queen by the Prime Minister and other senior Ministers. This is shown in the speech as the Queen will often use the words 'my Government will . . .'.

However, there is a problem of the amount of time available in Parliament. A lot of time has to be given to financial matters such as budgets and taxation; foreign policy is also discussed in Parliament, particularly at times of crisis, such as after the terrorist attacks in London in July 2005.

Other topics including education and health must also be given parliamentary time, so the time left for 'pure' law reform is limited.

19.1.2 Judges

When judges decide points of law in cases, they sometimes have to decide a new point. This allows them to 'make' law. Decisions by judges over the years have created the tort of negligence. This is the law that allows you to claim compensation when you have been injured by another person's negligence (see section 14.7). In the criminal law the judges have sometimes created new offences. An important example was when they created the offence of marital rape in *R v R* (1990) (see section 14.7).

The House of Lords can use the Practice Statement to alter the law when they think it is right to do so. This power is not used very often. However, it has been used when there has been a change of opinion or social values over several years so that the law did not match current expectations. An example of this use of the Practice Statement was *Herrington v BRB* (1972) (see section 14.3.2).

However, judges only create or reform law in a very small number of cases. Their job is to apply the law.

19.1.3 Public opinion

Where there is strong public opinion about a change to the law, the Government may bow to such opinion. This is more likely towards the end of a term of government when there will be a general election soon and the Government wants to remain popular with the majority of people.

Media

The media play a large role in bringing public opinion to the Government's attention. Where an issue is given a high profile on television and in the newspapers, then it also brings it to the attention of other members of the public and may add to the weight of public opinion.

However, in some cases this can be seen as the media manipulating the news and creating public opinion.

In addition, specific events may also play a role in formulating the law. A particularly tragic example was the massacre in1996 of 16 young children and their teacher in Dunblane by a lone gunman. An inquiry into the ownership of guns was set up and a pressure group organised a petition asking for guns to be banned. Eventually, Parliament banned private ownership of most handguns.

19.1.4 Pressure groups

Pressure groups may cause the Government to reconsider the law on certain areas. This was seen in 2000 when the Government finally agreed to reduce the age of consent for homosexual acts in private to 16. Another example of the Government bowing to public opinion and the efforts of a pressure group was the passing of the Hunting Act 2004 which banned hunting foxes with dogs.

Sometimes pressure groups will campaign against a proposed change to the law. This was seen when the Government tried to restrict the right to trial by jury. Pressure groups such as Justice and Liberty campaigned against this as they thought the changes infringed human rights.

There are also occasions when two pressure groups have conflicting interests and want opposing things. This was seen when the ban against fox hunting was being considered. The

League against Cruel Sports wanted it banned, but the Countryside Alliance wanted it to be allowed to continue.

Lobbying

Some pressure groups try to persuade individual Members of Parliament to support their cause. This is called lobbying (because members of the public can meet MPs in the lobbies of the House of Commons). If a pressure group is successful, it may persuade an MP to ask questions in Parliament about a particular problem. It is also possible that a backbench MP may use the Private Members' Bill session (see section 15.4.2) to introduce a Bill trying to reform the law in the way that the pressure group wants. However, it is very unlikely that such a Bill will be passed by Parliament unless there is widespread support for it.

 Internet Research

Look up websites of pressure groups such as Liberty **www.liberty-human-rights.org.uk** or Justice **www.justice.org.uk** or Greenpeace **www.greenpeace.org.uk**. Choose one and write a brief summary of any changes in the law it is suggesting or any success in changing the law that it has had.

19.2 The need for an independent law reform body

The problem with the above methods of law reform is that they do not look at the law as a whole. The Government has a political agenda. It will want certain policies for taxation, education, etc. Governments are less interested in 'pure' law reform. 'Pure' law means the law on different areas such as contract law, land law or criminal law.

Judges can only deal with the question of law in the case they are trying. They cannot deal with wider reforms of the law although in some cases judges have commented on the need for the Government to change the law.

Public opinion is not always based on accurate information. Also the topics that arouse public interest are not going to include the need to reform technical areas of law. Pressure groups are concerned with specific, and usually quite narrow, issues. Also pressure groups may be campaigning for the opposite thing as happened with fox hunting.

It is clear there needs to be an agency to consider reform of the law in a wider way. For this reason the Law Commission was created.

19.3 The Law Commission

The Law Commission was set up in 1965 by the Law Commissions Act. It is a full-time body and consists of a chairman, who is a High Court Judge, and four other Law Commissioners. There are also support staff to assist with research and four parliamentary draftsmen who help with the drafting of proposed Bills.

The Commission considers areas of law which are believed to be in need of reform. The role of the Law Commission is set out in s 3 of the Law Commissions Act which states:

> It shall be the duty of each of the Commissions to take and keep under review all the law with which they are respectively concerned with a view to its systematic development and reform, including in particular the codification of such law, the elimination of anomalies, the repeal of obsolete and unnecessary enactments, the reduction of the number of separate enactments and generally the simplification and modernisation of the law . . .

19.3.1 The way in which the Law Commission works

The actual topics may be referred to it by the Lord Chancellor on behalf of the Government, or it may itself select areas in need of reform and seek Governmental approval to draft a report on them.

The Law Commission works by researching the area of law that is thought to be in need of reform. It then publishes a consultation paper seeking views on possible reform. The consultation paper will describe the current law, set out the problems and look at options for reform (often including explanations of the law in other countries).

Following the response to the consultation paper, the Commission will then draw up positive proposals for reform. These will be presented in a report which will also set out the research that led to the conclusions. There will often be a draft Bill attached to the report with the intention that this is the exact way in which the new law should be formed. Such a draft Bill must, of course, go before Parliament and go through the necessary parliamentary stages if it is to become law.

@ Internet Research

Look at the Law Commission's website (**www.lawcom.gov.uk**) and make a list of three areas of law which the Law Commission is currently researching.

19.3.2 Repeal and consolidation

Repeal

There are many very old and sometimes ridiculous statutes which are still on the statute book, but have long since ceased to have any relevance. In order to remove out-of-date statutes, the Law Commission prepares a Statute Law (Repeals) Bill for Parliament to pass. Through this, more than 2,000 out-of-date Acts have been completely repealed. In addition, parts of thousands of other Acts have also been repealed. This 'tidying-up' of the statute book helps to make the law more accessible.

Consolidation

This is needed because in some areas of law there are a number of statutes, each of which sets out a small part of the total law. The aim of consolidation is to draw all the existing provisions together in one Act. This is another way in which the law is being made more accessible. For example, before 2000, the law on sentencing offenders under the age of 17 had been amended ten times and it was necessary to consult each of these Acts to get a full picture of the law. Much of the law on sentencing was consolidated in the Powers of the Criminal Courts (Sentencing) Act 2000.

The Law Commission produces about five Consolidation Bills each year, though it is perhaps true to say that as fast as one area is consolidated, another area is being fragmented by further Acts of Parliament! This has certainly happened with sentencing as, only months after the Powers of the Criminal Courts (Sentencing) Act 2000 brought most of the law together in one Act, Parliament passed the Criminal Justice and Courts Services Act 2000 altering some of the available sentences and creating new ones. Then in 2003 the Criminal Justice Act 2003 changed much of sentencing law again.

19.3.3 Codification

Codification involves bringing together all the law on one topic into one source. Codification was specifically referred to by s 3 of the Law Commissions Act 1965 as part of the Law Commission's role.

Indeed, when the Law Commission was first formed in 1965 an ambitious programme of codification was announced aimed at codifying family law, contract law, landlord and tenant laws and the law of evidence. However, the Law Commission has gradually abandoned these massive schemes of codification in favour of what

might be termed the 'building-block' approach. Under this it has concentrated on codifying small sections of the law that can be added to later.

19.3.4 Effectiveness of the Law Commission

In the first 10 years of the Law Commission's existence, it had a high success rate, with 85 per cent of its proposals being made law by Parliament. During the next ten years, however, only 50 per cent of its suggested reforms became law. This lack of success was due to the lack of parliamentary time and an apparent disinterest by Parliament in technical law reform. The rate hit an all-time low in 1990, when not one of its reforms was made law by Parliament.

Since then, matters have improved and the Government has enacted more reforms put forward by the Law Commission. Examples include:

- the Contract (Rights of Third Parties) Act 1999 which recognised that a person could have rights under a contract even though they were not a party to the contract
- the Land Registration Act 2002 which was important for anyone selling or buying a house, flat or any other building or land, as it modernised and simplified the method of registering land
- the Fraud Act 2006 which reformed the law on fraud and deception offences.

However, there are still many reports awaiting implementation. In fact, in 2006, the Law Commission stated that 26 reports were awaiting implementation. This was despite the fact that fourteen of them (the oldest dating back to 1991) had been accepted by the Government and were supposed to be implemented 'when parliamentary time becomes available'.

Criminal law

The reform of the criminal law has been slower than reform of other areas. Originally the Law

Key facts

Set up	By the Law Commissions Act 1965
Personnel	Chairman and four other Commissioners Support staff including Parliamentary draftsmen
Function	To 'keep the law under review' s 3 Law Commissions Act 1965
Effectiveness	First 10 years – 85% of proposals enacted by Parliament Second 10 years – 50% of proposals enacted 1990 – no reports enacted 1990 to 2007 – more reports enacted, but many still awaiting implementation
Recent reforms	Land Registration Act 2002 Fraud Act 2006

Figure 19.1 Key facts chart on the Law Commission

Commission hoped to create a criminal code which would cover large areas of the criminal law. They produced a draft Code in 1985 and a full Code in 1989. Because the Code was so large, it was obvious that Parliament would not have the time to deal with the whole of it at one time.

The Law Commission has since then published reports suggesting reform on parts of the criminal law. Some of these have become law, for example the Fraud Act 2006.

Other areas have either not been accepted by the Government or have not yet been made law. For example, the law on offences against the person is still awaiting reform. The Law Commission set out the lack of action in its annual report for 2006–07 when it wrote:

> Fourteen years ago [1993] the Law Commission published a report and draft Bill recommending an overhaul of the current legislation, which dates back to Offences Against the Person Act 1861. In 1997 the Home Office partially accepted these recommendations in principle. In 1998 the Home Office published a consultation paper setting out their initial proposals for reforming the law in this area, based on the Commission's report. In 2003, the Court of Appeal referred to the "need for radical reform" of section 20 of the 1861 Act. "

This shows how slow Parliament can be over taking action on the Law Commission's proposals. Clearly, the Law Commission can only be effective if the Government and Parliament are prepared to find time to enact reforms.

19.4 Other reform agencies

19.4.1 Royal Commissions

For some aspects of the legal system, the Government will set up a Royal Commission (a temporary committee) to investigate and report. For these Commissions, people with expertise in the area are consulted on the law. Once the Royal Commission has reported, its task is over and it is then disbanded.

Some Royal Commissions have led to important changes in the law. For example, the Royal Commission on Police Powers (the Phillips Commission) reported in 1981 and many of its recommendations were put into effect by the

Police and Criminal Evidence Act 1984.

However, the Government has not always implemented recommendations by Royal Commissions. In 1978, the Pearson Commission on Personal Injury made far-reaching proposals for changes to the way in which people are compensated for injuries. These recommendations have never been implemented.

In some cases the Government will bring in some proposals but not the full report. This happened with the Runciman Commission on Criminal Justice.

19.4.2 Reviews by judges

An individual judge may be asked to lead an investigation into technical areas of law and make proposals for reform. A key example of this was the Woolf Report on the civil courts system. This report led to major changes to the civil justice system being brought in, in 1999 (see section 2.6).

19.4.3 Other reviews

As well as using judges to carry out reviews of areas of law, the Government has in recent times asked business people to review the workings of some areas of the justice system. For example, Sir David Clementi was asked to report on the legal profession. His report was published in 2004 and led to the Legal Services Act 2007 (see Chapter 10) which will alter the way legal businesses are structured and the system for dealing with regulation and complaints.

Appendix

This appendix gives help with the activities on pages 6 and 228.

Distinguishing between civil and criminal cases (page 6)
Question 1 answer
Sources A and C are criminal cases. Sources B and D are civil cases. This information helps with the remainder of the questions in the activity.

Statutory interpretation and the case of *Fisher v Bell* (page 228)
The court used the literal rule in coming to the decision in this case. The court considered a technical legal meaning of 'offer for sale' and used this meaning in its literal sense. This meant that literally displaying knives in the window was not offering them for sale. As a result the court came to the decision that the knives were not 'offered for sale', and since they had not been sold or hired or lent either, the shopkeeper had not committed any offence under the Act. He was found not guilty.

Index

Notes: Page numbers in **bold** refer to key facts tables and figures